A DRUNKARD'S DEFENSE

ALCOHOL, MURDER, *and* MEDICAL JURISPRUDENCE *in Nineteenth-Century America*

MICHELE ROTUNDA

UNIVERSITY OF MASSACHUSETTS PRESS
Amherst and Boston

Printed in the United States of America

ISBN 978-1-62534-554-7 (paper); 553-0 (hardcover)

Designed by Deste Roosa
Set in Arno Pro
Printed and bound by Books International, Inc.

Cover design by Rebecca Neimark, Twenty-Six Letters
Cover art by Nathaniel Currier, detail from *The Drunkard's Progress,* hand colored lithograph, 1846. Courtesy of Prints and Photographs Division, Library of Congress.

Library of Congress Cataloging-in-Publication Data
Names: Rotunda, Michele, author. | Schrepfer, Susan R., honouree.
Title: A drunkard's defense : alcohol, murder, and medical jurisprudence in nineteenth-century America / Michele Rotunda.
Identifiers: LCCN 2020019502 | ISBN 9781625345530 (hardcover) | ISBN 9781625345547 (paperback) | ISBN 9781613767993 (ebook) | ISBN 9781613768006 (ebook)
Subjects: LCSH: Drunkenness (Crime)—Law and legislation—United States—History. | Defense (criminal procedure)—United States—History. | Schrepfer, Susan R.
Classification: LCC KF9243 .R68 2021 | DDC 345.73/04—dc23
LC record available at https://lccn.loc.gov/2020019502

British Library Cataloguing-in-Publication Data
A catalog record for this book is available from the British Library.

A DRUNKARD'S DEFENSE

In memory of
SUSAN R. SCHREPFER

CONTENTS

ACKNOWLEDGMENTS

Writing this book has been a long journey, incredibly challenging and yet so rewarding. I never could have even begun, much less finished, without the help of colleagues, advisors, friends, and family. I am grateful to many people for their encouragement, patience, and intellectual support. My first debt is to my teachers, especially the History Department at Rutgers University in New Brunswick and Newark, where I had the opportunity to receive advice and support from many brilliant scholars. I especially thank Gerald N. Grob, who sparked much of my early interest in the history of medicine, and Paul G. E. Clemens for his guidance and encouragement during my time in graduate school and afterwards.

The Alcohol and Drugs History Society has been a tremendous asset, and I appreciate the opportunities they have provided to publish and present parts of this project in various iterations. I first met Sarah Tracy through this group, and she has been a wonderful model and resource. The "I've Been to Dwight" conference in 2016 was one of the best I've been to, and I thank Sarah Lirley McCune for the scholarly conversations and for the short drive down Route 66.

I am incredibly grateful for the support and friendship of my colleagues at Union County College, who sustained me throughout this project. Phil Papas went above and beyond in providing invaluable criticism and suggestions, and I appreciate his forbearance given the many last-minute changes I threw at him. My thanks to Melissa Sande for her thoughtful reading of several chapters and to Mindi Norelli for always being my cheerleader. I am likewise indebted to my students, who provide me with deeper purpose and remind me every day why history is the most interesting subject in the world.

I also have the good fortune to be married to a man with a background in English and law enforcement. I owe Keith Delaney more than I could possibly acknowledge for reading various drafts of the paper, for acting as my unofficial legal consultant, and just for hanging out with me all these years.

ACKNOWLEDGMENTS

My greatest debt is to Susan R. Schrepfer, my advisor and friend, who I miss dearly, and to whom this book is dedicated. Her advice always managed to be both brilliant and kind, and I strive to emulate her example every day.

And of course, I take responsibility for all errors and omissions. As I was sober when I wrote this, I cannot plead the drunkard's defense.

A
DRUNKARD'S
DEFENSE

Introduction

Archibald James had been traveling by wagon through Maury County, Tennessee, on February 17, 1826, when he heard the "report of a gun." A quarter of a mile down the road, he approached a dwelling where he was greeted by a man whose hands were covered in blood. The man, later identified as James Bennett, declared that he "had caught the Villain at last." Inside the house, Thomas Callahan lay, still conscious and bleeding on the floor. The two men had reportedly been drinking together when Bennett accused Callahan of "pilfering" from him and shot his victim "a little above the Eleventh rib." Callahan died the next day. At his trial in June of the same year, Bennett, who was intoxicated at the time of the crime, put forth a defense that he was not guilty by reason of insanity. Friends, neighbors, and acquaintances were called upon to offer their respective opinions to the jury on Bennett's state of mind.[1] Was he insane or just drunk?

The judge seemed to see little ambiguity in the ability of lay witnesses to determine a distinction between insanity and drunkenness and thus instructed the jury

> that upon the subject of derangement, such was the structure of the human mind, that philosophers might forever speculate, upon the subject, but could not define in what it consists; but that if a hundred men should look at a drunken man, they would agree in saying he was drunk; and if a hundred men were to look at a deranged man, they would agree in saying he was deranged.[2]

In other words, as the saying goes, people "know it when they see it." The jury was convinced the defendant was drunk, a condition that provided no defense for his crime. Bennett was convicted, and his attorneys appealed to the Supreme Court of Tennessee, citing an error in the judge's instructions to the jury. The appeals court ruled that the charge was appropriate, agreeing that the application of an "intuitive principle" to distinguish between insanity and drunkenness was "very reasonable and probably very correct" even if "the reasons why the mind is insane cannot be defined in theory." The defendant's state of mind was a "voluntarily contracted madness by drunkenness." The order of execution was upheld.[3]

Intoxication, as far as it is understood to be a temporary, voluntary, and not uncommon condition, has not fit easily into medical or legal definitions of insanity. Those who have committed crimes while under the influence of alcohol have alternately evoked condemnation for their choice to drink or sympathy due to a perceived lack of intent behind their actions. Physicians and jurists, reformers as well as current and former drinkers themselves, have grappled with the question of how much control drinkers have over their behavior and even how much willpower certain individuals have over their desire to drink. Additionally, the suggestion that the choice to imbibe or refrain from alcohol does not come as easily to some as to others has been widely accepted, to admittedly varying degrees, within the past two centuries.[4] The question of how to define responsibility under the law for acts committed while under the influence is complex, and the answer susceptible to changes in the fields of medicine and the law as well as to changing cultural attitudes toward drinking.

As early as 1551, in the case of *Reniger v. Fogossa*, English common law proclaimed, "if a person that is drunk kills another, this shall be felony, and he shall be hanged for it." Even if the offender lacked "understanding or memory" of his crime, "inasmuch as that ignorance was occasioned by his own act and folly, and he might have avoided it, he shall not be privileged thereby."[5] That is to say, when the act of drinking is undertaken voluntarily, the resulting state of intoxication is predictable, so the offender bears full responsibility for his actions. The law in the United States likewise held that "drunkenness is no excuse for crime." The seeming forthrightness of the statement belies the reality of nineteenth-century courtroom scenes in which heavy drinking was often pled as a defense to a variety of heinous crimes, including murder. Even as prosecuting attorneys attempted to convince juries that drunkenness was no excuse under the law, physicians and defense attorneys often relied on that very same declaration, followed by an important "but" that negated its relevance in the case of their client. Arguments pointing out the lack of intent in an intoxicated defendant's actions were often supported by medical testimony for judges and juries to consider.

The drunkard's defense was generally one of last resort: to claim drunkenness as an excuse likely meant there was little reasonable doubt as to the details of the crime. Defendants may also have attempted to shift some of the blame by proclaiming "the Demon Rum" made them do it. The outcomes of these trials varied across time, place, and circumstance. More often than not, the "drunkard" was convicted; justice, and the cause of temperance, seemingly served. In other cases, juries were swayed by the argument that alcohol consumption did indeed affect the circumstances of crime and decided to acquit or convict of a lesser charge. In still other cases, an appeals court granted clemency.

Using a variety of court cases as evidence, *A Drunkard's Defense* focuses on several competing and often unresolved models of responsibility for crimes related to intoxication that emerged in nineteenth-century America. Like much of history, it is a story that does not follow a straight path. Drunkenness truly was "no excuse" for crime in the early years of the nineteenth century; however, changes in the fields of medicine, the law, and society created the circumstances under which such a defense became more viable and certainly more prevalent, if only intermittently successful, by midcentury. By the postbellum period, a backlash led by medical professionals and buttressed by an influential temperance movement materialized, but the groundwork had been laid for considering what today is more likely to be called a defense of "diminished capacity."

Broadly, this project connects two fields of historical research that too often remain disparate—the history of the insanity defense and a social and cultural history of alcohol consumption in the United States. Numerous scholars have written extensively on the insanity defense and the medico-legal question of responsibility.[6] Yet despite a meaningful overlap with the issue of insanity, the question of intoxication has too often been ignored or subsumed in the scholarship. The history of intoxication as a defense follows a similar trajectory to that of the insanity defense, which gained ground, linked to medical professionalization, in the early part of the nineteenth century and suffered a reversal by the century's end. However, by focusing exclusively on cases related to intoxication, this work recasts the narrative to provide broader insight into America's complicated relationship with alcohol.

An impressive array of literature exists already on the development of ideas of addiction and particularly alcoholism in this period.[7] The "hybrid" nature of excessive drinking, "part vice, part disease," as characterized by one historian, made it a particularly fruitful means for physicians to comment on physiological characteristics and broader social phenomena.[8] The primary literature reflects the ways in which the moral and medical sense of heavy drinking overlapped from the years of the early American republic. The historiography on alcoholism notes the process of incomplete medicalization that remains with us into the present day. More specifically, recent historians have demonstrated how ideas of individual agency have influenced medical models.[9] Other historians have demonstrated how the cultural function of drinking has impacted views on alcohol in American society.[10] It is in this intersection of medical knowledge and cultural understanding that I approached my research.

Interestingly, I did not set out at first to write about murder at all. Rather, I was intrigued by how physicians in this era defined a state of intoxication and how such knowledge was accepted or rejected by various members of society. Attitudes toward drinking, as well as drinking behavior itself, are determined, to some degree, by the cultural and historical moment.[11] Physicians brought their own ideas of scientific principles, as well as their specific social concerns related to gender, race, and class, to a medicalized sense of heavy drinking. Drinkers, their families, temperance workers, members of the legal profession, and others alternatively influenced and incorporated emerging medical sensibilities of alcohol use into their own sense of the impact of alcohol on American society. As I pored through the medical journals, I found myself drawn to physicians' descriptions of murder cases. The details themselves were compelling and quite revealing of nineteenth-century American life.

But more importantly, the adversarial system of a well-publicized trial provided a useful medium to explore a variety of opinions on the nature and impact of heavy drinking. The bulk of cases that form the backbone of this project tell of acts of murder that occurred while the offenders were, by their own admission, affected in some way by alcohol use.

Murder trials, in particular, offer a rich sense of competing viewpoints in American society. "Murder," cultural historian Karen Halttunen has noted, "thus demands some kind of cultural work through which the community can come to terms with the crime—to confront what has happened and endeavor to explain it, in order to move past the incident to restore order to the world."[12] The nature of a trial—the process itself—demands a variety of voices. In many of these cases, friends, neighbors, families, and the defendants themselves were granted an opportunity to offer their interpretations of events alongside those of legal professionals and expert witnesses. By the end of the eighteenth century, Halttunen observes, "the cultural authority to interpret murder diffused among a diverse array of new voices, as printers and hack writers, sentimental poets and even murderers themselves seized from the ministry the task of assigning meaning to the crime of murder for the American reading public."[13] The multitude of perspectives documented in a public trial point to a more nuanced understanding of the mental and physiological consequences of drinking that, at times, created room for sympathy and even an "excuse" for the intoxicated offender.

The number of cases to choose from is, sadly, prodigious. It was not unusual to be searching for information on a particular case in a historical newspaper only to be distracted by similar tales of murder and drunkenness that emerged in the search or even appeared on the same page as another act of violent crime. Generally, I took my cue from established medical and legal journals as I chose which cases to write about. Physicians and legal scholars were most vocal when there was a lack of consensus; for physicians, disagreement threatened their fragile professional status, and for jurists, precedent was essential. Newspapers provided an additional window into social and cultural perceptions. And while I'm sure the defendant would heartily disagree, the verdict was not always the most significant piece of evidence. A great deal was to be learned in the arguments, the testimony, and the instructions of the court. Defense attorneys noted the "insane" behavior of their clients; they pecked away at intent; they sought mercy from the jury for what they argued was a good man ruined by alcohol. Medical testimony could be significant, but it was clear that friends and neighbors often felt well qualified themselves to judge a man to be a deviant, a lunatic, or a victim of alcohol.

Society, however, weighed more than just the effects of alcohol in criminal cases; the social identity of the drinker was just as important. The nineteenth century has been characterized as a period in which a certain class of Americans (largely white and middle class) sought to bring order to what they viewed as an increasingly disordered world. Temperance was described as an essential quality for the self-made man, the breadwinner for his family, and alcohol undermined a middle-class family ideal based on male authority and economic independence.[14] Acts of murder provided particularly acute reminders of the dangers of alcohol use and its threat to this vision of society. Not surprisingly then, most of the cases in this book focus on defendants who were white and male as they were the ones most likely to be the object of temperance reform, the focus of medical theories related to alcohol, and the subject of a contentious trial. Despite their participation in temperance, Black men and women were more likely to be excluded from the mainstream movement and the traditional temperance narrative.[15] And especially for the crime of murder, Black Americans were much less likely to face a fair trial, be judged by their peers, or even make it to trial. The decision-making power of juries meant that decisions on guilt and punishment too often reflected racial prejudices as much as, or more than, they did the law.[16]

Cases of women murderers were certainly less common, especially those characterized by the physical and impulsive violence that too often accompanied drunken murder, and women were less likely to be able to effectively use drunkenness as a mitigating factor. The middle-class gender ideology that characterized the nineteenth century cast women as moral exemplars providing safe harbor from the male public sphere. Women's drunkenness was more likely to act as reaffirmation of an immoral character and was generally judged much more harshly in women than in men. In fact, Scott C. Martin has identified "a strand of misogyny" in temperance thought that at times was characterized by "denunciations of women as causes of intemperance and snares for men, or the celebration of their victimization."[17] Women were more likely to be portrayed as victims of men's intemperance.

The question of responsibility while intoxicated has undeniably been subject to competing meanings, particularly as social customs and moral judgments bump up against the particular circumstances of an individual case. The prevalence of drinking in nineteenth-century American culture, along with changes in the fields of medicine and the law, led to a probing of the still unresolved question of how responsible an individual should be for actions committed while under the influence of alcohol. The following chapters trace this history from a gradual expansion of the mitigating possibilities of drunkenness to a backlash against a defense based on intoxication by century's end.

The first chapter begins in the early years of the nineteenth century, when the law more definitively held that intoxication provided no defense to crime. The reasoning was that the decision to drink was voluntary; therefore, an individual was responsible for any ensuing actions. The only exception under the law and recognized by physicians was if a long-sustained habit of intemperance led to a settled, or permanent, insanity that was no longer distinguishable from any other type of insanity. The growing field of medical jurisprudence offered a path to medical professionalization and authority. Historian James Mohr describes how the spectacle of a trial offered an arena for the doctor to publicly use his knowledge and skills to act as a "hero" to the community. And while many physicians did obtain just such a role, for example, confirming the insanity of deceased family members who had left inequitable wills, the relationship between medicine and criminal law took place in a much murkier arena.[18] The "discovery" of delirium tremens, a temporary form of insanity caused by heavy drinking, physicians argued, required the expertise of the physician to diagnose. Delirium tremens became a viable defense to murder and set an example for a consideration of intent when the offender was intoxicated. However, delirium tremens remained subject to competing interpretations by the medical and legal fields, as well as by the general public.

Chapter 2 builds on the precedent set by these cases and examines the impact that the social and cultural perceptions of the "drunkard," promoted by temperance organizations, had on ideas of intoxication and responsibility. Stories of drunkenness were prevalent by midcentury in temperance tracts and works of fiction, as well as in real-life accounts of drinking and crime. Alcohol was cast as the "demon rum" in these stories, a force that brought down men and destroyed families. Narratives of uncontrollable behavior and violence served both as a warning for those who considered imbibing and as titillation for the public. Gender assumptions were central to most of these stories, as women were portrayed simultaneously as the voice of morality and the victims of the alcohol habit inasmuch as the "drunkard" was understood to be male. Temperance tales certainly did not excuse murderers from the consequences of their actions, but they did contribute to a framework in which to consider that guilt might be limited by, or shared with, intoxicating drink.

The third chapter builds on the exculpatory possibilities of intoxication by examining changes in the law. At the end of the eighteenth century, a number of states began to revise their statutes on murder, creating a system in which charges were divided by degree with corresponding sentencing. As the question of intent became more relevant to the charge of murder itself, the effect of intoxication on the offender became a key point of fact to be argued. A defendant who could convince a jury that intoxication had made it impossible to form the necessary mens rea required of the charge could face reduced punishment or even acquittal.

Turning back to the medical profession, chapter 4 focuses on the overlap between the rise and fall of moral insanity and medico-legal understandings of drunkenness. Medicalizing the alcohol habit became linked to the increasingly contentious atmosphere surrounding an expansion of the diagnosis of insanity, as it suggested that heavy drinking could be characterized as a mental condition that abrogated responsibility. Defenses based on moral insanity, and more specifically dipsomania, proliferated and were often accepted by courts of law and juries despite the factious and often public debates within the medical profession. Professional disagreement was most notably exemplified in the famous Gray-Ray debate between two leaders in the field of mental illness, John P. Gray and Isaac Ray.

Chapter 5 further reviews the expansion of diagnoses related to the alcohol habit concurrent with a continuing backlash against allowing drunkenness to potentially mitigate or even excuse crime. Attempts to diagnose heavy drinking were often characterized as a defense of immoral behavior, and what was viewed as a greater concern for society often took precedence over controvertible medical expertise. In many cases, juries rejected a defense based on diagnoses such as moral insanity or dipsomania as they weighed justice for the individual offender against protection of the social order. This chapter examines several cases that demonstrate how decisions were affected by the differing and complicated environments in which they were reached.

Finally, chapter 6 seeks to build a bridge to the twentieth and twenty-first centuries. The diagnosis of inebriety foreshadowed later conceptions of alcoholism as a somewhat unique diagnosis, generally outside the purview of insanity itself, at times challenged by and at times overlapping with ideas of vice and morality. The chapter ends with two murder cases in 1881, not coincidentally the same year that Charles J. Guiteau sought an insanity defense for assassinating President James A. Garfield. A comparison of these trials suggests the ways in which a defense based on intoxication, as well as the insanity defense more generally, had become less palatable by the end of the century.

Historically, intoxication has presented a unique challenge to the courts and today, according to one legal scholar, remains a "jumbled mess" in legal systems throughout the world.[19] This study certainly cannot straighten out that mess, but hopefully it will provide a greater understanding as to how it got that way.

Chapter 1

"Not the Intended Result of Drink"

In his pamphlet *An Enquiry into the Effects of Spiritous Liquors upon the Human Body, and Their Influence upon the Happiness of Society*, Benjamin Rush linked the use of "spiritous liquors," or distilled alcohol, to a "number of new diseases" observed by physicians.[1] First published in 1784 and intended for a popular audience, the *Enquiry* provided a mix of medical information on the effects of alcohol and practical advice to "reject spirits from being a part of our drinks."[2] His admonition against the excessive use of spirits relied on a detailed summary of its immediate and chronic physical effects, which included "a sickness of the stomach," "dropsy," "obstruction of the liver," "palsy," and "apoplexy." Speaking more directly to the mental effects of spiritous liquors and the concomitant social disruption, Rush noted it "unnecessary to describe" the disease of "Madness . . . with all its terrors and consequences," as it "is well known in every township, where spiritous liquors are used."[3]

Rush was one of the first and certainly one of the more well-known medical professionals in the United States to outline the harmful effects of alcohol. As a graduate of the University of Edinburgh, one of the signers of the Declaration of Independence, former surgeon general of the Continental Army, and respected professor at the University of Pennsylvania, Rush was a man whose opinions garnered attention. His *Medical Inquiries and Observations upon Diseases of the Mind*, published in 1812, was the first systematic textbook on mental diseases, later earning him the sobriquet "The Father of American Psychiatry."[4] Rush's publications and lectures also highlight the ways in which the practice of medicine began its transformation into a respected and influential profession in this period. Some of this nascent activity occurred in the development of medical societies, schools, and, eventually, licensure requirements.[5] Medical jurisprudence, existing as an inchoate field at the turn of the century, provided a fruitful outlet for securing a role for the medical profession. Rush manifested this budding interest in the contribution of medicine to law, speaking in 1810 on the issue of legal insanity in an important lecture, published the following year, at the University of Pennsylvania.[6] His long attention to the subject of the mind led him to view the subject of insanity as a fertile means to expand the medical profession just as it fueled his consideration of the effects of alcohol upon both body and mind.

Given the levels of heavy drinking Rush witnessed during the American Revolution and later in the backwoods country of Pennsylvania, it is not surprising to find that Rush supported temperance, both politically in his support of the tax on whiskey and in his medical practice. Furthermore, Rush's attention to intemperance reflected a number of significant trends in early America—adherence to Enlightenment ideas applied to medicine, faith in the principles of the Great Awakening, and a commitment to a republican form of government. Scientific observations provided ballast for both his medical conclusions and his political ideology. He feared that the use of spirits meant that "the republic would soon be in danger" from "men, chosen by intemperate and corrupted voters." He viewed intemperance as an avoidable social ill and called upon "ministers of the gospel" to "denounce, by your preaching, conversation and examples, the seducing influence of toddy and grog, when you aim to prevent all the crimes and miseries, which are the offspring of strong drink."[7]

Rush's understanding of the alcohol habit, along with many others of his time, reflected a complicated mix of the medical, moral, and personal. Throughout the course of his life, he had witnessed firsthand the effects of alcohol on his community and especially on the lives of his patients. That Rush believed these effects went beyond physical impairment is demonstrated by the chart "Moral and Physical Thermometer," which was added to the *Enquiry* by 1790 to increase the pamphlet's appeal to a general readership.[8] This "scale of the progress of Temperance and Intemperance" reinforced the consequences of intemperance, which were delineated into three categories—vices, diseases, and punishments. In one version, those who ventured past strong beer and ingested morning drams or rum might exhibit physical signs of epilepsy, melancholy or palsy, culminating in death. Vices escalated from "idleness" and "swearing" to "fraud" and "hatred of just gov't," eventually leading to murder or suicide. A similar range of punishments ended with the "gallows."[9]

The connections between violence and intemperance were apparent to Rush, who spoke of a man cured of the "desire for ardent spirits" after attempting to murder his beloved wife. "Upon being told of it when he was sober," recounts Rush, "he was so struck with the enormity of the crime he had nearly committed, that he never tasted spiritous liquors afterwards."[10] Alongside the chart, accounts such as these demonstrate a faith in providing warnings of both the physiological and behavioral consequences of drinking as a means to discourage intemperance. As Rush's examples suggest, the "habit" of drinking that attracted the attention and expertise of physicians in the early nineteenth century was both a social problem and a medical concern. And in the following decades, it would be in the hard-to-define line between insanity and intoxication where medical and legal determinations confronted one another in the aftermath of violent crime.

Criminal cases involving intoxication at first drew scant attention from physicians, including those who foresaw the value of medical expertise in a legal setting. At the turn of the century, insanity was only one aspect of an emerging field of medical jurisprudence in which physicians concerned themselves with a variety of matters including toxicology, causes of death, signs of rape, infanticide, and legitimacy.[11] A scientifically based inquiry into methods of poisoning, the nature of wounds, and even the timing of a pregnancy often served as key evidence in civil and criminal cases. Determining mental competence likewise proved imperative in matters of contracts and wills.[12] Criminal matters, however, posed a greater challenge. An evaluation of a suspect's mental state that offered the possibility of a mitigated sentence or even an acquittal suggested a

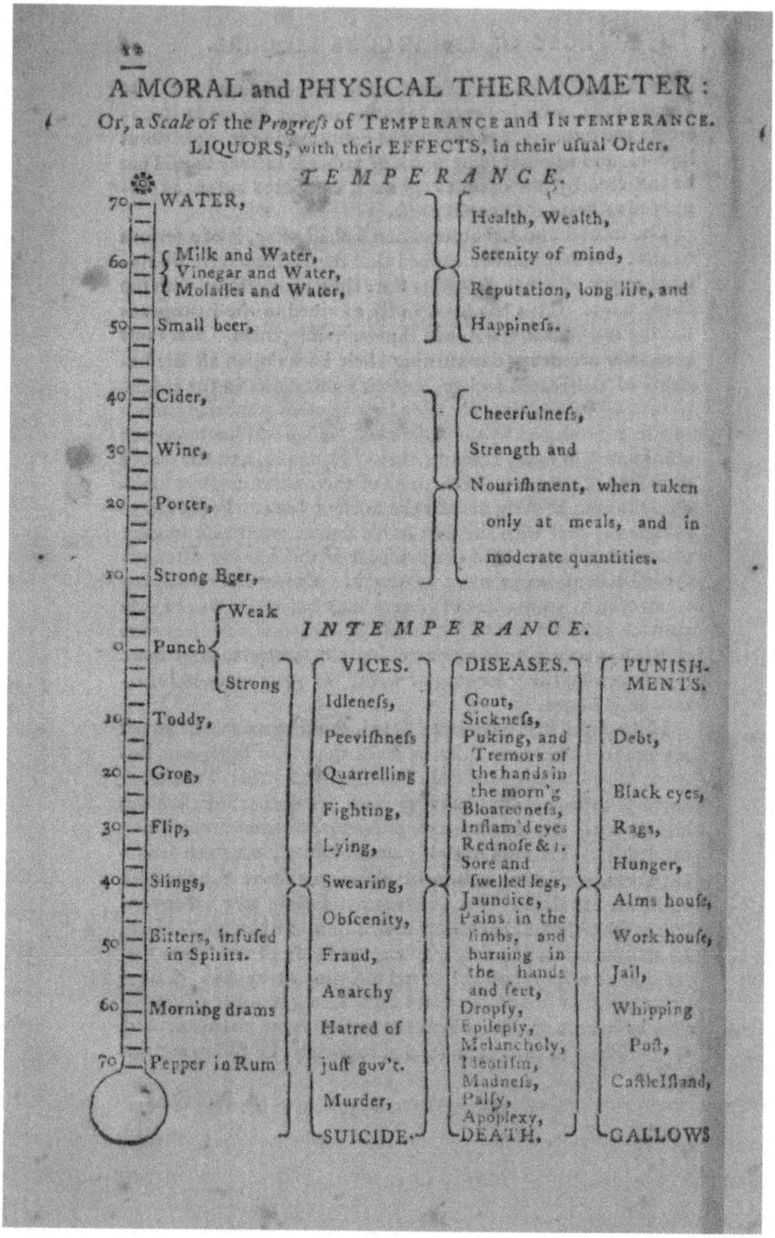
12

A MORAL and PHYSICAL THERMOMETER:

Or, a *Scale* of the *Progress* of TEMPERANCE and INTEMPERANCE.

LIQUORS, with their EFFECTS, in their usual Order.

TEMPERANCE.

	Liquors	Effects
70	WATER,	Health, Wealth, Serenity of mind, Reputation, long life, and Happiness.
60	Milk and Water, Vinegar and Water, Molasses and Water,	
50	Small beer,	
40	Cider,	Cheerfulness, Strength and Nourishment, when taken only at meals, and in moderate quantities.
30	Wine,	
20	Porter,	
10	Strong Beer,	

INTEMPERANCE.

	Liquors	VICES.	DISEASES.	PUNISHMENTS.
0	Punch — Weak / Strong	Idleness,	Gout,	
10	Toddy,	Peevishness	Sickness, Puking, and Tremors of the hands in the morn'g	Debt,
20	Grog,	Quarrelling	Bloatedness,	Black eyes,
30	Flip,	Fighting,	Inflam'd eyes	Rags,
40	Slings,	Lying,	Red nose & f.	Hunger,
50	Bitters, infused in Spirits.	Swearing,	Sore and swelled legs,	Alms house,
60	Morning drams	Obscenity,	Jaundice,	Work house,
70	Pepper in Rum	Fraud,	Pains in the limbs, and burning in the hands and feet,	Jail,
		Anarchy	Dropsy,	Whipping Post,
		Hatred of just gov't.	Epilepsy,	Castle Island,
		Murder,	Melancholy,	
			Idiotism,	
			Madness,	
			Palsy,	
			Apoplexy,	
		SUICIDE.	DEATH.	GALLOWS

FIGURE 1. Benjamin Rush, "A Moral and Physical Thermometer," *An Inquiry into the Effects of Spiritous Liquors on the Human Body and the Mind*, 1790. Courtesy of the Library Company of Philadelphia.

different medical conception of individual responsibility. Few physicians sought to challenge existing legal tenets and prevailing cultural norms.

Theodric Romeyn Beck, an early and influential expert in the field of medical jurisprudence, included the topic of insanity in his 1811 dissertation at the College of Physicians and Surgeons in New York City. He was motivated by the hope that a careful study of insanity would result in a more humane system of care and treatment for patients.[13] After more than a decade of a relatively unremarkable career, Beck gained notoriety in 1823 with the publication of *Elements of Medical Jurisprudence*, which served as a reliable guide not only for the American medical profession but the legal one as well. Filling a palpable need for a summary of the current field of medical jurisprudence, the text received overwhelming praise and attention, becoming the "national standard" as a medico-legal reference in the courts.[14] The *American Jurist and Law Magazine* affirmed that before Beck's publication, "there was no systematic work in our language, which could be recommended to the student at law" on medical jurisprudence. By this point, scientific knowledge had become essential to an understanding of "the nature of diseases, the effects of violence upon the human system, and the vast variety of causes which produce death." Issues of insanity, particularly, it was noted, "form a most important class."[15]

Alcohol use, however, remained peripheral to the field of insanity and the concerns of medical jurisprudence. In Beck's two-volume set, an entire chapter was dedicated to the issue of "Mental Alienation"; less than two pages of that chapter address the issue of intoxication. According to Beck, intoxication exists as one of the "inferior degrees of diseased mind" that also include delirium of fever, hypochondriasis, hallucination, epilepsy, and nostalgia. Each of these is listed by name in the table of contents, and its relation to a determination of legal insanity is explicated in the text. While "repeated intoxication" was noted as one of the "remote causes" of insanity, the medico-legal definition of insanity offered by Beck explicitly excluded intoxication as a distinct form of insanity: "Intoxication—its presence does not excuse from guilt of crimes—a frequent cause of insanity." Beck acknowledged the medical wisdom of the time, which accepted habitual drunkenness as a potential cause of insanity, but he exhibited some trepidation that intoxication might be equated with legal insanity.[16] He validated the current rule of law, stating, "It is a well known and salutary maxim in our laws, that crimes committed under the influence of intoxication, do not excuse the perpetrator from punishment." A staunch proponent of the value of medical expertise in legal matters, Beck recognized the complexity of the issue as he predicted that "the partition line between intoxication and insanity may hence sometimes become a subject of discussion."[17] Here Beck is quite prescient if ultimately understated.

The problematic distinction between intoxication and insanity is exemplified in the case of William McDonough, who was found guilty of murdering his wife, Elizabeth, in Massachusetts in 1817.[18] According to testimony from the trial, the defendant reportedly suffered from bouts of insanity due to "a severe injury of the head" years earlier, but a determination of McDonough's responsibility under the law was complicated by his drinking habit. In a discussion of the case, Beck concluded that "the use of spiritous liquors immediately induced a return of the paroxysms, and in one of them thus induced, he murdered his wife." He did not dispute that a condition of insanity existed, but he did argue that this state of mind, induced by drink, was well known to the defendant and thus not unanticipated. Beck was therefore in agreement with the guilty verdict because McDonough knowingly brought a state of drunkenness upon himself that led to his insanity at the time of the crime: "The *voluntary* use of a stimulus which he was well aware would disorder his mind, fully placed him under the purview of the law."[19] In this early reference, the voluntary nature of the act of drinking, along with the assumption that the consequences were known to McDonough, negated any exculpatory influence that his insanity may have otherwise had under the law. The perceived willfulness in the decision to drink tipped the scale from insanity to drunkenness and, consequently, legal responsibility.

Additional accounts of the trial suggest that the court similarly struggled with the distinction between insanity and intoxication as the testimony of friends, neighbors, and medical experts offered a careful parsing of McDonough's behavior. According to Charles Fiche, who had been present earlier on the evening of the murder, McDonough was "very intemperate," and had already been drinking when his wife arrived home around nine o'clock. Fiche saw no signs of "peculiarity" in the defendant's behavior, affirming, "when sober, he was harmless; when drunk, he quarreled with nobody but his wife."[20] Fanny Johnson also appeared uninclined to accept McDonough's claim of insanity. Blaming his bad behavior on seemingly nothing more than the effects of drinking, she noted, "he was often intoxicated and troublesome among the neighbors."[21] However, Joseph Stokes, for whom the defendant worked, testified that "Mac" was "not in his right senses" and, along with several other witnesses, observed that McDonough would stamp, strike his head, tear his hair, and unexpectedly start and stop when telling stories. There did seem to be a general agreement that McDonough was easily affected by alcohol, but whether his actions were a result of a disordered mind was not clear. Stokes suggested that McDonough was particularly affected by alcohol due to his head injury; however, in the end he was unable to provide a definitive assessment, noting, "He was odd; but I could not say whether it was the effect of drinking or not."[22] Daniel Kidder, similarly unsure, stated, "I supposed he was intoxicated but upon better examination thought he was in a delirium."[23]

The counsel for the defense, appealing to expert knowledge, called on Dr. George Parkman to "distinguish insanity from drunkenness." Parkman, later the infamous victim of John Webster, had authored two papers, *Remarks on Insanity* and *The Management of Lunatics,* that same year and testified that McDonough's symptoms and medical history were consistent with a diagnosis of insanity. Observable symptoms, Parkman assured the jury, such as "staggering and thick speech" and an attempt to "hide the obscured state of his intellect," separated the drunkard from an insane person. The defendant's behaviors, as described by witnesses, such as shaking his head and starting suddenly, he noted, were common symptoms in such cases. McDonough had also relayed a history of treatment for mental disorders which Parkman assessed as reliable. The defendant had been injured at the age of twelve and was in and out of St. George's Hospital in London where he was bled and treated with diet. When questioned by the chief justice, Parkman could not confirm McDonough's insanity was due to the injury but responded that he "discovered nothing else in his history from which it is likely to have originated." In the end, however, it fell to the jury to weigh all of the testimony to determine "the line between sanity and insanity." They returned a verdict of guilty.[24]

In 1818 Michael Clarke was tried and also found guilty for the shooting murder of his wife in Washington, D.C., Clarke had a history of drinking and was intoxicated at the time of the crime. The defense argued for insanity claiming that the defendant "from long and settled habits of intemperance, had become disordered, both in body and mind, and subject to fits which affected both his mind and body." Although chronic intemperance was recognized by physicians as a possible cause of a settled state of insanity, the defense had the onus of proving that Clarke was "at all times, when not under the influence of liquor, of unsound mind."[25] It was critical to establish that the insanity was permanent and not brought on only when Clarke had been drinking. The judge, however, created an even greater burden of proof, suggesting that the defendant's state of mind during the commission of the crime must be clearly and solely attributable to insanity and not intoxication. The judge instructed the jury that "they should be satisfied, by the evidence, that the prisoner at the time of committing the act charged in the indictment, was in such a state of mental insanity, not produced by the immediate effects of intoxicating drink, as not to have been conscious of the moral turpitude of the act." The jury, thus charged with the mind-boggling task of separating the influence of alcohol from the influence of insanity on the defendant's behavior, returned a guilty verdict and a sentence of death.[26]

In the cases of McDonough and Clarke, intoxication not only failed to provide an excuse for crime; it served to negate what may have been an otherwise effective insanity defense. The complicating circumstances of drunkenness at this time were more likely to undermine a defense based on insanity, given not only the difficulty of separating one from the other but the reluctance of juries to do so. Even before the adoption of the 1843 M'Naghten rule, the courts often considered the defendant's ability to distinguish right from wrong as a key element to prove a defense based on insanity—unless of course it was alcohol that had clouded that judgment.[27] The assertion that alcohol provided no excuse to crime presupposed that the decision to drink was voluntary and that the resulting state of intoxication was foreseeable. Despite arguable similarities between the irrational behavior exhibited under conditions of insanity and intoxication, the "fault rationale" meant the latter condition was an exception to the law governing insanity.[28]

As medical experts turned their attention to a study of the more insidious effects of alcohol, they began to highlight symptoms that were sometimes unanticipated and beyond the control of ordinary drinkers, challenging a legal system that assumed intoxication was voluntary and predictable. In his oft-cited article, Harry Gene Levine has argued that before the late eighteenth century, "the assumption was that people drank and got drunk because they wanted to, and not because they 'had' to." The drunkard's actions were perceived to be the consequence of a decision made by one who knew right from wrong when sober, and thus intoxication provided no exculpatory value. By the turn of the century, however, the alcohol habit was more likely to be viewed as "a progressive disease—the chief symptom of which is loss of control over drinking behavior." This conception rested not only on the increased scrutiny of physicians but on the fears of a middle-class society seeking to emphasize individual responsibility.[29] It also had the effect of challenging a more straightforward sense of individual volition and responsibility as early advocates struggled to differentiate between vice and disease.[30] The field of medicine began to expand further just what could be considered the unintended consequences of intoxication.

Early references to drunkenness as a disease were expounded by British physician Thomas Trotter, who first wrote on the subject in 1804 for his University of Edinburgh MD dissertation, *An Essay, Medical, Philosophical, and Chemical, on Drunkenness and Its Effects on the Human Body*. Recognizing that a medical study of drunkenness was a novelty, he maintained that it was an important topic of research because the "habit of inebriation" was "so common in society, to be observed in all ranks and stations of life." Furthermore, "the physical influence of custom, confirmed into habit, interwoven with the actions of our sentient system, and reacting on our mental part" made the mental effects of habitual drinking a proper subject for physicians.[31] Trotter acknowledged "the difficulty of fixing on any symptom, or even concourse of symptoms, that are invariably present," but he did place particular emphasis on the delirium of drunkenness, characterized by "imbecility of intellect, erroneous judgment, violent emotions; and loss of sense and motion."[32] Rush similarly noted that intemperance could pose a challenge to individual volition: "The use of strong drink is at first the effect of free agency. From habit it takes place from necessity."[33] It is likely an overreach to too closely correlate early conceptions of the alcohol habit with modern understandings of alcoholism. At this early date, medical descriptions, like those provided by Rush, were presented primarily as an impetus to change for the drunkard and a warning for others who might imitate the habit.

As physicians were progressively exploring the mechanism of habitual drinking and contributing to the development of the field of medical jurisprudence, observations of the disease of delirium tremens began to appear in the medical records. Delirium tremens was first categorized as a form of insanity caused by heavy drinking in the late 1810s and was referred to by a variety of different names, including *mania a potu*, *mania a temulentia*, and *febris temulenta*.[34] The development of this particular disease aspect of heavy drinking straddled an earlier acceptance of excessive drinking as a remote cause of settled insanity and a developing sense of an uncontrollable "habit" or "craving" for alcohol. While physicians had already established that insanity could be caused by excessive drinking, such insanity, once settled, was not clearly differentiated from any other type of insanity resulting from a myriad of other causes. Delirium tremens, on the other hand, existed as a distinct and temporary form of insanity clearly attributable to excessive and habitual intoxication. It was a form of alcoholic insanity, yet one that did not always limit itself to the symptoms of withdrawal with which it is associated today. Attention to the physical and mental symptoms of delirium tremens further expanded the purview of medical knowledge on the consequences of heavy drinking. Intemperance became not just one of many possible causes of insanity, but one that could create a distinctive mental state that required the expertise of a physician to diagnose and treat.

In 1818 Dr. Joseph Klapp described the pathology of a form of temulent disease produced by "the inordinate use of ardent liquors."[35] Klapp's detailed cases reveal how a diagnosis of delirium tremens contributed to emerging medical understandings of intemperance as a disease. Unlike other types of insanity, dissections revealed that those "who have died with madness from intemperance" carried "no mark of disease whatever . . . in the brain, when both the liver and stomach have been inflamed." Rather, he observed the similarity of the gastric nature of the disease brought on by intemperance and those brought on by "other irritants."[36] Up to this point, diseases had generally been classified according to their symptoms, and mental illness could potentially result from a variety of causes, including intemperance; delirium tremens, on the other hand, historian Matthew Warner Osborn notes, was "unique" among diseases because it was classified according to "a singular cause: habitual heavy drinking."[37] Klapp professed optimism in the possibility of achieving a cure through medical knowledge; noting "dyspeptic symptoms," and a connection to "gastric pathology," in relying on a treatment of emetics.[38]

Delirium tremens, as a medical pathology, was a subject of interest for physicians and, as a form of insanity, fell under the purview of the growing field of medical jurisprudence.[39] Describing an "insanity produced by intemperance," an 1830 article in the *American Jurist and Law Magazine* explained the essential, if somewhat murky, legal distinction between intoxication and insanity caused by excessive drinking: "The law discriminates between the delirium of intoxication and the insanity which it sometimes produces. While the drunkenness continues, the person under its influence is responsible as a moral agent, though reason in the meantime has lost her dominion; but when the intoxication ceases, if insanity immediately follow as a consequence of the vice, he is, in the eye of criminal justice, no longer amenable for his acts."[40] While drunkenness itself did not obviate legal responsibility, insanity caused by intemperance, it was argued, should be treated as any other form of insanity under the law. Even as demarcating the boundary between insanity and drunkenness had proved to be quite challenging, as in the cases of McDonough and Clarke, the new disease of delirium tremens began to expand the circumstances under which an individual might make a case for an involuntary and exculpatory lack of intent. The state of delirium tremens here was described as "a species of madness which often deprives the sufferer of the power of distinguishing between right and wrong" but crucially exists apart from a state of intoxication.[41] Unlike insanity, it was not a permanent or "settled" state of mind, but unlike intoxication, it was not deemed a foreseeable consequence of intemperance. Drunkenness continued to be no excuse for crime, but the resulting disease of delirium tremens, a condition that required the expertise of medical men to recognize, might absolve one of legal responsibility.

The *American Jurist* article continues to discuss one of the earliest cases to successfully employ delirium tremens as a legal defense in the United States, the case of *U.S. v. Drew*. Alexander Drew, the commander of the whaling ship *John Jay*, stood accused of killing his second mate, Charles F. Clark, on September 1, 1827. When Clark responded to a request to go on deck by declaring that he would first finish his breakfast, Drew stabbed him with a knife he had concealed under his jacket. He then fired his pistol, but missed, at the ship's cooper, George Galloway, before being restrained by the crew. Clark died later at a Spanish port.[42] If Drew had been merely drunk, his resulting mental state would be considered irrelevant or even an "aggravation" of the crime. If Drew were insane, he could be exonerated; however, a number of factors suggested that a traditional defense of insanity would have been ill suited to this case. The defendant had no history of insanity and was described as a "respected" man of "fair character," and "a man of humane and benevolent disposition." He also had a reputation as a heavy drinker. Two witnesses who had been present on board ship and had observed Drew's actions in the days before the crime testified that the captain had been drinking heavily in the last days of August 1827, noting that Drew "often indulged to excess in spirituous liquors" and specifically "for weeks during the voyage had drunk to excess." The captain also seemed to have regained full use of his faculties several weeks later, when he "appeared to be in his right mind." His drinking and subsequent intoxication, dating back several months, appeared voluntary in nature.[43]

However, the defense argued not that Drew was insane from intoxication when he committed the crime, drunkenness providing no excuse, but rather that he was insane due to delirium tremens, a condition that arises after intoxication has ceased.[44] Crucial testimony established that, at some point during the voyage, Drew apparently made a resolution to abstain and subsequently ordered that all liquor be thrown overboard. It was two or three days later that he began to manifest odd behavior including being unable to eat or sleep, countermanding his own orders, and exhibiting verbal outbursts and paranoia. Such actions, it was observed, suggested "physical weakness and alienation of mind," rather than drunkenness. On the night of August 31, Drew attempted to jump overboard but was stopped by Galloway, who testified as the first witness in the case. Additional evidence of insanity was proffered by a witness who described Drew's appearance as "that of a foolish person" and noted that, after being seized, bound, and placed under guard by the crew, "his whole demeanor, for some time after, was that of an insane person."[45]

After hearing the first two witnesses, Judge Joseph Story stopped the proceedings, opining that "the indictment upon these admitted facts cannot be maintained" because the "prisoner was unquestionably insane at the time of committing the offence." At this time, Story, a renowned jurist who is most remembered for his decision in the *Amistad* case in 1841, was serving as a member of the U.S. Supreme Court but continued to cover the New England circuit. The judge's opinion on the exculpatory nature of insanity was unequivocal: "insanity is an excuse of the commission of every crime, because the party has not the possession of that reason, which includes responsibility." He acknowledged that intoxication is an "exception" to the rule of law concerning insanity because it allows "a man to avail himself of the excuse of his own gross vice and misconduct," but such an "exception" applies only when the crime was committed as "the immediate result of the fit of intoxication" rather than as a consequence of insanity caused by heavy drinking. At this point, there was little argument from counsel on either side, and the jury returned an immediate verdict of not guilty.[46] Story's record demonstrates that he ordinarily had little sympathy for the inebriate criminal, and in an earlier case he asserted that he viewed drunkenness as an "aggravation" of crime.[47] Clearly, Story accepted that the period between Drew's cessation of drinking and the crime created a delay that allowed for a clear distinction between the effects of drunkenness and a state of insanity. The circumstances in this case are certainly unique in that the inability to obtain alcohol, after Drew's disposal of the ship's supply, was more probable at sea than in most other cases.

Physicians had long held that chronic intemperance was one of many causes that could lead to a state of insanity—a determination that was accepted under the strictures of medical jurisprudence. From a legal point of view as well, the cause of a state of established insanity was largely irrelevant, as "the law looks to the immediate, and not to the remote cause; to the actual state of the party, and not to the causes which remotely produced it." Yet according to the testimony at the trial, Drew's insanity had not been established more than a few days before the incident, and he was described as "in his right mind" just a few weeks later. The judge ruled, nevertheless, that this manifestation of mental disease fell under a definition of insanity that precluded legal responsibility. Drew's particular form of insanity in this case was viewed as a "remote consequence" of intoxication despite its seemingly temporary nature. While questioning the morality of indulgence in liquor, the judge determined that Drew was not intoxicated at the time of the crime but rather was "merely insane from an abstinence from liquor" and thus should be acquitted.[48]

The influence of the developing field of medical jurisprudence, buoyed by Beck's publication, is apparent in this case even as the source of medical expertise lay outside the courtroom itself. Story's decision appears to be based on a contemporary medico-legal understanding of delirium tremens. While the judge did not employ "delirium tremens" or any of its related medical terms in his decision, subsequent interpretations of the case were clear.[49] Drew's condition was specifically characterized as "delirium tremens" in contemporaneous publications, and the case of *U.S. v. Drew* was used as an early example of "the effect of delirium tremens on responsibility, the principles and practice of American courts" in Isaac Ray's later *A Treatise on the Medical Jurisprudence of Insanity*.[50]

Previously physicians had seemed reluctant to suggest that the effects of intoxication could mitigate responsibility unless a clear state of settled insanity was the result. Beck concurred with the guilty verdict in the McDonough case because of the voluntary nature of the act of drinking, which incited the resulting insanity. Clarke, likewise, was found guilty because of the difficulty of separating the effects of insanity and intoxication. However, a diagnosis of delirium tremens, defined as neither intoxication nor settled insanity, suggested that heavy drinking could induce a mental condition that did not fit comfortably in either category.

Judge Story relied on this third option, in which the vice of heavy drinking led to an unintended consequence, delirium tremens, for which the individual could not be held accountable, to rule for an acquittal for Alexander Drew.

The verdict in *U.S. v. Drew* represents a reconciling, albeit uneasy, of a moral condemnation of intemperance and a nuanced medico-legal definition of responsibility. Most newspapers reporting on the case ended their coverage of the trial with the acquittal. The *Christian Watchman*, however, included an account of the judge's words after the verdict: "The Judge then gave the prisoner a very solemn admonition on the effects of intemperance, reminding him that although not held responsible by law to a human tribunal, he would be to one infinitely higher at the last day, and ordered him to be discharged."[51] A report of the case also appeared in an 1833 collection of criminal cases subtitled "An awful warning to the youth of America being an account of the most horrid murders, piracies, highway robberies." In a presumed attempt to emphasize the tragic nature of the crime, the account is provided under the heading "Charles F. Clark," Drew's victim.[52] Yet the description of the case follows, virtually word for word, those of other public accounts and ends with the acquittal. While this report of the crime was meant to act as a cautionary tale, one might also suspect that any potential moral lessons in this case competed with an evolving medico-legal sense of intent as it related to drunkenness.

An understanding of the effects and consequences of heavy drinking precariously straddled moral, medical, and legal interpretations. As physicians expanded their purview to the study of the effects of heavy drinking within the field of medical jurisprudence, their conclusions held some influence within the legal arena. Yet juries, and the public more generally, were often reluctant to accept the latest medical wisdom on the effects of habitual drinking. Daniel Drake, a well-known physician and temperance advocate, was one of the early contributors to the medical literature on delirium tremens, concurring with Klapp and others, that this disease represented a disorder of the stomach. Displaying the growing professional attention to the connections between alcohol and disease, he also recognized delirium tremens as one of "the mental diseases produced by intoxication" and professed faith in medical treatment.[53]

Drake's career exemplifies the expansion of the medical profession in America—both professionally and geographically. Characterized as "physician to the west" by one historian, he is today perhaps best known for his expansive study *A Systematic Treatise, Historical, Etiological, and Practical, on the Principal Diseases of the Interior Valley of North America.*[54] Although he had already completed a physician's apprenticeship and operated a successful medical practice in Cincinnati by the age of twenty, Drake traveled to Philadelphia to study under Benjamin Rush at the University of Pennsylvania. He received his medical degree in 1816 and then accepted an appointment to the faculty of the medical department at Transylvania University in Lexington, Kentucky. He later returned to Cincinnati, where he helped organize the Medical College of Ohio in 1819 and founded the *Western Journal of the Medical and Physical Sciences* in 1827.[55]

Drake took up the cause of temperance reform in the late 1820s. His interest in the subject, like that of his mentor Rush, reflected a complicated mix of medical and moral sensibilities fed by an awareness of American development. While Rush, influenced by his Revolutionary experience, was most concerned with political culture, the Western physician Drake included observations on the American environment and character in his scientific writings. Such a correlation would not have been unfamiliar to his fellow Americans who often fused the interaction of body and the environment in what one modern historian has referred to as a "geography of health."[56] Drake's ideas on intemperance were particularly informed by his concern over the increase in drinking in cities as well as by an assumption of the superiority of the white Anglo-Saxon race.[57] In an 1831 oration, Drake reassured his audience, "It is now generally admitted, that the use of Ardent Spirits, among the respectable classes of the eastern, middle and western states, has greatly diminished."[58] In fact, the "civilized life" could be explained by knowledge of human physiology, and the desire for stimulation that could be achieved with the consumption of alcohol was characterized as natural to humans. Drake observed, "In the savage state, the means of gratifying this desire, are few and feeble, in civilized life, they are diversified and abundant; and we find the desire for their use, correspondingly energetic. Their action upon us increases the appetite for them, and too often raises it to a state of morbid and ruinous importunity. This is conformable to an original law of our nature."[59]

Medical attention to the issue of intemperance built on an existing interpretation of alcohol consumption as a natural craving and a voluntary action, but one that was implicitly understood through developing nineteenth-century reform ideology. When faced with the question of what could be done to promote sobriety, Drake responded, "I answer, on the same basis, upon which the moralist rests his efforts, against the inordinate indulgence of any other propensity."[60] The cause of temperance was increasingly bolstered by scientific proof, long observed, of the physiological destruction wrought by alcohol. Some physicians even formed their own temperance organizations, and in 1841 Drake organized the Physiological Temperance Society of the Louisville Medical Institute to investigate the effects of alcohol on the system.

Included among the physical consequences of excessive drink were those that impaired the mental state. Drake reminded the public that intemperance "impairs the power of observation, weakens attention, renders the memory treacherous, excites the imagination, and subverts the understanding. Neither the observations nor the judgments of one in this condition, are to be trusted." Habitual intoxication, in particular, could result in a drinker becoming one who is "actually *insane*; and should no longer be held responsible, for his actions." The significance of these effects, especially as they persisted past a clear state of intoxication to challenge volition, was the point most hotly debated. Drake lamented that his view had not always been adopted in the criminal courts which "have confounded the *insanity* of drunkards, with their fits of *intoxication*, from which it is distinct; and punished the offences of both states, in the same manner."[61]

Drake's exposition on the consequences of alcoholic indulgence was surely meant to rally his audience to the temperance cause and not excuse the behavior of drunkards. He insisted that "Drunkenness in all its stages . . . should be met with appropriate penalties. The personal rights of those who practice it, should be restricted; their political consequences abridged; their children placed under guardians, and their property transferred to trustees. By the fear of these penalties, thousands would be deterred from becoming intemperate; while the friends and families, of those who might still drink to excess, would be screened, in part at least, from the calamities, which, in the absence of all protecting legislation, never fail to overtake them." Yet as his subject turned to the issue of medical jurisprudence, the argument shifted subtly. The drunkard, according to Drake, should be punished under the law, but "*he who is insane shall not be punished*," even when that insanity resulted from drinking.[62] How is the public to reconcile the call for punishment with the exception for those who have seemingly drunk themselves into a state of insanity? As delirium tremens was becoming increasingly accepted as a form of dementia by the medical community, physicians were suggesting that an exculpatory state of insanity might not only come on the heels of intoxication but also could be temporary in nature.

By the end of the 1820s, delirium tremens as a defense was embraced by a number of prominent physicians and members of the legal profession, but it was contentious and often discounted by the public. For Drake, a faith in temperance as a moral virtue and a commitment to reform were consistent with his advocacy of delirium tremens as a defense to murder. Drake was able to reconcile a condemnation of the alcohol habit with the belief that delirium tremens, the sometimes result of this habit, could render a criminal offender not responsible in the eyes of the law. He was dismayed to find in the trial and subsequent guilty verdict of John Birdsell that the public did not always share this point of view.[63]

In 1829 John Birdsell murdered his wife "by cutting through her neck from side to side, with a narrow axe, at a single blow" and faced a jury with the defense of insanity, that he was suffering from *mania a potu* (delirium tremens). A man of about fifty years of age and a resident of Harrison, Ohio, he had been married to his second wife for approximately twenty years at the time of the murder. Witnesses recounted that Birdsell had a history of intoxication dating back several years and had exhibited a variety of "physical and moral symptoms" that Drake viewed as consistent with a diagnosis of delirium tremens. Among these were tremors, paleness, red eyes, perspiration, and visual and auditory hallucinations. At times Birdsell believed he was surrounded by snakes and other reptiles, heard trumpets and vocal music, and imagined himself the subject of conversations. In particular, he experienced a profound fear that others were attempting to harm him. Most relevant to the crime was "his prevailing maniacal conception" that his wife was conspiring with others to kill him.[64]

The defendant's actions in the days leading up to the murder were presented as especially significant to distinguishing a state of delirium tremens from that of drunkenness. Birdsell drank and was intoxicated on the Sunday before the murder. There was no evidence that he continued to drink over the next three days, and on Wednesday evening he was ill complaining of stomach cramps but was described as rational. By the next day, Thursday, March 5, "his family thought him crazy." He told two different witnesses that he believed his wife was making plans to kill him, and he kept an ax by his side. By evening, he accused his wife of causing the deaths of thirty thousand men and believed others were in his loft making ropes with which to hang him. Later, after pacing about the room, Birdsell grabbed his ax and struck his wife dead in front of several of their children. He struck her twice more in the face before his oldest daughter began a struggle with him for the weapon. The younger children opened the latched door so that she could escape unharmed.[65]

That Birdsell did kill his wife was undisputed. In fact, Birdsell's past behavior and drinking habits, as well as the horrific nature of the crime itself, were intended to support the defense's argument that Birdsell was insane. Despite the success of the defense of delirium tremens in the case of Drew, there were two significant hurdles to a similar verdict for Birdsell. The court needed to not only accept that Birdsell was insane during the commission of the crime but also that this state of insanity, a consequence of his use of alcohol, was sufficiently distinct from the state of intoxication. It appears that the jury was convinced of neither. It was no easy feat to prove a murderer insane. The insanity defense was controversial throughout the nineteenth century (and remains so today). Despite the wild accusations Birdsell had leveled against his wife, witnesses also testified as to his rational behavior after the crime, so marked that Drake admitted "that many of the witnesses could not believe him deranged." The defendant exhibited some regret, noting he felt "bad" when his youngest child, held in his arms, "exclaimed, 'mamma bleeds!'" Yet he also swore "that he ought to have done it nine months sooner; and that if he had it to do again, he would strike two blows where he only struck one." Furthermore, Birdsell purportedly admitted shortly after the murder that he knew he would be hanged for the crime, an acknowledgment that he did indeed understand the consequences of his actions.[66]

At this point physicians had been describing delirium tremens as both a mental disease produced by intoxication and as a category of a variety of temulent diseases caused by gastric infirmity. In so doing, they looked beyond the cause to the symptoms that suggested delirium tremens was a form of insanity, and therefore one suffering from this illness should be held non compos and not responsible for his crimes in the eyes of the law.[67] Three physicians testified at trial that Birdsell was suffering from the disease of delirium tremens which, they argued, should be treated as insanity rather than intoxication under the law. Drake himself later testified for the defense at a motion for a new trial which was ultimately denied.[68]

It appears likely, however, that evidence of Birdsell's drinking history, intended by the defense to support a case of delirium tremens, cemented the idea that the defendant was responsible for his own bad habits. The decision of the jury, Drake recounts, was such "that they were not called upon to give an opinion, whether *Mania a potu* would, under any circumstances, be an excuse for the commission of a crime, but they feel no unwillingness to express their opinion, that if the insanity was the offspring of intemperance and the prisoner *knew* that intoxication would produce it, he could not plead it as an apology."[69] The court recognized that Birdsell had voluntarily become intoxicated and, as he had experienced the condition of delirium before, concluded that his state of mind should have been foreseeable. One newspaper reporting on the denial of a motion for a new trial dismissively suggested "that habitual insanity, produced by habitual drunkenness, constituted no better apology for the commission of a crime than drunkenness itself."[70]

Drake expressed regret that the case did not result in an acquittal on the basis of *mania a potu*; yet he was less concerned about the defendant than the state of medical jurisprudence, later clarifying that he was "indifferent" to the fate of Birdsell himself.[71] Drake was particularly dismayed at the ambiguity of the legal decision, insisting that "if the Court could not say what the law is, they might have said what it ought to be." Furthermore, "I am likewise unable to ascertain, whether the jury convicted the prisoner, because, in their opinions, his insanity was not made out; because the act which he perpetrated was not connected with his disease; or because they would not allow insanity, from drink to constitute an excuse."[72] He was further outraged at the idea that delirium tremens could not be argued as a defense to crime. "If this variety of mental alienation cannot constitute a valid defence," he argued, "it can only be from the character of its remote cause." He argued that the court had no right "to travel behind the testimony which establishes the insanity, to inquire into its causes, and estimate the culpability of *non compos*, not by the degree of his alienation, but the criminality of those causes."[73] Drake's medical knowledge of delirium tremens led him to place it in the same category as insanity, which could result from a variety of remote causes that included intemperance.

More importantly, Drake emphasized the point that not only is delirium tremens a condition distinct from intoxication, it is a form of insanity that upsets a sense of right and wrong. "It must be shown," he stressed, "either that the culprit is insane on all subjects, to such a degree as to pervert his affections and destroy his estimate of right and wrong; or that his crime had some natural connexion with the subject of his hallucination. *Submitting to these requirements*, the subjects of *Mania a potu* seem fairly entitled to plead their alienation, when arraigned for crimes."[74] Drake's experience told him this was a true form of insanity and should be considered as such under the law. Having studied and written on the issue for ten years, he expressed faith in the ability of the medical profession to discern the difference between intoxication and *mania a potu*, "a new and distinct delirium."[75] He did not argue that delirium tremens in and of itself was a defense to crime but rather that it should be held to the same standard as other forms of mental alienation. Drake's medical, moral, and legal interpretation of delirium tremens rested squarely on his understanding of this condition as an unintended consequence of drinking and a remote cause of insanity.

As physicians expanded their provenance in this period, medical and legal interpretations of drunkenness as a disease that affected state of mind increasingly overlapped. Beck did consider those who had become insane due to the "remote cause" of persistent drinking to be permanently and legitimately insane, but he had been reluctant to excuse McDonough's crime, medically or legally, *because* the offender was intoxicated. McDonough had freely engaged in the consumption of alcohol and was aware of the uncommon effect of producing insanity it would have on him. The initial and voluntary decision to drink was cast as a point of no return that held the defendant responsible for all actions that followed. Thirteen years later, Drake revisited the decision in the McDonough case, asking, "A great variety of causes are *known*, among other sinister effects, to produce insanity. Suppose an individual do not avoid these causes, is he *therefore* to be held accountable when he becomes insane?" He agreed that intoxication brought on the "paroxysms of insanity" that led to the murder; however, McDonough "could not have foreseen this, or any other criminal action; he did not, therefore, drink with malice prepense; and his crime seems to have been, merely that he did not refrain from that which promoted the recurrence of the paroxysms, but involved no malice, and is not prohibited by our criminal law."[76]

As a committed temperance advocate, Drake considered the beneficial effects to the cause of temperance and the safety of society in punishing all actions that follow voluntary drunkenness. Ultimately, however, he viewed punishment for acts committed under a state of delirium tremens as ineffective: "But I cannot bring myself to believe, that this desirable end can be thus attained.—Few men, perhaps none, when presented with the prevailing temptations to drunkenness, are likely to anticipate consequences so remote, or contemplating, will be deterred by them." Drake's understanding of delirium tremens as an unintended and unanticipated consequence of heavy drinking allowed him to acknowledge its exculpatory impact in a court of law. He further questioned the efficacy of the law in deterring drunkards in the first place and suggests the greatest value of punishment is in "preventing bad men from real or simulated intoxication, as an excuse for the crimes which they desire to perpetrate."[77]

Interpretations of the Birdsell case provide a particularly telling example of the divide that often existed between scientific, legal, and lay observations of intoxication. The dichotomous verdict system of "guilty" or "not guilty" belies a much more complicated sense of the relationship between drunkenness and responsibility. One can imagine that Drake's support of temperance reform could have led him to condemn Birdsell, as the jury ostensibly had, for his years of drinking. In the end, Drake's scientific worldview held sway in arguing the irrelevance of intemperance as the remote cause of what he viewed as a legitimate case of insanity. The jury, on the other hand, appears to have viewed a history of drinking as an incriminating factor in that Birdsell should have foreseen the consequences of his actions.

Legally, jurors were often asked to draw what may have appeared to be an arbitrary distinction. The defense in Birdsell's trial was careful to inform the jury that "drunkenness cannot be plead as an apology for crimes." Yet in this oft-repeated phrase, there was usually a "but" not far behind. Birdsell's state, the defense argued, was not drunkenness, which patently provided no defense, but rather insanity caused by alcohol, and he therefore was due "all the immunities of a *non compos* from any other cause."[78] Addressing what was viewed as a disappointing verdict in the Birdsell case, one medical journal contrasted the actions of the drunkard with those of the sufferer of delirium tremens experiencing the "paroxysm of intoxication." The drunkard, acting from inherent immoral impulses, was fully responsible under the law: he "is only exhibiting his true character, stripped of the disguise which in his sober intervals he is able to throw over it, he is not the less a moral agent, and answerable for his conduct." On the other hand,

> Whatever may be thought of the soundness of this philosophy in view of the ebrious paroxysm, it is evident that it does not at all apply to the subject of delirium tremens. He exhibits nothing of that exaggerated state of the passions, of that boisterous violence which marks the drunken man; he is timid, watchful and jealous; and much more disposed to apprehend injury from others, than wantonly to inflict it on them. Such was the state of the individual in the case alluded to, and surely there is none which renders a man more truly and deservedly an object of compassion.[79]

An association between criminal behavior and delirium tremens complicated the contribution of medical knowledge and challenged the utility of distinguishing between disease and immoral behavior. This ambiguity presented a profound stumbling block to participation in a judicial system that required clear legal strictures. The law made unambiguous characterizations of a defendant's mental state essential if medical jurisprudence were to have any value in criminal cases concerning drinking and insanity.

Events after Birdsell's trial also reveal that the public did not necessarily view Birdsell's case in the stark choice of verdict required by law. A week before Birdsell's scheduled execution, a number of citizens of Cincinnati submitted a petition requesting a commutation of the death sentence. The request was granted, although initially Birdsell refused and was brought out to the gallows. Only after ascending the platform did he change his mind, and he was ultimately confined to the penitentiary.[80] Supporters of the commutation were described as "respectable citizens," perhaps those more likely to embrace the medical interpretation of events. Some newspaper accounts did note that the commutation was a "disappointment" to those who had gathered "to witness the delightful spectacle."[81]

As physicians maintained that delirium tremens and insanity caused by chronic intemperance existed as diseases distinct from common drunkenness, categories often blurred. Drake supported the idea that the sufferer of delirium tremens was worthy of compassion. He asserted that delirium tremens rarely resulted in violence, since it most often occurred "in old inebriates, whose constitutions are broken down" and were "far more disposed to flee from danger, either real or imaginary, than to face it."[82] One medical journal praised Drake for "showing that the cause of humanity is compatible with the soundest views of medical science and ethical philosophy."[83] Another author, quoting legal scholars Francis Wharton and Moreton Stillé, pointed out that "'delirium tremens is not the intended result of drink in the same way that drunkenness is'"; it is "shunned rather than courted by the patient."[84] The heroic contribution of physicians, in their own eyes anyway, was to provide a means to separate the immoral drunkard from the inebriate patient.

Medical expertise, physicians argued, would provide clarity and a higher quality of justice to legal proceedings. Drake hoped that the case of Birdsell would "incite our physicians and lawyers, to a closer study of mental alienation, particularly of *Mania a potu*, in reference to the laws of the different states."[85] One of the objections to according an exculpatory factor to drunkenness was the fear that criminals would either feign drunkenness or purposefully drink to excess before committing a crime in order to receive a reduced sentence. Delirium tremens was thought near impossible to feign. Drake assured his readers that a trained physician could render an accurate diagnosis. In the case of Birdsell, Drake noted the manifestation of observable physical symptoms such as an elevated pulse and incessant spitting as proof that the defendant's mental state was consistent with this condition.[86]

Some years later, Isaac Ray used the Birdsell trial to criticize the discretion that juries held in determining insanity over the opinions of trained medical men. He described the case as one that "furnishes another instance of the deplorable consequences of obliging a body of men, most of whom are utterly unacquainted with the phenomena of insanity, to decide the question of its existence in a given example." He rejected testimony regarding Birdsell's rational behavior after the crime because those witnesses "knew as little of insanity" as the jury. Furthermore, anyone who believed Birdsell to be sane "must have derived his notions of this disease from some other source than the wards of the hospital and asylum." Ray highlighted this case as an example of the divide between medical knowledge and legal interpretation as he suggested a greater emphasis for the former in the courtroom.[87]

Although the Birdsell verdict generated considerable debate and outrage, it was the case of Alexander Drew, found not guilty due to delirium tremens, that ultimately proved a more significant medical and legal precedent. In 1838 Ray referred to the decision of the court in the Birdsell case as "untenable" and ended his discussion of delirium tremens, suggesting, "it is scarcely necessary to pursue this train of reflection any farther."[88] However, in later editions of this work, Ray followed these words with the assertion that the decision in the Drew case "has unquestionably settled the law on this point in this country." He also included descriptions of several later cases in which delirium tremens provided a satisfactory defense.[89] Another physician, writing on delirium tremens in 1875, ignored

Birdsell altogether and characterized Drew's trial as "the great American case."[90] As far as physicians had been able to define delirium tremens as a condition distinct from intoxication, the diagnosis became an acceptable and often successful defense to criminal acts. Physicians, by the end of the 1830s, were not only epistemologically convinced of delirium tremens; the habit and resulting behavior of heavy drinking itself were increasingly receiving medical attention as a form of disease. Beck, who in 1818 had been so reluctant to accept McDonough's insanity because of the complicating factor of intoxication, later retracted his support for the guilty verdict in that case.[91]

Delirium tremens initially presented a problem for legal systems and juries because of the overlap with the issue of intoxication. Delirium tremens occupied a place between permanent insanity, in which heavy drinking was considered one of a number of possible remote causes, and intoxication, whose effects were viewed as both immediate and foreseeable. This middle ground provided physicians an opportunity to expand their purview over issues of drinking as part of an intensifying concern with the effects of intemperance on American society. In the next decades, a broader array of the consequences of heavy drinking became legitimate fodder for medical interpretation.

Chapter 2

"A Victim of Intemperance"

In his 1831 oration on temperance to the town of Columbus, Ohio, Daniel Drake made a plea for the recognition of the special circumstances related to the "mental alienation of habitual drinkers." Intemperate habits, he proclaimed, could lead to a madness in which the drinker became "the victim of every kind of delusion" and was no longer able to "distinguish between right and wrong." Friends and family faced the possibility of becoming "the prey of vindictive and murderous designs." Such an individual, he argued, is "actually insane; and should no longer be held responsible." Despite his position as a staunch temperance advocate, Drake expressed dissatisfaction with the stark distinction required by the courts between insanity and drunkenness. He urged that even a delirium caused by drunkenness "should be plead in mitigation of punishment; for the individual often does that, when intoxicated, from which he would recoil with horror, in his sober moments; and this should be the test."[1]

The contemplation of how much control habitual drinkers had over their behavior was not just a question for medical jurisprudence experts but one that drew the attention of a growing temperance movement. An emerging sense that the violent acts of the drunkard could be an unintended consequence of intemperance competed with legal and moral principles that held individuals responsible for their actions. Inchoate medical definitions of drunkenness and responsibility overlapped with changes in the legal field and the exhortations of reformers, with competing groups seeking to each create their own public narrative of the alcohol experience. Arguably, both physicians and temperance advocates had in common the goal of establishing a certain societal authority based on their respective, and sometimes overlapping, world views. The alcoholic narrative that emerged in this period was one that was both contentious and familiar, and no easy answer existed as to what to do with the inebriated criminal.

Since the colonial period, alcohol had been an integral part of American life serving various economic, social, political, and even nutritive purposes. High levels of drinking characterized life in the colonies, and after the Revolution, alcohol consumption continued to rise steadily, reaching an annual peak of more than five gallons per capita by 1830. Improved distilling technology and the proliferation of untaxed distilled spirits, such as whiskey, contributed to this growth.[2] However, by the first decades of the nineteenth century, alcohol was increasingly viewed as being at odds with a more modern way of life. American society, it was believed, was more demanding on its citizens, from reasons ranging from its climate, democratic system, and, as the century progressed, higher rates of urbanization and industrialization. In response, temperance efforts and medical study of the issue increased over the course of the nineteenth century and effectively reduced rates of drinking by midcentury.[3]

One of the early and more influential temperance reformers was Lyman Beecher, a Presbyterian minister who advocated abstinence as the only effective means of preventing the alcohol habit.[4] He was certainly not the first to do so, but the moral mandate to abstain fit in especially well with the emphasis on moral perfectibility that characterized the Second Great Awakening.[5] In 1826 Beecher, along with fellow Presbyterian minister Justin Edwards, founded the American Temperance Society, which in the span of five years grew to include 2,200 chapters and more than 170,000 members. In his *Six Sermons on Intemperance*, Beecher described both the moral and physical degradation of the drinker. He preached that intemperance is "a sin which excludes from heaven" and that the decision to engage in ardent spirits, even in limited amounts, would lead to the "moral ruin" of the individual. The physical symptoms of the disease were laid out in detail as additional warning for the sinner, who could expect to suffer any of a number of bodily infirmities including "nausea at the stomach," "obstructions of the liver," "epilepsy," "gout," "consumptions," "coughs," and "insanity." Conceiving of the alcohol habit as a disease drew attention to both the manifest physical effects of heavy drinking and the often uncontrollable compulsion to drink. The correlation between heavy drinking and physical and mental disease was utilized quite effectively by both moral reformers and medical men and provided a reciprocal reassurance of the soundness of their respective views. The equation of intemperance with disease additionally provided a means for Beecher to rally the community to the cause: "Intemperance is a disease as well as a crime, and were any other disease, as contagious, of as marked symptoms, and as mortal, to pervade the land, it would create universal consternation."[6]

Recognizing a compulsion to drink whereby "men become irreclaimable in their habits," Beecher proclaimed that abstinence was necessary to avoid the point whereby "the habit is fixed, and the hope of reformation is gone." This of course meant that the proper target of reform was the moderate drinker or even the prospective drinker rather than the irredeemable drunkard. Beecher, in fact, went so far as to claim "that habitual tippling is worse than periodical drunkenness," and the message to reject alcohol and its "injurious effects" was broadly aimed and designed to muster national support.[7] American Temperance Society members readily "took the pledge," promising to abstain from drinking as the only effective means to avoid the sinful path of the intemperate. The temperance movement sought to limit drinking, whether through moral suasion or, later, legal coercion, with a convincing and universal portrait of the drunkard as a threat to society. By the time one became a drunkard, it was believed there was little hope of moral redemption; his or her only purpose was to act as a "warning" to those who might still be saved. Beecher and his followers certainly did not argue that the degenerated state of the drunkard excused criminal behavior. These actions were a result of what they would characterize as a sinful indulgence in alcohol, but they did portray the drunkard as a "ruined animal" unable any longer to make a moral decision.[8]

This characterization provided some resonance with medical jurisprudence arguments that weighed the level of intent and potentially limited responsibility of a drunk offender. According to temperance advocates, the choice to abstain was the moral one; the choice to drink was sinful. However, the reality of the habit of heavy drinking and the resulting state of intoxication complicated traditional notions of individual moral responsibility. The initial choice to imbibe was considered to be one based on free will, even as the resulting desire for alcohol was often described with words such as "overpowering" or "irresistible"—suggesting a state of mind that interfered with rational decision making.[9] A number of historians have suggested that the uncontrollable compulsion to drink had been recognized by ministers dating back to at least the eighteenth century, and by the 1830s the loss of control associated with alcohol became a common trope among moral reformers, physicians, and jurists.[10] Temperance advocates professed that the decision to drink was a voluntary sinful act, yet both their descriptions of drunkards' lives spinning out of control and their resistance to try to reform actual drunkards suggested a limit to free will if not individual moral responsibility. Moral reformers could and did condemn the drunkard for the initial decision to drink even as they acknowledged one might no longer have the power to resist the urge.

By the 1830s, as medical and legal authorities contemplated the relationship between criminal responsibility and intoxication, the temperance movement similarly focused on narratives of crime and alcohol. Temperance tracts, real and fictional, underscored the effects of men's drinking habits on their families, highlighting stories of brutality against wives and children as the consequence.[11] These acts of horror simultaneously provided their audiences with titillating descriptions of violent crime and an opportunity to weigh the moral consequences of drink. The shocking details of crime that nineteenth-century society used to highlight the monstrous effects of the alcohol habit on ordinary men may also have been the same ones that indicated an exculpatory lack of intent. Would he have done it but for the alcohol? The range and conflicting nature of opinions on drunkenness and murder are reflected in the medical, legal, and public commentary on Theodore Wilson, who was found not guilty of killing his wife by reason of insanity.

On June 10, 1835, Wilson was arrested on the charge that he had murdered his wife in Kittery, Maine. Earlier that Wednesday morning, Wilson, who had a history of drinking, had complained of feeling ill and accused his wife Sally of attempting to harm him. Shortly before the murder, he removed his clothes, left his home completely naked, and began to walk down the road, "throwing up his arms, and making a wild, howling noise." His wife, after failing to get assistance from one of the neighbors, followed him and attempted to persuade him to return home. Wilson reacted by throwing her on the ground and beating her on the head with a sharp stone, causing her immediate death. He then proceeded to a nearby house, pounding on the doors and breaking windows as he threatened to kill the two women inside. Wilson, who had grievously injured himself as he broke the windows with his bare hands, reportedly rubbed blood along the side of the house, claiming he was sealing it with the blood of his wife. The women were able to fend him off with an ax until help arrived, and Wilson was arrested. Wilson's defense at trial was based on a claim of insanity.[12]

The brutal nature of the murder was not disputed by any of the parties. The indictment against Wilson read that he "did strike, beat and kick the said Sally Wilson, with his hands and feet, in and upon the head, breast, back, belly, sides and other parts of the body." He then threw her on the ground and, using "a certain stone there situated with great force and violence," caused "one mortal wound on the left side of the head of her the said Sally Wilson, of the length of three inches and of the depth of three inches."[13] Newspaper reports printed around the country called the murder an act of "extraordinary barbarity" and a "horrid deed," as they conveyed the grisly details to the public, including the fact that Wilson used the same stone he had used to kill his wife to break the windows of the women's house.[14] His wife's body was described as "mangled" and "truly frightful" in appearance, and Wilson's own injuries were described as considerable, with one newspaper erroneously reporting that he had succumbed to them.[15]

At this point, delirium tremens provided the strongest legal defense that a habitual drinker was not responsible for his actions, that he did not intend the resulting state of mind that led to murder. For this defense to be effective, it was vital that insanity be proven as something other than ordinary intoxication. A diagnosis of delirium tremens did not necessarily resonate with a public who felt confident enough to themselves expound on what it meant to be drunk, as Drake had learned in the Birdsell case. The question of when Wilson, a man of admittedly intemperate habits, had last had a drink became crucial to determine whether or not he was laboring under some form of alcoholic insanity, delirium tremens, or mere drunkenness. Wilson admitted buying rum on Saturday and drinking all of it the next day; however, according to an account by Isaac Ray, "it did not appear that he drank any more after this, and circumstances render it probable that he did not." Ray bolstered his conclusion that Wilson was not acting under the immediate effects of intoxication by describing, in a situation reminiscent of that of Alexander Drew, how five years earlier Wilson had become "deranged" on a fishing voyage in which he had been "deprived of spirits" for three days.[16] Here Ray appears to interpret Wilson's actions as consistent with the effects of delirium tremens, what was by that time a medically and legally accepted form of insanity.

Situating the details of the crime alongside the consequences of heavy drinking meant that such actions could be potentially defended by shifting some of the blame to the effects of alcohol. Wilson was known to have "abused and beaten his wife when intoxicated" in the past, yet his actions on the morning of the murder certainly seemed further out of the realm of the ordinary. He was described as "raving" and "traversing the road *naked*." He beat his wife "in the most shocking manner" and then attempted to attack another woman as "blood ran profusely from his hands and wrists, which were lacerated with deep gashes made by forcing them through the glass." As three men seized him, he made "little or no resistance."[17] To the jury, Wilson's "shocking" behavior may have suggested a state of mind affected by more than the predictable effects of intoxication. The deliberations of the jury are not known, but Ray recounts that "the court in charging the jury observed that it was not material for them to determine what *species* of insanity it was under which the prisoner had been suffering, if satisfied with the fact of its existence."[18] Ultimately, in Wilson's case, the court seemed quite tolerant of implementing a broad definition of insanity. Wilson was found not guilty, "he laboring under insanity at the time of the act."[19]

Outside of the trial, however, others had their doubts. One newspaper reported that Wilson "had not been seen to drink any spirit for three days previous to the murder, although there is no reason to doubt but he was under its influence at the time of the horrid deed, as it was his custom at times to keep liquor secreted."[20] Another was more unceremonious, reporting, "Theodore Wilson, of Kittery, Me., murdered his wife on Wednesday, by beating her head with a stone. He was drunk at the time."[21] One newspaper account attributed Wilson's behavior to a combination of immoral character and the effects of drunkenness, arguing against the legitimacy of an insanity defense by suggesting "no symptoms of insanity had ever been observed in him, excepting when under the influence of spiritous liquors."[22] Wilson was condemned for his drinking, which was viewed as sufficient enough cause to explain his criminal behavior.

Despite some conflicting details in the press, reports of the Wilson murder were remarkably consistent and widespread, as newspapers across the country routinely lifted news items virtually word for word. By the 1830s hundreds of newspapers existed across the United States, reprinting stories of interest in what one historian has described as a "chain-letter version of national and international news."[23] The penny paper had become a ubiquitous presence in American cities and towns, and crime reporting was its bread and butter. Even in large cities where a thriving press had already existed, the penny press was able to build on the appeal of reports of violent crimes that were not always covered in the more respectable newspapers. Inexpensive publications were readily available and appealed to a largely literate working-class readership in search of entertainment, but, as a public medium, newspapers also helped build community and often played a key role in social and political change.[24]

Published stories of intemperance and violence shaped perceptions of the effects of alcohol even as they reflected experiences that were too often not unknown in the lives of their readers. Through graphic illustrations and detailed narratives of shocking behavior, murder pamphlets served the dual purposes of providing a moral lesson and entertaining the public.[25] It was not unusual for newspapers and pamphlets to include expert testimony from medical witnesses or statements from the criminal, although the veracity of the latter especially was sometimes suspect. "The drunkard's story," literary scholar Thomas Augst observes, "generated larger contests for moral authority that were waged between professional elites and ordinary people within relatively new forms of mass communication such as the newspaper and the popular lecture, as well as across the evolving literary genres of sermon, novel, autobiography and stage melodrama."[26] Horrific crimes, such as that perpetrated by Theodore Wilson, provided an opportunity to extemporize on the subject of heavy drinking.

After describing the lurid details of the "shocking" crime, one Christian paper declared the murder of Sally Wilson "another horrible result of intemperance."[27] For some, intemperance was a character flaw, an expected indication of a dissolute character. Theodore Wilson was characterized in one newspaper as "a farmer of 52 years of age, of bad disposition and habits" and in another as "a man of notoriously irregular habits, and possessed of a fiend-like disposition."[28] Another paper, however, confirmed the insidious nature of the alcohol habit, designating Wilson a "victim of intemperance." Such accounts were not intended to suggest that Wilson was a sympathetic figure but rather that his actions should serve as a lesson to others who might consider the drinking habit themselves. The fact that Wilson "manifested no penitence or concern at what he had done" emphasized his depravity in a number of published accounts. Yet attributions of blame directed solely at Wilson existed uneasily alongside temperance warnings, with one of the most provocative reportedly coming from Wilson himself, who shifted blame to the retailer who sold the rum, charging him with being the "cause of the murder." He declared, "'I should not have killed my wife if *that* man had not sold me Rum—had not sold me *Rum* out of his store.'"[29] The modern reader may be skeptical as to whether or not Wilson actually uttered these words the morning after his arrest. In either case, whether by Wilson himself or the newspaper writer, the real-life murder was transformed into a lesson on the evils of drink.[30]

Acts of drunken murder made for a poignant temperance lesson, as they suggested the powerful transformative role of alcohol on an individual's character as well as the threat posed to the dominant social structure. The murder of the "innocent victim," often the wife, made the crime especially appalling, but it also demonstrated the power and influence of alcohol in causing a man to kill the woman he had once loved.

Wilson's "barbarity" and "bad disposition" stood in stark contrast to the "exemplary" character of his wife and certainly made his crime all the more abhorrent.[31] Yet the presumably unintended nature of the crime also turned the murderer himself into "a victim of intemperance." Would it have happened if not for the rum? These accounts were powerful not just because they were shocking but because they were all too familiar. The perpetrators of domestic violence in temperance stories were likely to be native, hardworking men whose intemperate behavior destroyed their own lives and livelihoods and created a greater sense of urgency to the cause of temperance.[32] If the drunkard were portrayed as inherently venal or somehow innately inferior, the cautionary nature of the tale, the possibility of identification with the protagonist, would be lost.

The Washingtonians were especially adept at utilizing the horrors of alcohol abuse to convey an anti-drinking message to the common man. In 1840 a group of habitual drinkers from Baltimore formed the Washington Temperance Society, which boasted a half-million members within just a few years. Invoking George Washington, who had freed the country from British rule, the Washingtonians sought independence from "King Alcohol," and their 1841 manifesto proclaimed "all men are created temperate."[33] Unlike evangelical groups such as the American Temperance Society that directed their message to the general community, Washingtonian societies aimed their efforts toward the drunkard himself. Their members also advocated total abstinence, but they presented their case through emotionally charged personal anecdotes and public confessions of their own alcohol-related experiences. Their orations were a mix of lived experience and fiction that outlined the destruction alcohol wreaked on the drunkard, his family, and society.[34]

Graphic stories of delirium tremens added to a narrative that demonstrated the consequences of heavy drinking and the extent of the compulsion to continue the habit. John Gough, one of the society's leaders and most well-known speakers, offered explicit accounts of drunken behavior and the experience of delirium tremens. A former actor with little formal education, Gough became known as "the poet of the d.t.'s," and would often physically reenact the scene of a man in the throes of delirium tremens for his audience. Born in England in 1817 and sent to America by his family at the age of twelve, Gough worked on a farm and then entered the bookbinding trade. His mother and sister eventually joined him, but he later recounted a difficult life in which his mother's death spurred a drinking habit that consequently led to the loss of employment and an ongoing struggle to support himself.[35]

Gough epitomized the style and appeal of the Washingtonians, who were largely working-class men, utilizing a "homespun eloquence" to reach out to an audience that was simultaneously entertained and uplifted.[36] Attempting to describe the emotive effect of one of Gough's lectures in New York, the *New York Times* observed, "Words, when from his mouth, and accompanied by his gesticulation, are not as when they fall from other men," especially noting "his power over the sympathies of his fellow man."[37] Gough's stories were a mix of fact and fiction meant to both enthrall his audience and warn them of the dangers of alcohol consumption. He became enormously popular as a public speaker, delivering more than nine thousand lectures over the course of his life. The difficulty of resisting the compulsion to drink, however, was too often acted out in real life by members of the Washingtonians. By 1845 Gough personified the notorious backsliding of the group with his own highly publicized alcoholic binge, contributing to the precipitous decline of the Washingtonian movement.[38]

Timothy Shay Arthur, perhaps best known for the temperance novel *Ten Nights in a Bar-Room and What I Saw There*, initially found fodder for his temperance message in the stories of the Washingtonians. Arthur's background was a modest one, and his interest in the condition of the drunkard may have been inspired by some of his own past encounters, in particular, an early friendship with notorious drinker and drug user Edgar Allan Poe. Arthur published *Six Nights with the Washingtonians* after reporting on the Washingtonian experience meetings for the *Baltimore Merchant* in 1840. These stories brought greater attention to the burgeoning movement and helped establish Arthur's career as a writer. Originally appearing as a series of articles, the collection was published as a book in 1842. A few short years later, a version was produced that included George Cruikshank's eight-panel series *The Bottle*, which visually highlighted the ravages of alcohol on the family. In each image, the intemperate father and

PLATE VII.—THE HUSBAND, IN A STATE OF FURIOUS DRUNKENNESS, KILLS HIS WIFE WITH THE INSTRUMENT OF ALL THEIR MISERY.

FIGURE 2. *The Bottle*, seventh plate by George Cruikshank, 1847. Courtesy of the Boston Public Library, digitalcommonwealth.org.

husband descends further—from first glass to destitution, the murder of his wife, and eventually insanity—as his plaintive children look on.

Arthur's writings reflected a sense of working-class community alongside an affirmation of the prevailing moral sensibility that stressed personal accountability and traditional gender roles shaped by the middle class. Arthur would build on this sensibility, later writing for *Godey's Lady's Book* and other women's magazines. It is not surprising that the Washingtonian movement held a literary appeal for Arthur. The life stories of these men depicted their descent into drunkenness through transgressions of the domestic ideal, and in turn it was these very same acts of cruelty and violence that led to a realization of the possibility of individual redemption.[39]

Additionally, for Arthur, the strength of the Washingtonian stories lay in the fact that they had actually happened: "it is because they are not mere fictions that they have any power to awaken a corresponding interest in the mind of the reader."[40] In *Six Nights* he recounts stories of men who neglected and abused their wives and children, descended into poverty, fell ill, and died. In one particularly disturbing passage from a story titled "The Reclaimed," a man recounts how he beat his sick child who was vexing him with her crying:

> But little Mary did not hush. Then I caught her up madly by one arm, and commenced beating her with all my strength—the strength of a nervous man inspired by intoxication and anger, exercised on a delicate child but two years old! One blow, such as I gave her, were enough, it would seem to have killed her. The poor child ceased crying on the instant; but I was in a rage and ceased not my blows until her mother, terrified at the scene, sprung forward, and snatched the little creature from my hand that held her high above the floor. To this I responded with a powerful blow on the side of my poor wife's head, and she fell senseless to the floor, and at the same moment, I kicked my child who was clinging to her mother's garments, half across the room.[41]

While his wife and child survived the beating, the man noted that afterwards his "little one seemed to me to have a sad expression in her dear young face," and his wife eventually died "from the agonies of a wounded spirit" caused by his drinking. By the end of the story, however, this same man, was sober, gainfully employed, and had regained the care of his children.[42]

Despite Arthur's commitment to temperance, his portrayal of these men was quite sympathetic with Arthur admitting he "felt with the actors." The man who attested to beating his wife and child in the above passage, was described as "a middle-aged man, with a thoughtful intelligent countenance."[43] Arthur made no further comment on his actions. Rather, the story is conveyed in the man's own words, for the man's guilt and agony are as essential a part of the temperance lesson as his reclamation at the end of the tale. The warnings against alcohol were likely to fall flat if the victim of alcohol was not a relatable figure. The "this can happen to you" point of the story made little sense if the drunkard was depicted as an unimaginable monster; rather, it was the alcohol that made such men act as they did. Even as evangelical temperance advocates often cited a moral weakness in the character of the drunkard, the purported overwhelming impact of alcohol use left room to form a sympathetic picture of the drunkard as a victim of his habit.

What is initially most striking in these stories is the frightful set of circumstances that accompany heavy drinking. Part of this certainly reflects the literary conventions of the time. Murder narratives displayed and promoted a fascination with the horrific details of crime that emerged by the end of the eighteenth century. The explicit depictions of criminal behavior found in these stories on one level catered to a public demand for entertainment; however, they were also cautionary tales of the dangers of intemperance. The Washingtonians employed graphic stories of families destroyed financially, morally, and even violently by a drunkard husband and father. However, unlike the sinful intemperate individual described by the evangelicals, the Washingtonian vision of the drunkard was that of a good man destroyed by the alcohol habit. The evocation of sympathy was for both the drunkard and his family, and the point was that the possibility of individual reformation lay within reach.[44] Other temperance advocates employed a similar style. As the publisher explained in his introduction to Lucius Sargent's *Temperance Tales,* "The perusal of some one of these narratives is well known to have turned the hearts of many persons of intemperate habits, from drunkenness and sloth, to temperance and industry."[45] Alcohol appeared as a monster in literary form, a destroyer of lives in Washingtonian speeches, and a cause of physical and mental illness that was supported by the medical literature. However, casting drink as the true villain of the story created a more ambivalent meaning of the drunkard as the palpable focus on alcohol, buoyed by temperance and medical writings, provided some explanation for seemingly incomprehensible acts.

Given the critical implications and cultural prominence of intemperance, it is not surprising to consider that the temperance narrative had a profound effect on American culture.[46] Real-life stories of alcohol and murder existed alongside equally sensational temperance novels that charted the drunkard's devolution from ordinary man to irredeemable criminal and were often indistinguishable in form. Benjamin Rush had already suggested that intemperance could lead to crime and murder, but he provided few of the grisly details found in nineteenth-century temperance tracts. This "movement toward the sensational" in temperance literature can be traced to the early 1830s as temperance writers sought to compete against the increasingly lurid and tremendously popular stories in the penny press.[47] Despite the immediacy and mass appeal of the penny paper, other published works also looked to real-life events as the source of their stories, and as in the case of Timothy Shay Arthur, the career trajectories of journalists and authors often intersected. Mark Canada has described this "sibling rivalry" between journalism and literature in the early nineteenth century as both sought to convey their own "sense of the truth."[48] Increasing sensationalism in literature and the press combined with the profound impact of temperance reform on society, and the temperance movement, broadly defined, became "a fertile source of literary themes and images."[49] Temperance novels, many of them not much longer than a short story, were enormously popular in this period, and by one estimate more than one in eight novels published in the 1830s had temperance as its subject.[50]

Nonfictional tales of murder, whether temperance lessons or newspaper reports, were similarly constructed to appeal to a popular audience. Cultural historian Karen Halttunen notes that murder literature, dating from the mid-eighteenth century, began to adopt a more detailed and realistic writing style that reflected a new way of viewing immoral behavior and criminals themselves.[51] Earlier crime literature had come out of the Puritan tradition and was accompanied by moral lessons to serve as a warning to the potentially sinful. By the 1820s purpose and literary convention began to change. "The cult of horror" that emerged, she argues, "had largely replaced an earlier view of the condemned criminal as sympathetic moral exemplum with a view of the murderer as moral alien."[52] Halttunen characterizes these works as "overwhelmingly secular" as compared to the inherent moral lessons found in earlier accounts. The murderer was clearly the villain of the story, yet, as the subject turned to crimes committed against home and family, that distinction was less defined. That sense of the murderer as "monster" and "alien" was complicated when the crime occurred within the domestic setting: "For the domestic-Gothic tale of murder quite literally brought the horror and the mystery *home*, showing readers that sometimes the moral monster was not an alien creature of the wicked world outside, but an intimate companion at the family fireside."[53] This sense of familiarity was often a key element of the temperance narrative. Yes, the drunkard who murdered members of his family was a monster, but the act was more horrifying and thus a more effective warning against intemperance, when he was also recognized as a husband and father.

In much of the temperance-influenced literature of this period, alcohol appeared as an independent actor terrorizing the lives of drinkers and their families. Fictional works, such as *The Catastrophe* and Edgar Allan Poe's "The Black Cat," often culminated in the drunkard's murder of his wife to demonstrate the depths to which alcohol had brought him. *The Catastrophe*, published in 1833, recounts the story of Edward L——, once an upstanding member of a dry community who succumbed to alcohol and, "driven to a frenzy by drink," murdered his wife with an ax.[54] Some of Poe's stories perhaps best demonstrate the ways literary horror was influenced by temperance discourse. The vivid hallucinations and imagery of delirium tremens, in particular, provided fodder for "Metzengerstein" and "The Black Cat," stories in which the protagonists suffer alcohol-related delusions that respectively led to the death of one and the murder of the other's wife.[55]

Descriptions of the symptoms of delirium tremens resonated broadly within a society increasingly concerned with yet often fascinated by the consequences of heavy drinking. Medical accounts of delirium tremens were not only influenced by the wider culture but, after becoming part of the medical canon, reentered popular culture in American literature. Confirmation of the disease often rested on the presence of nausea, vomiting, hallucinations, paranoia, and even a sense of vermin crawling over one's body. The symbolism of these accounts casts light on the fears of an urban middle class over attendant social and economic changes. "Reflecting doctors' concerns with the threat liquor posed to individual psychology," Matthew Warner Osborn states, "here and elsewhere accounts vividly portrayed supernatural horrors lurking just beyond the fragile walls of middle-class selfhood, walls that spirituous liquors threatened to dissolve."[56] Intemperance, its reformers could argue, simultaneously threatened both the individual and society.

"The Black Cat," a story of intemperance and violence intertwined, was first published in 1843. The narrator is introduced as a "destroyed" man on the day before his death by hanging. He describes his "tenderness of heart" as a child and his early love for animals. His change in character, he explains, is due to the effects of drinking: "for what disease is like Alcohol!" His transformation is symbolized by his mistreatment of his cat—first gouging out its eye and then hanging it. This deed comes back to haunt him when he later encounters and adopts a very similar cat. Wracked with guilt and tortured by the presence of the animal, he attempts to kill it with an ax but is stopped by his wife. The narrator becomes enraged by her interference and instead "buried the axe in her brain," where she "fell dead upon the spot."[57] "The Black Cat" is particularly illustrative of the ways the lurid progression of alcohol abuse was portrayed through a description of the symptoms of delirium tremens alongside moral consequences. While the tragic ending of the drunkard and his family was conveyed with moral purpose in the temperance tale, Poe was able to utilize the disjunction between tranquil family life and the resulting brutality that accompanied heavy drinking to a successful narrative purpose in constructing a tale of horror.[58]

Within the context of a more boisterous temperance movement, publications expounding on the descent of the drunkard through alcohol-related violence permeated popular culture. Nathaniel Currier, one of the founders of the successful printmaking firm Currier and Ives, created dozens of lithographs related to temperance. *The Drunkard's Progress*, published in 1846, is perhaps the best known of these. The image depicts the drinking man's "steps" from respectability to ruin in what John Crowley has called "the masterplot for hundreds of temperance tales, in which the hope of domestic bliss is cruelly dashed by chronic inebriety."[59] In the first steps, a well-dressed man partakes in "a glass with a friend," then "a glass to keep the cold out," leading to "a glass too much." By step 5, he is "a confirmed drunkard," and by step 8, he has turned to "desperation and crime." The last step depicts his "death by suicide." Underneath the steps, a weeping woman and a young girl, the family of the drunkard, are depicted walking away as their presumably once-happy home burns in the background.[60]

FIGURE 3. *The Drunkard's Progress,* 1846.
Courtesy of Prints and Photographs Division, Library of Congress.

This valence of sentimentality in both fictional and journalistic accounts of alcohol and violence was fed by changes in the American domestic ideal from one that rested on economic productivity to one that saw the home as haven from the harsh reality of the world.[61] The ideal family of the nineteenth century held traditional gender roles at its foundation as women from middle-class families saw a diminishing economic role in the household by the early decades of the century. The American Revolution failed to bring about significant legal or political changes for women who found themselves restricted to the domestic sphere. By the 1830s women's economic role took on a less obvious, if not always less important, presence in American society as the household economy gave way to the industrial wage economy. These changes fueled the "romance of family culture" that characterized middle- and upper-class domestic life in this era.[62] As murder was, and is, far too often a crime of familiarity, of blood as well as blood relation, the murder narrative provided a window into familial relations, revealing the reality of tangled social relationships and deviant behavior.[63] Accounts of murders committed in the domestic sphere, generally wife murder, drew a picture of the criminal's home life, and "turned the domestic lives of ordinary men into a new kind of public spectacle."[64]

The temperance movement's focus on a "separate spheres" ideology of family served to elevate public awareness of men's drinking as it further stigmatized women drinkers, who were generally perceived as lower class and lacking in virtue. In the earlier part of the century, women's participation in temperance was most visible in an auxiliary role. The Washingtonians, for example, did accept women drunkards as members, but they were not allowed to speak publicly, thus denying them the camaraderie that came of shared experience and limiting their ability to reshape the public image of the drunkard as a male. Generally, women who were members of the Martha Washington societies provided food, clothing, and other forms of tangible relief along with general moral support for the men. Most of the Martha Washingtonians were from the lower classes, often the wives, daughters, and sisters of intemperate men, who might have found that embracing domestic ideology in this context provided a level of affirmation and influence.[65]

It is difficult to get an accurate portrayal of the numbers and lives of women drinkers, as the social consequences of primarily men's drinking were highlighted. Prevailing ideals may have indeed discouraged some women from drinking, and women could more acceptably partake of a variety of patent medicines and opium derivatives. Gender assumptions also served to limit resources and even acknowledgment of women's drinking habits. Because women were employed as victims of men's intemperance, the recognition of the woman drunkard could actually undermine temperance arguments. Even as women reformers agitated for greater legal rights to protect them from the violence of drunken husbands, temperance warnings of the graphic violence committed against women served to emphasize the value of men's abstinence. As Scott C. Martin has argued, temperance discourse, as it highlighted violence against women to warn against the effects of alcohol, ultimately "placed a positive value on female victimization by emphasizing its didactic usefulness."[66] Both male and female reformers drew on this narrative to condemn men's intemperance and to eventually demand tangible rights for women. At a women's temperance convention in 1853, Clarina Howard Nichols defended her right to speak by characterizing women as the victims of men's drinking: "Woman, who is herself not addicted to this vice, suffers more than man." Nichols utilized traditional gender roles as a powerful critique against intemperance and in support for legal and political reform for women.[67] However, little room was left to envision a woman drunkard.

More commonly, in tales of drunken murder, a sense of astonishment at the incongruity between the horrific violence of the crime and the womanly virtue of the victim was relayed to the reader. In 1833 the widow Mary Hamilton was murdered by Joel Clough, a resident at Hamilton's mother's boarding house, who, after having allegedly unsuccessfully pursued her affections, turned to drink and murdered her. A popular pamphlet titled "The Authentic Confession of Joel Clough" used melodramatic and sexualized language to contrast the innocence of the victim against the depravity of her killer. Hamilton was described as "chaste, beautiful, urbane, and lively, and as pure as the unclouded sky," and when her bloody garments were displayed in court, reportedly only the prisoner was able to look upon them without shame. The testimony was reported to be "of the most thrilling and touching character. The description of her (Mrs. Hamilton's) delicate person—her amiable character—her piercing shrieks, and her death struggles, while he held and pushed still deeper and deeper, the murderous dirk into her bosom, was truly affecting." The disjunction between violent murder and womanly virtue was further highlighted through the inclusion of a letter Clough purportedly wrote to his mother just days before his execution assuring her of his "spiritual welfare" as he faced death.[68]

Despite the narrative dissonance between violent crime and the domestic ideal, few Americans in this era were unacquainted with domestic violence, either through direct experience or public accounts. And, not unlike today, the connection between domestic violence and alcohol was easily observable. One study of crime in eighteenth-century Pennsylvania noted that roughly half of all murders claimed family members as victims, and homicides in which alcohol played a part routinely involved family,

FIGURE 4. *Trial, Sentence, Confession and Execution of Joel Clough*, 1833. Rare Book Collection, Lillian Goldman Law Library, Yale Law School.

friends, or neighbors as their victims. Surveys conducted in 1829 and 1853 revealed that members of the legal profession viewed a strong connection between violence and intemperance, particularly within families. As one respondent observed, "domestic happiness is generally destroyed by drunkenness," and many of these lawyers drew on their professional experiences to assert that at least nine-tenths of domestic violent crimes were a result of excessive drink.[69] Even as temperance literature exposed the reality of home life for some, the potency of the temperance message rested on the disjunction between the ideal of the domestic home and the savage violence that took place within, between virtuous wives and unrestrained husbands. How could such a monster infiltrate the core of American domesticity, the theoretically inviolable sanctuary of family? A key player in this drama was often alcohol, "demon rum." Drunkenness served simultaneously as an indicator of the husband's failure to live up to his end of the domestic bargain as a sober and productive man and as an explanation for what was considered an unthinkable crime.

The early goal of the temperance movement was not to provide a cure or even redemption, despite its emphasis on medical descriptions and legal consequences for the drunkard, but rather to limit the consumption of alcohol. By the late 1830s, the increasing focus on absolute abstinence, meaning not even wine or beer was tolerable, had caused some of these groups to lose members. Yet in this same era the consequences of heavy drinking were felt more keenly than ever before, as Jacksonian political reforms meant that this behavior posed a potential threat to political freedom. As liquor flowed freely during political campaigns and all classes of men gained the right of suffrage, alcohol was viewed by many as a "national evil."[70] The growth of cities, changes in the nature of work, and an increase in immigration in this period likewise contributed to a loss of faith in the ability of moral suasion to change behavior. The popular outreach efforts of the Washingtonians had influenced temperance groups that had previously been more concerned with promoting an already largely teetotal membership to "take the pledge"; however, unlike the Washingtonians, a number of temperance organizations began to embrace political action. As early efforts based on moral suasion proved less effective than advocates had hoped, the movement turned toward advocating for legal restrictions on alcohol. This shift reflected a growing belief, increasingly fueled by nativism and degeneracy theory, that those most likely to drink excessively were the least likely to heed moral and medical arguments, no matter how well crafted. The legal prohibition of alcohol, therefore, was necessary because, it was believed, too many men lacked the moral capacity and individual sense of responsibility to abstain.[71]

The movement to legally restrict access to alcohol, however, rested on the assumption that the act of drinking itself was so insidious that it could easily become an irresistible habit to those who did not embrace abstinence and that the ready availability of the product acted as further temptation. This characterization could in turn raise questions about legal responsibility, and in much of the temperance literature, "demon rum" and the "rum-seller" often joined the drunkard as accomplices in crime. A short item titled "The Effects of Intemperance" in the *Christian Secretary* noted the trial of a man named Barlow for murder in 1828. Barlow's wife and victim, not specifically named, was described as "a pious and affectionate wife, who has borne him five children: the youngest two weeks old." Mrs. Barlow's gentle nature contrasted sharply with the actions of her husband, who "beat his wife until he thought she was dead" and then, when she attempted to escape, "pursued her and beat out her brains with a stone!" The dubious claim that the couple "had previously lived in perfect harmony" served to highlight the horrific effects of intemperance and possibly bolster a claim of insanity. How else to make sense of such a crime? In this particular case, Barlow was acquitted on insanity "induced by drunkenness."[72] A similar report in the *Christian Watchman*, this one titled "Awful Effects of Intemperance," went so far as to suggest that the preacher who had supplied Barlow with spirits in the weeks before the murder was himself an "accessory to murder and to the death of the soul."[73] Barlow's guilt was one that was shared with "demon rum" and its purveyor.

In 1836 the evangelical-based American Temperance Society merged with the American Society for the Promotion of Temperance to form the American Temperance Union. This group advocated abstinence through a mix of religious rhetoric and legal action, and the *Journal of the American Temperance Union* routinely included reminders to take the temperance pledge intermixed with arguments that the law must likewise reflect a high moral standard. It was argued that alcohol, when sanctioned by the law, lost its proper sense of revulsion and its status as a moral transgression.[74] Not only was intemperance portrayed as a sin, but the sale of alcohol was characterized as "purely evil," and it was proclaimed that the rum seller builds a "fence between himself and heaven." The warning that alcohol use could lead to violent actions had been used both to dissuade the potential drinker and to bolster a sense of personal responsibility on the part of the offender who should have anticipated possible criminal results. However, temperance advocates argued that the drinker did not act alone. Reverend Beecher preached that "the commodity which the rum-seller deals out, murders not only the man who takes it, but it often instigates to the murder of *others*; and the rum-seller *knows* it."[75] The purveyors of liquor, they argued, act with full knowledge of the consequences of their actions. A Connecticut man who murdered a young woman with an ax and then killed himself was described as having been "infuriated by rum, sold by a man licensed to sell for the public good."[76] Government sanction of the sale of liquor added insult to injury.

In his autobiography, John Marsh, corresponding secretary and editor of the American Temperance Union, included numerous examples of the ways in which American society embraced the temperance movement's condemnation of the rum seller as well as the drunkard. In 1845 a "respectable mechanic" in Pittsfield, Massachusetts, "made drunken by liquor sold contrary to law," was accidentally killed on the railroad tracks, putting his family in a "destitute condition." Governor George N. Briggs assigned responsibility to the "vendor of intoxicating drink, the man who, in defiance of all laws, human and divine, scattered around him the seed of temporal and eternal death." And even as he excoriated the deceased man, who, he noted, was soon to face judgment, Reverend John Todd urged those who sold liquor to understand the lethal consequences of their actions: "Don't you see the blood on it? In your bar-room, by the cask, don't you see that mangled body? Don't you hear the steps of the naked feet of the orphans? Don't you see the wild eye and the pale face of the broken-hearted widow?"[77] The deaths of such men were often laid squarely at the feet of the rum seller, with some temperance tracts going so far as to label a drunkard's death "murder" to highlight the need for laws to end the sale of alcohol.

The complicity of the rum seller was at times extended further to the criminal actions of the drunkard. One minister suggested that the manufacture, sale, and even the consumption of alcohol met the "legal and scriptural definitions of murder and manslaughter."[78] Edward L. Youmans, the founder of *Popular Science Monthly*, insisted that drunkenness is no excuse for crime since it was "voluntarily brought on," but he did name an accomplice in asking, "is not society, is not every individual who makes, sells or patronizes the use of Alcohol, and leads the wretch to temptation and death responsible also?"[79] Another article in the *Journal of the American Temperance Union*, titled "The Traffic, the Traffic," recounted the stabbing murder of Jemima Morgan and the sorry state of her husband and killer as he awaited his fate in prison. The author concluded with an admonition against the legal sale of alcohol: "Such, we are obliged to repeat, are the bloody effects of the license system."[80] To the extent that the drunkard's decline was predictable, evil was found not only in the moral lapse of the intemperate but also in the calculated business of those who promoted it.

Temperance reformers condemned drinking and increasingly embraced abstinence and even prohibition. Their goal was not to excuse behavior but to employ it as a warning, yet their inclusion of the "demon rum" as accomplice potentially provided some legal cover for defendants, many of whom also blamed strong drink themselves. Of course, part of the opprobrium cast on the rum seller can be attributed to political expediency. To effectively end intemperance, it was necessary to stop the sale of liquor. The 1851 Maine Law, which would become a model for other state prohibition campaigns and eventually the Eighteenth Amendment, was the first to effectively ban both the manufacture and sale of alcohol. This law became a model of success for the temperance movement, and by 1855 thirteen states had their own version of the Maine Law.

Somewhat ironically, the demonization of alcohol and those who sold it allowed for a narrative that mitigated the actions of the drunkard himself. This is not to say that temperance advocates did not hold an individual drinker responsible for his behavior—for he is the one who made the decision to imbibe. And, by the mid-nineteenth century, few could claim ignorance of the warnings on the dangers of drink, whether they learned of them through temperance sermons, the penny press, or personal witness. Yet, according to many, the drunkard did not act alone. If the drinker could not be persuaded to refrain, perhaps his accomplices—the demon rum and the rum seller—could be interdicted. In one article, the zeal for intemperance was compared to defending the nation from a "foreign enemy," wreaking havoc on society. Certainly, the greatest sympathy was for sober society and the families of drunkards; however, those who chose to imbibe were compared to being taken into a "hopeless captivity" by this "potent and insatiate destroyer."[81]

Justin Edwards in his *Temperance Manual* provides especially graphic evidence of both the medical and moral consequences of drinking, which destroys "the bodies and souls of men." While his condemnation of the drunkard is palpable, citing stories of a man who killed his wife "while nursing her babe" and a father who beat out the brains of his "little child" with a bootjack, his efforts to deter individuals from taking even a single drink led to a characterization of the violent effects of alcohol almost as an inevitability: "Temptations to the commission of crime, which the mind when not under the power of strong drink will withstand, will lead it, when it is, to commit the crime. Iniquity, from which the soul before recoiled with abhorrence, becomes the element of its delicious revel; and crimes, from the thought of which it revolted, it now commits with greediness." He blames the manufacturers and sellers of liquor, who "teach the fatally erroneous doctrine, that the drinking of it is right" and who "corrupt the character and feed the vices of his fellow-men."[82]

When Edwards turns to the law, he suggests not only that the suppliers of alcohol are accomplices but that they may even hold a greater share of the guilt:

> Ask that widowed mother who did her the greatest injury, he who killed her long lost, drunken husband; or he who made a drunkard of her only son, the hope of her youth and the support of her declining years? Ask those orphan children, who did them the greatest injury, the man who made a drunkard of their kind affectionate father, and thus blasted all their hopes; turning home, sweet home, into an emblem of perdition; obliging them and their sick mother to flee at the dead of night, in the midst of winter, without a covering or a shelter, till she was going down with a broken heart to an untimely grave; or the man, who, after long years of this unutterable anguish, sold him the last glass which closed his eyes, and caused in that long tumultuous habitation, a great calm? Can you doubt which of the two did that lovely family the greatest mischief? If the guilt of the latter may be that of murder, what must be that of the former?[83]

Could such a man, a son or a father, be held entirely responsible for his actions under the influence of alcohol? This picture of an individual incapacitated, made irrational by alcohol, was not only supported by medical and temperance authorities, but it also paralleled simultaneous developments in the legal field regarding the potentially mitigating effects of alcohol on state of mind.

Chapter 3

"Not Capable of Entertaining This Specific Intent"

As accounts of alcohol-fueled murders became ubiquitous in popular culture through temperance rhetoric, newspaper accounts, trial reports, and literature, the public exhibited a fascination with the chilling details. The murderer's behavior before, during, and even after the act became a means to speculate on motive and intent. Did the decision to drink sufficiently constitute intent to commit crimes that took place while in a state of intoxication? To what extent was an offender's state of mind at the moment of the crime relevant to his guilt? Evidence of alcohol use did not necessarily excuse crime, but it did raise questions that complicated legal proceedings. Juries often held intoxicated offenders fully accountable for their actions, but in other cases, they shifted some of the blame to the pernicious effects of alcohol. This latter judgment may have reflected an influential temperance message that blamed alcohol for putting men on the road to ruin, but it also mirrored changes in an American legal system that increasingly required the establishment of intent.

Historically, drunkenness had provided no excuse for crime. Legal precedent and medical opinion held offenders who had voluntarily made the decision to drink responsible for their actions because the resulting state of mind was foreseeable, even if the specific acts were not. Settled insanity and delirium tremens proved exceptions because those outcomes were deemed not to be an intended result of drinking. However, a heightened focus on the issue of intent within the legal field called these strictures into question. Over time, the possibility of a compromise verdict that weighed intent alongside criminal actions emerged, as the charge of murder in many states was delineated into degrees with corresponding levels of punishment. While drunkenness did not form the only basis from which to argue for a mitigated charge, intoxication did provide one of the more powerful examples of a state of mind that rendered a person incapable of forming the requisite intent to commit first-degree murder.

The significance of intent to a criminal act lay in the legal doctrine of mens rea, or "guilty mind." English common law dating back to the mid-seventeenth century provided the precedent for this concept with Sir Edward Coke's assertion "actus non facit reum nisi mens sit rea," the idea that a guilty act requires a guilty mind. However, before the nineteenth century, courts were not particularly invested in exploring the inner working of a defendant's mind: the concept was not clearly defined, and the nature of the criminal act itself often served to sufficiently demonstrate guilt. Insanity proved an exception, but a state of insanity that was recognized under the law was not subtle. By the eighteenth century, British courts generally employed what was referred to as the "wild beast" test for an insanity defense. A person would be held not responsible for crimes only if "totally deprived of his understanding and memory, and doth not know what he is doing, no more than an infant, than a brute, or a wild beast."[1] Temporary states of insanity or an altered state of mind, which included intoxication, provided no excuse for crime. It was accepted that as the initial decision to drink was presumably made by a sane and sober individual, the resulting intoxication did not by definition meet this test. Yet the distinction between legal insanity and mens rea existed at best as an "uneasy entente," according to modern legal scholars.[2] As questions of intent began to be more seriously contemplated in criminal trials, the doctrine of mens rea provided a significant point of entry for medical knowledge in cases of insanity and criminal behavior resulting from drunkenness.

Legal doctrine in the United States, given its history as an English colony, was shaped by English law, most notably by Blackstone's *Commentaries on the Laws of England*, which sold out in its first printing in the American colonies in 1771–72. Blackstone held that laws governing men were "immutable" and discernable like scientific laws, a position that influenced the recognition of the "self-evident" truths and "unalienable rights" found in the Declaration of Independence. The concept of mens rea reflected an Enlightenment faith in reason and individual free will. In a legal consideration of who could be held responsible for committing crime, Blackstone stated, "All the several pleas and excuses, which protect the committer of a forbidden act from the punishment which is otherwise annexed thereto, may be reduced to this single consideration, the want or defect of will. An involuntary act, as it has no claim to merit, so neither can it induce any guilt."[3] In other words, a crime must be accompanied by an intent to do harm, what Blackstone called a "vitious will." While this phrase has routinely been interpreted as "vicious will," legal scholar Gerald Leonard has pointed out that "vitious" is more properly defined as "vitiated"—"unlawful" or morally corrupt. This meaning is more consistent with Blackstone's assertion that an actor was responsible for the consequences, foreseeable or not, of "an unlawful act." The evil intent and moral blameworthiness of the defendant was generally sustained by the harmful outcome of the offense. This position was consistent with English law at the time, which held voluntary drinking, to the extent that it caused public harm, did not excuse crime. An individual with a "vitious mind" was one whose behavior was at odds with the interests of society.[4]

By mid-nineteenth century, however, the legally defined "vicious mind" was less likely to be one in which the offender did not have the best interests of society at heart than it was to be one in which the offender manifested a specific unlawful intent. Legal scholars of this period reflected an optimistic faith not only in the objective nature of the law but also in a system that would mete out moral justice. The American legal system was in the throes of a shift from a framework that was "harm-oriented" to one that was "act-oriented." Earlier legal theorists weighed the threat of criminal acts on society as a whole as they considered individual volition, but changes in the legal system, buoyed by medical interest in diagnosing mental function, meant that a determination of intent became more narrowly defined.[5] While consideration of a "vitious mind" meant examining the broader social consequences of a willful action, a determination of a "vicious mind" meant a greater consideration of the specific mental state of the individual at the time of committing the act, and, consequently, an expanded consideration of the insanity defense. A determination of individual intent therefore became essential to the decision of an appropriate charge and commensurate punishment.

American legal authority Joel Prentiss Bishop asserted that establishing mens rea was a means of ensuring that punishment corresponded to the malicious intent exhibited by the offender with the goal of what has been characterized as "awarding of punishment in accordance with moral desserts."[6] Describing the general doctrine of intent in his 1858 *Commentaries on the Criminal Law,* Bishop noted that, unlike in civil law, "crime proceeds only from a criminal mind" and that "neither in philosophical speculation, nor in religious or moral sentiment, would any people in any age allow, that a man should be deemed guilty unless his mind were so." He rejected the argument that deterrence should be a consideration, questioning how the punishment of one "who meant no wrong" could be in the public good.[7] Characterized by one biographer as "driven by an inseparable mix of religious inspiration and empirical study," Bishop accorded great weight to legal scholarship and the significance of judicial decision over the rigid application of precedent. His jurisprudence was informed by both a deeply held religious sense and an abiding faith in a system of law modeled on natural science and empirical knowledge. Bishop was an influential scholar whose background of relative poverty and limited schooling made him typical of most middle-class lawyers of his time. Despite the lack of formal education, his legal writings reflected a knowledge of the mainstream psychology of his day. This approach cast Bishop as representative of jurists of his age who more purposefully weighed individual morality against a determination of intent and as such provides an example of the legal system's shift away from classical jurists "who prided themselves on separating law from morals and on divorcing law from society."[8]

Bishop came of age during the period of the Second Great Awakening, and early reformers were similarly influenced by Enlightenment beliefs that behavior derived from rational thought and that humans could exert free will in shaping their destiny. The potential conflict between the actions of the individual and the greater good of society was not immediately apparent as evangelical reformers simultaneously foresaw an improved society on earth and a heavenly reward for those who followed the moral course. However, the general vagueness of the concept of mens rea meant that actions were often subject to competing interpretations by legal actors, physicians, and even the public, who often applied their own interpretations of human nature to evaluate criminal responsibility. The distinction between the "vitious will," under which only the actual commission of an unlawful act was proved, and the "vicious will," under which a specific unlawful intent was proved, was not always apparent, nor was it always contemplated in the wake of potential social harm.

The focus on mens rea in this period reflected the growing public and professional concern over the issue of insanity. If the mind of the defendant was in some way impaired, there was an argument that there was no legal responsibility. However, what of the mind of the drunkard? Initially, the problem of drunkenness, and drunken criminal behavior in particular, seemed to pose little challenge to prevailing beliefs and institutional responses. The drunkard, in exercising his free will to drink, constituted a threat to society; thus, punishment was both moral and practical. The law even went so far as to note exceptions for those who had been made drunk accidentally or against their will.[9] Early rulings continued to hold that drunkenness was not a defense to crime. To the extent that the act of drinking itself was made through free will, individuals were wholly responsible for the consequences of their actions. However, the element of mens rea provided an argument that drunkenness did indeed affect intent and therefore responsibility.

It is not difficult to imagine an alternative scenario in which the sustained focus on temperance and the campaign for legal prohibition of alcohol furthered arguments that drinking, as a willful act, was by definition irrelevant, or even an aggravating factor, to criminal responsibility. This interpretation would follow the model of strict liability in which individuals are responsible for their actions regardless of intent or fault. For example, the element of strict liability was applied to the crime of statutory rape in the mid-nineteenth century, with courts ruling that an offender be held strictly liable for knowing the age of the victim. For this particular crime, a lack of intent to commit wrongdoing, for example, based on a mistaken belief concerning the age of an underage girl, was not an adequate defense: the crime was defined by the action alone. In this circumstance, public interest held sway over concerns for moral justice for the individual.[10]

Debates over the appropriate punishment for the drunken offender similarly represented a negotiation between private justice and public interest. This tension existed within an unsettled nineteenth-century legal climate that has been described as one in which "varieties of consequentialism—defining a self-consciously 'public' approach to criminal justice—dominated the language of criminal theory, while never entirely crowding out concerns for individual moral and legal justice."[11] Before the 1830s, evidence regarding a defendant's use of alcohol had been relevant only as a remote or unintended cause of a disordered mind where the result was either settled insanity, in which case the cause became irrelevant, or delirium tremens. However, changes in the law provided another means of introducing intoxication as a possible legal defense to crime. As intent became relevant to the determination of a criminal charge, a state of drunkenness could provide a possible defense or serve as a mitigating factor.

In 1794 Pennsylvania became the first state to distinguish between degrees of murder. The impetus behind this change sprang from reforms in the criminal justice system, in particular, a move toward rehabilitation and a reaction against capital punishment. Pennsylvania had abolished the death penalty for robbery, burglary, and sodomy eight years earlier. Justification for reforming the law pertaining to murder is found in the statute, which observed that the offenses to be defined in the law "differ . . . greatly from each other in the degree of their atrociousness." Murder in the first degree was a capital crime and was defined as "willful, deliberate, or premeditated killing" or murder committed during the course of another serious crime such as arson, rape, robbery, or burglary. Crimes that did not meet this definition were considered murder in the second degree under the law. The establishment of mens rea was required in order to convict an individual of first-degree murder and hand down a sentence of capital punishment.

Throughout the nineteenth century, other states began to similarly divide the crime of murder into degrees, with some including the charge of manslaughter in their penal codes. This change provided even greater discretion to juries who were now faced with a variety of charges and corresponding punishments to consider.[12] By 1858 Massachusetts had joined a dozen other states which already included a variety of statutes defining degrees of murder in their laws. First-degree murder was characterized by "deliberately premeditated malice aforethought"; second-degree murder fell short of this definition. The specific requirement of premeditation or intent meant that the criminal's state of mind before and during the act was relevant to the charge and eventual punishment, and the new law was praised by legal authorities for providing "certainty and humanity" to the courts.[13]

The requirement of premeditation meant intoxication was potentially relevant and mitigating evidence. The defendant who was drunk during the commission of a crime, however, still faced a substantial challenge in using a state of intoxication as an effective defense. Drunkenness, and increasingly drinking itself, were considered wrongful acts, and as Bishop observed, "when a man intending one wrong does another unintentionally, the intention and the act coalesce." Therefore, the "wrongful intent" required by the law could be found in the voluntary decision to drink. Yet noting that the charge of murder was divided into degrees in some states, Bishop did allow that drunkenness could prove that the offender was "not capable of entertaining this specific intent" as defined in first-degree murder and would be rightly convicted of murder in the second degree.[14] Thus the possibility that a state of intoxication could statutorily mitigate criminal responsibility emerged within those legal systems that required malice aforethought in order to prove first-degree murder. As one legal historian asked, "Could you, then, be so far gone in liquor that you could not make the grade as a first-degree murderer?"[15] Descriptions of the effects of intoxication found in writings on medical jurisprudence suggested that drunkenness could prove incompatible with the "wilful, deliberate, malicious and premeditated" killing that defined first-degree murder.[16] Punishment was to be meted out in line with the appropriate degree of guilt.

Even as the law continued to insist that drunkenness was not a defense to crime, American courts slowly and steadily began to rule that drunkenness should be considered in determining state of mind and subsequently an appropriate criminal charge. In 1819 the relevance of drunkenness to intent had been contemplated in English law in *Rex v. Grindley*, which stated, "Though drunkenness cannot excuse from the commission of crime, yet where, as upon a charge of murder, the material question is whether an act was premeditated or done only with sudden heat and impulse, the fact of the party being intoxicated is a circumstance proper to be taken into consideration." The question, however, was far from settled. Some judges later disagreed with this ruling, and the relation of drunkenness to intent was fiercely debated in England as well as in state and federal courts in the United States.[17]

The 1851 *United States Digest*, a summary of decisions rendered in courts of common law and admiralty, asserted that "drunkenness is no excuse of crime" but then continued to address those circumstances in which drunkenness should be considered as part of a valid defense. Here legal authority conceded that "evidence of drunkenness to an extent that absolutely incapacitates the defendant from forming such a deliberate and premeditated design is admissible for the jury, to show that the offence has not been committed." The standard evoked here was a high one, but it did establish that drunkenness could prove a viable defense to the charge of murder in the first degree, which was defined as "a deliberate, formed design to take life."[18] Drunkenness would not excuse from murder, but it could serve as evidence of a lack of the requisite intent outlined in the charge of first-degree murder. However, just because drunkenness was viewed as consistent with establishing state of mind did not mean that it always served to mitigate the charge. There continued to exist a great deal of reluctance to allow what was already considered bad behavior to excuse greater crimes. Additionally, early in the century, courts resisted considering drunkenness as an excuse because of fears that criminals would plan their crimes in such a way as to take full advantage of the law.

Courts in Tennessee debated the impact of intent and state of mind on criminal culpability in the years before passing a statute establishing separate charges for murder in 1829. The trial of Burrell Cornwell in Tennessee provides an early example in which the defense of drunkenness was raised to argue that the defendant could not have formed the intent legally required to convict of murder. The prisoner's counsel had requested that the court charge the jury to consider intoxication "a circumstance of excuse or mitigation" if it had caused Cornwell to act under "a temporary suspension of reason" or if "intoxication were not intended at the time of drinking." However, without the distinction between first- and second-degree murder yet in place, the court set the bar high, requiring that only a case of settled insanity was a viable defense and charging that "if his insanity or bad conduct arose from drunkenness, it was no excuse." Only when the habit of drinking resulted in permanent insanity could it properly be considered. Cornwell was convicted of murder.[19]

In setting precedent and instructing juries, the courts struggled with the broader implications of allowing drunkenness of any sort to act as an exculpatory or mitigating factor in criminal prosecution. In the case of *Cornwell v. State,* the appeals court seemed especially troubled by the fact that the accused was witnessed drinking with another man, Moses M'Clanahan, who had sworn his enmity against the victim, Owen Hughes, just before the murder. While defense counsel doubtless hoped this testimony would substantiate the claim that intoxication had caused temporary insanity, the court instead viewed the act of drinking in contemplation of a crime as a voluntary step toward greater malice. The court agreed that intoxication was potentially relevant but only in those cases in which there was an "entire prostration of intellect immediately occasioned by drunkenness," noting these were rare. Rather, they relied on what was viewed as the more likely scenario: "It is generally the drunken man acting out the sober man's intent." They especially feared that criminals would take advantage by intentionally drinking alcohol prior to the commission of a premeditated act. The history of criminals, it was argued, demonstrates that such men are known to rely on liquor to quiet any lingering moral qualms and to "screw his courage to the sticking point." The court noted, for example, another case in which a murderer planned to get drunk before committing a "horrid murder" and "inquired of a grocery-keeper, what kind of liquor would make him drunk soonest." If the justice system were then in turn to view such behavior as exonerative, it would mean that murderers could calculatingly use drunkenness as "a shield to protect from punishment."[20] Similarly, in *State v. Turner* in Ohio in 1831, the jury was warned that allowing drunkenness to serve as an excuse would mean that "the most hardened criminal would escape punishment, and the corrupt, and profligate and revengeful, would only have to intoxicate themselves to be exonerated from liability for crime, and to acquire the right to commit any act, however shocking and horrid, with impunity."[21]

In seeking to reach a practicable definition, the courts considered the impact of allowing drunkenness to serve as a mitigating factor not just in terms of individual justice but in service to the greater social good. Temperance organizations grew increasingly influential throughout the nineteenth century, and their admonitions against drinking would not have been unfamiliar to either judges or juries. An argument that drunkenness abrogated mens rea could be challenged by the assumption that the choice to drink was both a moral failing and a social ill; thus, the prisoner was rightfully punished. In the aforementioned Ohio case, the judge affirmed, "The habit of intoxication is highly immoral and vicious, tending to the destruction of the best interests of society."[22] In the Cornwell case, the court observed that "all civilized governments must punish the culprit who relies on so untenable a defence; and in doing so they preach a louder lesson of morality to all those who are addicted to intoxication, and to parents, and to guardians, and to youth, and to society, than 'comes in the cold abstract from pulpits.'" Significantly, it was noted that during the current term of the court, three cases of murder and one case of intent to murder by perpetrators who were drunk had already been heard. The conclusion that the choice to drink, to engage in a "degrading and disgraceful, yet too common" vice, was a lapse in moral judgment simultaneously served as a sign of the defendant's weak moral character as well as a temperance lesson on the evils of drink.[23]

However, the distinction of first-degree murder from second-degree murder, gradually adopted by the states, set up a framework in which drunkenness was considered relevant in a court of law. The courts increasingly accepted the idea that "if a man's intoxication is so great as to render him unable to form a wilful, deliberate and premeditated design to kill, or of judging of his acts and their legitimate consequences, then it reduces what would otherwise be murder of the first degree to murder of the second degree."[24] A writer in the *American Law Journal* who feared "that some unfortunate prisoners have gone to the gallows for want of a proper explanation of the law" praised a Pennsylvania judge who "humanely" explained the requisite conditions for first-degree murder—even though in the end it "did not save the lives of the prisoners."[25] The changes in statutes establishing degrees of murder were intended not to redefine the crime of murder but rather to act as a guide to appropriate punishment. A successful argument that drunkenness mitigated degree would effectively result in reduced punishment rather than acquittal.

Despite the risk of highlighting their clients' immoral habits, nineteenth-century defense attorneys not infrequently requested that the jury be allowed to consider a defendant's drinking in their determination of guilt. Intoxication became an important tool for the attorney defending a criminal drunkard when there was little chance of proving innocence otherwise. By midcentury a number of state courts were more vigorously debating the proper application of the insanity defense and the significance of state of mind to determining the degree of culpability on the part of the criminal. Intoxication would prove to be a key factor in this determination. Ordinary intoxication was no defense to crime, yet it was increasingly viewed as admissible evidence in determining a state of mind that would establish a proper charge. While the drunk criminal might still be convicted of murder, a charge of second-degree murder rather than first generally meant the difference between life and death. If a jury could be moved by a degree of sympathy for an individual acting under the effects of alcohol, the court had virtually no means by which to question the reasoning behind the decision. Ideally the legal system hoped for impartial jurors, but in reality decisions might be based on newspaper accounts, prior prejudices, misunderstandings of the law, or outside influence.

Juries could and did engage in their own sense of "popular justice" to enact vengeance or dole out mercy.[26] The law had long held that verdicts could not be impeached based on the decision process of the jurors themselves. Such an undertaking would not only be time consuming and fraught with uncertainty, but it would also represent a betrayal of the confidentiality of jury deliberation. Appeals therefore often revolved around the specific instructions given to the jury and provide insight into the legal consideration of the relevance of intoxication in determining culpability, since attorneys and judges were limited in the extent to which they could question the jury. A challenge to the instructions given to the jury, technically a point of law, could be a means to challenge the mindset of the jury without infringing upon the sanctity of the jury system itself.[27]

As drunkenness and crime progressively became subjects of scrutiny by legal scholars, physicians, and reformers, a growing body of experts in medical jurisprudence began to more carefully delineate between states of drunkenness through the observation of physical, mental, and moral symptoms. Perhaps the troubling question of responsibility and intoxication could be answered by the medical expert. Isaac Ray noted in his 1838 *Treatise* that "it has become a question of considerable delicacy in some cases to decide how far legal responsibility is diminished" by the effect of drunkenness on the mind.[28] A more "scientific" understanding of drunkenness and its effects, it was believed, was needed because of the difficulty in determining the impact of alcohol on the mental state.

Jurists similarly sought to reconcile scientific evidence with the law seeking to delineate not only degrees of crime but degrees of drunkenness. One author noted that the common practices of inquiry into the quantity of alcohol consumed were unreliable because individuals can be affected quite differently by drink. Rather he suggested that the grade of drunkenness should be defined by an informed observation of its physical and mental effects. Here, like many others including medical experts, legal scholars relied on Hoffbauer and Macnish, contemporary authorities in criminal psychology, who outlined three stages of "voluntarily, wilful drunkenness" in order to consider their relevance to state of mind and criminal responsibility.[29] The first was described as a state of mild intoxication in which the "intellectual powers remain in their normal equilibrium, and the use of his understanding is not diminished."[30] While it "stimulates men to the commission of crimes," it did not affect moral or legal responsibility.[31] The description provided was of an individual who voluntarily became drunk and was assumed to retain sufficient control over his faculties and reasoning abilities to be held legally responsible, even as it was acknowledged that the alcohol may have contributed to the likelihood that he would commit a crime. In contrast, the third stage was one in which there is "an entire loss or disorder of the consciousness," thus "imputability ceases."[32] Another author described this state as one in which "reason is gone" and the individual virtually unable to act: "As to the legal responsibility of one in this latter state no inquiry is necessary, for there can be little possibility of one who is 'dead drunk' injuring anybody."[33] Certainly, an individual in this state was considered unable to form the requisite intent to commit a crime, but presumably he was also so close to a state of incapacitation that such a scenario was unlikely.

It was the second stage of drunkenness, in which senses were "enfeebled or distorted," that was deemed the appropriate concern of the court, a stage that "renders a man 'unable to form a wilful, deliberate and premeditated design to kill or of judging of his acts and their legitimate consequences.'"[34] In this stage, physiological symptoms indicating state of mind were observable. The drinker might exhibit greater muscular strength or confused perception, as well as "stronger pressure of the blood" and "increased nervous irritability," rising to a "state of passion" and "increased excitability." This condition did not necessarily abrogate responsibility, but it might suggest the justness of a reduced sentence for the sufferer: "we cannot consider responsibility as at an end; but, on account of the deceived and confused consciousness, it is just, that there should be a diminution of the punishment for crimes."[35] Of course assumptions about character influenced this determination. One who was easily angered was thought more likely to commit a crime in the first stage in which responsibility is clear, while one known to have a normally peaceful temperament who committed a crime under the influence of alcohol could be more easily regarded as having entered the second stage of drunkenness. It was this second stage of drunkenness that became a subject of contention in courtrooms as the appropriate verdicts and punishments were meted out to drunk offenders.

Courtroom debates over criminal intent and appropriate punishment mirrored broader debates over responsibility and mental state among physicians, jurists, and reformers. Since the turn of the century, medical jurisprudence had proven itself useful in civil courts as a "sound mind" was required in order to execute a valid will or contract. By the 1820s an expanded sense of the diagnosis and treatment of insanity, which included a burgeoning focus on the effects of drunkenness, was making a similar impact in the field of criminal law. As the physical and mental effects of alcohol were studied and described by physicians, medical evidence could either support or undermine traditional ideas of responsibility. For example, the temperance movement relied on both physiological and psychological evidence to bolster their claims of the ill effects of drink, presumably hoping to convince members of society to make the moral choice to abstain. Juries regularly considered the mental state of those who, under the effects of intoxication, perpetrated untold violence on their friends and families. If the results of drink were so pernicious, was there "wiggle room" for the drunkard who had committed a crime to argue for a lesser, if not absent, sense of responsibility?

In 1827 Tennessee justices had dismissed Cornwell's intoxication as a mitigating factor, but subsequent trials reflected changes in Tennessee statutes and established that intoxication was relevant in determining intent. The circumstances of the March 1842 murder of T. G. Moore were pretty well substantiated. Wade Swan, the defendant, and Moore, his victim, had been working together rolling logs, and at some point during the day, both became intoxicated. Following dinner and a brief interaction between the two, Swan left, ostensibly to go home. Instead, he returned a few minutes later with a hand-spike he "could have killed a horse with" and struck Moore, who was sitting down leaning against the wall, two or three times, "giving him a deep cut over the left eye, two or three inches long, and breaking the bone over the eye." Moore died the next morning. Swan was arrested and admitted that he delivered the blows after being treated "damned badly" in a dispute over whether or not a twenty-dollar bill was counterfeit.[36]

The significance of Swan's intoxication was not clear under the law. The defense asked that the charge to the jury include a statement that Swan's drunkenness reduced his crime to murder in the second degree "as a matter of law," but the court refused. Swan's actions were characterized by the judge as murder in the first degree defined by "the existence of a settled purpose and fixed design, on the part of the assailant, that the act of assault should result in the death of the party assailed; that death being the end aimed at, the object sought for and wished." The circumstances of the case from choice of weapon to Swan's own sense of being wronged, it was held, reflected a "deliberate design and purpose" to take Moore's life and thus proved intent. The decision to hold Swan's intoxication as irrelevant was consistent with earlier English law establishing that "voluntary drunkenness can not excuse," as the appeals court affirmed. However, a full reading of this decision, which ultimately went against Swan, does suggest a greater willingness on the part of the court to consider intoxication as relevant to the determination of charge:

> To regard the fact of intoxication as meriting consideration in such a case, is not to hold that drunkenness will excuse crime, but to enquire whether the very crime which the law defines and punishes has, in point of fact, been committed. If the mental state required by law to constitute the crime be one of deliberation and premeditation, and drunkenness or other cause excludes the existence of such mental state, then the crime is not excused by drunkenness or such other cause, but has not, in fact, been committed.[37]

Blackstone's "vitious will" had held that an actor was responsible for his actions, foreseeable or not, in a definition of guilt that conflated moral and legal judgment. The introduction into the penal code, however, of differing degrees of murder based on intent allowed for a more flexible interpretation of culpability and a greater consideration of the role of intoxication.

The proliferation of legal arguments that intoxication served as a mitigating factor or even a defense to murder provides insight into a culture that simultaneously weighed the deleterious impact of heavy drinking on individuals against the harm such behavior inflicted on their families and American society. A defendant whose counsel maintained that the effects of intoxication indicated a lack of mens rea faced a substantial challenge in presenting drunkenness as an exculpatory factor, but by midcentury, a significant number of trials and appeals hinged on just such an argument. A consideration of mens rea to determine degree of murder meant, at a minimum, that the defendant's mental state, perhaps one influenced by heavy drinking, was relevant to the charge. On the other hand, the case against mitigation relied both on traditional law that held "drunkenness is no excuse" and a broader mission to protect society from the consequences of such behavior.

In the Alabama case of *State v. Bullock* in 1848, the defendant was found guilty of intent to murder—a charge that was upheld on appeal in the Alabama Supreme Court. However, at least one judicial observer questioned the verdict, suggesting that "possibly this case may have gone too far in refusing to allow drunkenness to be given in evidence upon the question of intention."[38] On the day in question, James Bullock, the assailant, and Henry W. Robertson, the victim, were "deeply intoxicated . . . with spiritous liquors" when Bullock "with a certain large knife . . . did cut, thrust, and stab" his drinking companion. In this case, because the victim Henry W. Robertson survived the attack, the question of intent to commit murder was a key element in the charge. The indictment read that the defendant intended "feloniously, wilfully, and of his malice aforethought, to kill and murder." The defense sought to convince the jury that Bullock's actions sprang more from his drunkenness than from any malicious intent. As noted in the bill of exceptions, the defense asked that the court charge the jury "that although drunkenness does not incapacitate a man from forming a premeditated design of murder, yet, as drunkenness clouds the understanding and excites passion, it might be evidence of passion only, and of a want of malice and design." The court refused to so charge, and Bullock was found guilty and sentenced to five years' imprisonment. The actions of the court became part of the subsequent appeal.

The judge in this case, J. Chilton, agreed that the question of malice was one to be considered by the jury; however, he instructed that "malice may be inferred from the deadly character of the weapon used in the commission of the act." The judge also considered the further implications of this type of crime, suggesting that had Bullock "slain his victim," his drunkenness would not have reduced the charge to manslaughter—essentially providing an "excuse" for murder. He cited precedent in cases in which a mitigation of charge from first degree to second degree had been argued, conceding the significance of "mental status" but claiming "that these decisions do not apply to the case before us." Even as Chilton accepted the legal relevance of drunkenness in establishing malice, he defined this evidence very narrowly.[39]

The debates and decisions to charge one degree of murder over another reflected convoluted ideas about responsibility, intoxication, and punishment. Statutes distinguishing between degrees of murder allowed for a greater consideration of the effects of intoxication on criminal actions. Arguments for lack of intent could be undermined by a belief that drunkenness should not serve as a defense to crime; on the other hand, a more expansive sense of the effects of intoxication could, almost by definition, preclude proving the intent necessary for a conviction of first-degree murder. A finding of murder in the second degree for an individual who committed murder while intoxicated suggests a compromise between acknowledging the debilitated state of mind that accompanies drunkenness and the general approbation against intemperance. For example, in the 1849 case of *Pirtle v. State* in Tennessee, the defendant was indicted for "commission of murder in the first degree by stabbing." The jury, convinced that Pirtle's "use of ardent spirits" prevented him from forming the requisite intent, decided a conviction of murder in the second degree was more appropriate. Pirtle appealed, arguing that the correct charge was the lesser one of manslaughter, given his state of mind. The appeals court, however, upheld the verdict, asserting drunkenness was relevant "not to mitigate the offence, but in explanation of the intent."[40]

Even when it was accepted as evidence by the courts, drunkenness generally was determined to be relevant to state of mind only for determining the applicability of first-degree murder, but rarely was it admissible to lessen a charge of second degree or manslaughter. Some judges attempted to limit the extent to which intoxication could mitigate the degree of crime even further and continued to see drunkenness as a potentially aggravating factor. In the case of *Haile v. State,* also in Tennessee, the judge, setting a high bar for the lesser charge, instructed that voluntary intoxication is "an aggravation" of crime and only relevant "if the defendant was so deeply intoxicated by spirituous liquors at the time of the killing, as to be incapable of forming in his mind, a design, deliberately, and premeditatedly to the act"—and even then it was argued that at best the killing could be ruled murder in the second degree. The jury subsequently found Haile guilty of murder in the first degree. An appeal was made to the state supreme court in 1850. That court disagreed, determining that "any degree of intoxication" was relevant to determining mental state: "We know that an intoxicated man will often, upon a slight provocation, have his passions excited and rashly perpetrate a criminal act. Now, it is unphilosophical for us to assume that such a man would, in the given case, be chargeable with the same degree of deliberation and premeditation that we would ascribe to a sober man perpetrating the same act, upon a like provocation." The judgment of the lower court was reversed.[41]

Legal and medical definitions were up for debate, literally, in an adversarial system of justice that required juries to rely on their own judgment. Ideally, under the law juries reach decisions through a careful assessment of the facts of the case and a thoughtful application of the law, yet undoubtedly they are also influenced by their own experiences as well as prevailing social norms. Before the nineteenth century, few opportunities for jury discretion existed, particularly in murder cases, where the instructions of the judges tended to be quite direct and the choice was "guilty" or "not guilty," with only limited and specific circumstances allowing for a determination of insanity. However, an expanded sense of legal insanity combined with the classification of murder charges into degrees created a plethora of decisions and increased discretion for the jury.

Expert medical witnesses often found their expertise challenged in the courtroom from both professional rivals and popular opinion on a variety of issues relating to medical jurisprudence. For example, one of the more pronounced challenges dealt with issues of sexuality, in which "myths, fears, and unscientific misconceptions" characterized the views of many Americans. It was not uncommon in the early decades of the nineteenth century to believe pregnancy resulting from a sexual assault demonstrated volition on the part of the woman or that sex with a virgin could cure sexually transmitted diseases.[42] Similarly, some physicians sought to disabuse the public of their traditional ideas on drunkenness. Yet here medical and legal opinions were sometimes divided, and the line between common knowledge and expert opinion was not always clear. Some juries condemned the use of alcohol and simply refused to consider drunkenness as evidence of a lack of intent. In other cases, as one legal scholar complained, juries acted "as if they were privileged to return a verdict of murder in the second degree in case they find that the defendant, when he gave the fatal blow, was at all under the influence of liquor."[43] Questions of character, intent, and responsibility seemed as subject to social consideration as to expert opinion.

Members of juries often felt themselves sufficiently qualified to form their own opinions on the nature of drunkenness, despite the testimony of medical expert witnesses and judges' often specific, and arguably leading, instructions to juries. By midcentury, most Americans were routinely exposed to stories of true crime and were well versed in the conventional temperance narrative. Tales of murder, particularly ax murders, contributed to the appeal and expansion of early mass media. Even as the penny editors relied on sensationalism, they promoted themselves as tools of self-improvement and learning for the working classes. Benjamin Day, editor of the *New York Sun*, argued that "'the public have as good an opportunity of forming as correct an opinion' on public matters as the jury or the authorities," as well as a "'right to express that opinion, whatever it may be.'" For the popular press, the "Court of Public Opinion" was just as important as official pronouncement.[44] The drunkard's defense often relied on a combination of the insanity defense and statutes that allowed for lesser included offenses that obliged juries to weigh individual actions against intent, but this defense was also argued within a very specific societal context.

On July 22, 1845, in Avon, Connecticut, Orrin Woodford murdered his wife, Diana. The choices before the jury, under Connecticut law, were acquittal based on insanity, guilty of murder, or guilty of manslaughter. An examination of the testimony in this case reveals conflicting opinions on drunkenness, insanity, and intent. Neither Woodford's insanity nor his drinking on the day of the murder were clearly established at trial. Alongside an extensive closing argument, which drew on both legal precedent and medical evidence, to establish his client's insanity, the defense attorney offered an additional option—manslaughter. He informed the jury that "This kind of homicide is 'the unlawful killing of another without malice, express or implied. There may be an intent to kill, and yet the offence may be manslaughter only, as where the act is done in a sudden transport of passion."[45]

Alerted by the Woodfords' son, Daniel, Dr. Samuel Brown was first on the scene, where he discovered the body of Diana Woodford lying on the bed. He observed an extensive set of injuries that included a "large wound on the left side of the head" and two more blows to her face, noting "the scull was fractured over a space of about three inches one way and three and a half another, and the bone depressed—a portion of it an inch deep." The cheekbone was broken, and there was a "wound over the stomach four and half inches long, which was cut entirely into the stomach, and through which I found a portion of the stomach had protruded." The likely weapon was the ax that was found in the home.[46] There was little doubt that her husband had killed her; the appreciable point of contention, among both the medical experts and local witnesses, was whether Woodford's "apparent insanity" was real or feigned, and how to distinguish signs of insanity from "the effects of cider." Woodford himself claimed he had not been drinking: "I have had no drink; we have no drink in the house." But others were less sure, and he had an established history of intemperance.[47]

There was no clear agreement among the medical experts at the trial, who contemplated testimony regarding the defendant's aberrant behavior such as digging for gold and silver in his chimney and accusing his wife of trying to poison him. Physical symptoms, such as the "wildness of his eyes," were also deemed meaningful. Brown acknowledged there were actions that "might be consistent with insanity" but then equivocated, noting he was uncertain if it was "real or feigned." Dr. R. H. Tiffany also hedged on a definitive assessment blaming "the effects of cider."[48] Agreeing that the use of alcohol complicated a diagnosis, Dr. E. K. Hunt, who was associated with the Insane Retreat at Hartford, testified, "In case of an abstemious man, it would be evidence of insanity. In case of a man in the habit of drinking, I should say that it might be the result of that habit, but coming short of aberration of mind."[49] Dr. John S. Butler, superintendent of the Insane Retreat at Hartford, lamented he had no empirical evidence, such as "the condition of the pulse," to form a "conclusive opinion." He felt confident that the prisoner exhibited signs of

A FULL REPORT OF THE

TRIAL OF ORRIN WOODFORD,

FOR THE

MURDER OF HIS WIFE,

At AVON, Conn., July 22d, 1845.

[Likeness of ORRIN WOODFORD, from a Daguerreotype by CAREY & STANCLIFFE.]

BY N. H. MORGAN,
KEEPER OF THE HARTFORD COUNTY JAIL.

HARTFORD.
PUBLISHED BY ELIHU GEER, 26 STATE STREET.
AND FOR SALE BY PETER COOKE, and ABRAHAM ROSE, HARTFORD;—T. H. PEASE, NEW HAVEN;—J. D. LYMAN, MIDDLETOWN;—SAFFORD & PARK, NORWICH;—W. W. KINGSLEY, NEW LONDON;—WM. TAYLOR & CO., 2 Astor House, BURGESS & STRINGER, corner Broadway and Ann Streets, WM. H. GRAHAM, Tribune Buildings, and GEORGE DEXTER, 30 ANN ST., NEW YORK; HOTCHKISS & CO., and REDDING & CO., BOSTON;—WM. B. BROCKETT, SPRINGFIELD;—ZEIBER & Co., PHILADELPHIA; GEORGE JONES, ALBANY, N. Y.; LEVI WILLARD, TROY, N. Y.; D. M. DEWEY, ROCHESTER, N. Y.;—ROBINSON & JONES, CINCINNATI, OHIO.

1846.

FIGURE 5. *A Full Report of the Trial of Orrin Woodford, for the Murder of his Wife*, 1845. Rare Book Collection, Lillian Goldman Law Library, Yale Law School.

insanity before the act and diagnosed him with "monomania with hallucinations" but stopped short of providing unambiguous support for the defense, noting "evidence as to his insanity at the time of the act and afterwards, is not, in itself, so conclusive to my mind."[50]

Despite the disagreement on Woodford's insanity, Woodford's actions and state of mind were viewed through the lens of the expected character and qualities of a man. Butler in particular weighed evidence of insanity through these assumptions. Observing that "men are not apt to admit, that they are insane," he was suspicious of Woodford: "His declaration that he was insane when he did it, I look upon as indicative of sanity." However, he did consider Woodford's purported abuse of his wife to be more likely due to an altered mental state, finding it an unsurprising fact "for a coarse rude man, under such an hallucination, to beat his wife if he thought her prostituted; should expect it." Furthermore, he held that "his beating of his wife to make her acknowledge guilt, is evidence of insanity." Diana Woodford's past contention that this abuse was actually a result of intemperance was dismissed by Butler, "As to his wife's saying that he was kind to her when himself, but abusive when under the influence of liquor, I regard it as of no weight. She was probably, no very competent judge of such insanity, and not perhaps suspecting it herself, she would naturally attribute his conduct to some other cause."[51]

More unequivocally, however, a report in the *Journal of the American Temperance Union* blamed Woodford's drinking and proclaimed this a "Horrid Murder from the Use of Rum and Cider."[52] Several of the women who testified agreed and vociferously asserted that Woodford was feigning insanity. Brown admitted that initially his "attention was called to the condition of the prisoner's mind in consequence of some remark about his feigning to be crazy, made by one of the women."[53] Three neighboring women who were present at the scene shortly after the murder were consistent in condemning Woodford for his drinking and the abuse of his wife. Nancy Hawley, who lived nearby, testified that on the afternoon of the murder, "I thought he appeared some as he did once before when he abused her—would walk about; seemed somehow as if he had been angry, or drinking." Sara B. Walker noted Woodford admitted to killing his wife and confronted him, asking, "how long is it since you told me you would not abuse her again? what have you done?" Similarly challenging Woodford when he tried to deny his wife was dead, Hannah Woodruff stated, "you need not try to make me think you are insane, you are no more insane than I am; if you are, cider and rum has made it."[54]

The topic of temperance allowed women to add their perspective to an existing narrative of the drunkard. As historian Carol Mattingly points out, temperance women often created effective rhetorical arguments using "comfortable, familiar language," evoking ordinary experiences to promote nontraditional reforms in temperance as well as in women's rights. Unlike the testimonials of the Washingtonians, these accounts were not used to compel the transformation and redemption of the drunkard but rather to argue for greater rights for women to protect themselves against a domestic ideal gone wrong. This narrative of intemperance came not from sober and reformed men but from women who shared powerful stories of abusive men well entrenched in the habit of drinking.[55] To the extent that temperance women advocated against liquor and for greater rights for women, they railed against demon rum and the rum seller, but they rarely lost sight of the evil actions of the drunkard himself. Woodruff, upon seeing the body of her dead friend, lamented, "oh dear, why didn't she go away?"[56] But Diana Woodford likely had few options, and intemperance highlighted the dangerous consequences of women's limited legal rights. In the 1850s Carrie Bloomer expanded her cause from the temperance movement to marriage reform, painting a decidedly unsympathetic portrayal of the alcoholic marriage in which "a pure-minded, gentle woman" is bound "to a loathsome mass of corruption."[57] It was these experiences of "ordinary" women, increasingly publicized, that highlighted the abuse and neglect that accompanied the alcohol habit in an effort to gain legal safeguards for women.

In this case, however, the women's condemnation failed to resonate. The jury did not accept the defense claim of insanity, but Woodford was only convicted of manslaughter, sentenced to ten years, and fined fifty dollars. The judge had defined a condition of insanity in which "the prisoner was so far insane when he committed the act, either from general insanity, or from partial delusion only, as to have been unconscious, either of the act itself, or of its criminal character." And given the inconclusive testimony on Woodford's state of mind, it is perhaps unsurprising he was not acquitted under this defense. A verdict of murder applied unless the prisoner was "unable clearly to distinguish between right and wrong; or to impair, in any essential degree, his force of conscience, or his knowledge as to the full guilt of the transaction." Manslaughter, characterized by the judge as "partial insanity," perhaps offered a way to acknowledge the defendant's strange behavior, whether due to mental illness or intoxication, yet still hold him responsible to some measure.[58]

In the murder trial of Terence Hammill in 1855, the court seemed persuaded that alcohol bore at least some of the blame for the death of Eliza Hammill, also deciding that her husband was guilty only of manslaughter. The first newspaper report of the murder appeared in the *New York Daily Times* under the headline "Murder of a Wife by Her Husband." The language reinforces that such acts of violence, "another horrible murder," were not uncommon and were routinely covered in the press. In fact, two other stories on the same page reported on alcohol-related crime. In one case, a man attempted to defend himself against charges of robbery, stating, "I am not guilty. I was drunk at the time." Another recounts a "probable murder and suicide" between two men gambling in a groggery. In the case of the Hammills, the domestic nature of the violence seems to have not been unanticipated. The couple was described as having lived "in a very unhappy state, on account, as is alleged, of the ill-nature of the husband, he having been constant in his abuse to his wife, occasionally beating and kicking her in a shameful manner." On New Year's night, Terence Hammill, forty years old and from Ireland, reportedly "went home in a beastly state of intoxication" and then proceeded to beat and strike his wife until she "fell to the floor a corpse." The newspaper also recounted how Hammill attempted an escape but was thwarted by neighbors, though some witnesses claimed he was found next to his wife in the apartment.[59]

Later reports provided a more sympathetic portrayal of Hammill, painting a picture of a good man done in by drink. At his arraignment, he was described as having "deeply regretted the death of his wife, but that he was intoxicated at the time, and did not know what happened." Further details revealed that he was at one time employed in "a good situation" at a warehouse but was "left penniless." Nonetheless, he retained the support of friends, who raised the money to pay for his defense.[60] In the resulting case of the *People v. Hammill*, attorney Henry L. Clinton portrayed his client as a character in what seemed to be the classic drunkard's tale: a man "strictly temperate" on most occasions but made so "infuriated and ungovernable" by drink that he "killed the wife of his youth and the mother of his children." The defense counsel certainly took care in selecting the jury, relying on peremptory challenges and spending a great deal of time interrogating jurors who would be asked to judge Hammill's actions.[61]

The question before the jury was not whether Hammill had killed his wife, for his own defense admitted that he had, but rather the effect his intoxication had on his intent to kill her. The prosecution presented a case that Hammill was a habitual drinker and that he had purposefully killed his wife. On the opening day of the trial, medical testimony was provided to emphasize the ferocity and presumed murderous intent of the injuries inflicted on Eliza Hammill. A neighbor, Thomas Malone, testified to a history of "drunken scrapes" between the couple and claimed that Hammill confessed that not only had he "meant" to kill his wife but that he "was sorry he did not do it long ago." The district attorney described Hammill's drunkenness as an unremarkable fact, noting the existence of "thousands and thousands" of other habitual drunkards in the state, and he quoted Shakespeare alongside legal authorities to note that such a habit provided "no excuse" for crime.[62]

A good part of the defense's case depended on establishing that Hammill's behavior when drunk was not indicative of his usual character or a rational state of mind. While intoxication might prove a mitigating factor, convincing the jury that Hammill's condition resembled a state of insanity offered the possibility of an acquittal. A number of witnesses for the defense emphasized that Hammill behaved as a "crazy" man when drunk. One witness noted that "very little liquor made [the] prisoner quite crazy," and another described Hammill as being "of a wild disposition and a terror" when drinking and related previous incidents in which the defendant was "drunk naked in the street." A friend and co-worker of four years similarly noted that Hammill was "wild or crazy" and "very passionate" when under the influence of alcohol. This witness, like others, testified to a remarkable personal acceptance of Hammill's seemingly violent proclivities when drinking. He noted that Hammill, when drunk, would "hunt me for my life" and "I had to run to get out of his way," yet he seemed surprisingly tolerant of such behavior, insisting the two remained "always on good terms." A local police officer similarly dismissed Hammill's drunken behavior as out of line with his true character. After describing several run-ins with an inebriated Hammill, the officer concluded, "I do not think that he knew what he was about" when intoxicated, and "when sober he was a very peaceable and quiet man." In fact, many witnesses asserted that Hammill was known to be "very kind to his family." Additional testimony, including that of his fourteen-year-old daughter, also revealed that he had suffered from a blow to his head a number of years back. While such evidence suggested that Hammill's drunken behavior was not typical, that he was perhaps inordinately affected by drink, no medical testimony was offered on this point, and the connection appears to not have been made explicit to the jury.[63]

The court's charge to the jury noted that this case was "an unusually painful one" because

> the prisoner is not a man who has been familiar with vice or hardened by crime. Though in the humble walks of life he is proved by men of the highest standing who have known him well, to have sustained the most irreproachable character for honesty, integrity, and industry, and on all occasions, except when infuriated by intoxication, for kindness and attention and affection to all his family. With that single exception, no better character in all these respects, or for quietness and unobtrusiveness of manners, could have been shown than has been established for him.

This remarkably sympathetic depiction stood in stark contrast to the details of the crime. Hammill was found "in the act of stamping upon his wife" while wearing "heavy iron-nailed shoes." His wife "exhibited marks of the most brutal violence, the head and chest being covered with bruises and blood," and died within minutes.[64] Clinton defended his client as lacking a motive and asserted he was "for the time at least insane" under the influence of liquor. The defense argued for manslaughter in the second degree, citing Hammill's otherwise good character and the fact that he did not intend to *kill* his wife, who was also derided as having been "in the habit of drinking freely" and intoxicated at the time of her death.[65]

Arguments of character and intent were accepted as legitimate points of fact to be determined by the jury. On the question of intent, the court charged, "But if his judgment was in part obscured and his only intention was to severely beat his wife, but with no thoughts that death was either certain or possible, then the jury must convict of a less offence." The fact that Hammill chose to strike his wife with kicks and blows rather than with a "deadly weapon" such as a rifle, bowie knife or poison, it was argued, spoke to his lack of intent to cause her death. An argument was also made that Hammill's state of drunkenness precluded the formation of intent. Presumably, it was noted, he was less aware of the effects of his blows due to a state of intoxication, which "clouds and obscures the judgment" and affects "the whole nervous organization" to the point of mitigating intent, even if the same act "in a state of entire sobriety" indicated "a murderous mind." Likewise, Hammill's reportedly upstanding character was relevant to the issue of determining intent, as the court added, "but where the intent is not certain, where the minds of the jury feel that the scales are nearly poised, then the jury may do that which the prisoner humbly asks them to do here, throw the weight of his good character into the scales and thus secure a preponderance in his favor. In cases not free from doubt, the law allows it." Despite the barbarity of the act, the jury was convinced that Hammill did not *intend* to kill his wife, and he was convicted of manslaughter in the second degree.[66]

The sentencing seemed to speak more as a lesson on the evils of drink than to the facts of the case. Through his attorney, Hammill threw himself on the mercy of the court, claiming no memory of the "lamentable and horrible death of his wife." While not denying the crime, he "attributes [it] solely to the use of intoxicating drinks" and proclaimed himself now a redeemed man, promising to never again "touch spiritous liquor." The court agreed, attributing the paradox of Hammill's upstanding character and the "dark deed" he had committed to "that maddening poison," which was to be blamed "partially at least, if not entirely," for the current situation. Like the verdict, the sentencing seemed remarkably lenient:

> The Court have taken into consideration your circumstances, and the condition of your little children, who appear to be wholly dependent on you for support, and are disposed to treat your case with leniency, in the hope that, now that you have had this severe experience, and have seen the danger and the peril in which you put yourself by taking into your system a stimulus that lowers you from a man almost to a level with the brute, you will, when you emerge from the prison to which you will now be consigned, come with a full determination to abandon the use of intoxicating liquors, to live the life of a reputable man, and to do all in your power to retrieve your character.[67]

In sentencing Hammill to four years and six months in prison, a mere half-year more than the minimum term, the court accepted intoxication as a mitigating factor and asserted a faith in redemption that echoed the tales of the Washingtonians.

Despite the prevailing insistence in American law that drunkenness provided no excuse for crime, by midcentury a murderer who was drunk during the commission of his deed could employ a variety of defense options to mitigate, if not excuse, his crime. A number of key precedents had been established: settled insanity caused by the habit of drinking was regarded as any other type of insanity; delirium tremens was accepted as a legitimate insanity defense; and now evidence of intoxication was considered relevant to establishing mens rea and degree of crime. Cases, like those of Orrin Woodford and Terence Hammill, demonstrate an unprecedented potential to establish that intoxication could, under certain circumstances, significantly mitigate responsibility under the law. Nevertheless, intoxication continued to hold an uneasy place in medical jurisprudence, and the chasm between vice and mental illness meant that drunkenness only infrequently served as a legitimate excuse for crime.

Chapter 4

"The Broad Resemblances between Insanity and Drunkenness"

Under the American legal system, in which the ultimate determination of guilt is made by a jury of the defendant's peers, a defense based on intoxication rests on a blend of legal, medical, and popular perceptions of the causes and effects of heavy drinking. The consequences of intemperance were of practical concern in a culture that was weighing the social costs of alcohol consumption in terms of crime, self-control, domestic relations, and health. A reliance on intoxication as a defense both depended on and challenged the legitimacy of medical and legal experts, as "ordinary" people felt qualified to speak on the all-too-common issue of drunkenness. Contemporary ideas on intoxication served to shape the debates surrounding the legitimacy of diagnoses and legal definitions.

It was difficult in the nineteenth century, and arguably today as well, to separate the social utility of characterizing chronic drinking as a disease from its nascent medical and legal sense. A great deal has been written on the controversies surrounding the insanity defense in this era, with the history of the medico-legal debates over alcohol subsumed within this narrative.[1] By the second half of the nineteenth century, the emergence and subsequent debate over moral insanity created a bridge between immoral acts and disease that allowed for greater consideration of intoxication in criminal cases. Medical science offered a profusion of diagnoses, backed by testimony from medical experts, that could support a plea of not guilty based on insanity. The inclusion of excessive or uncontrollable drinking within the lexicon of psychiatric terms was touted as proof of the illegitimacy of the concept of moral insanity, a diagnosis that was often condemned as nothing more than an excuse for bad behavior. An intractable craving for alcohol and compulsion to drink, what was frequently called dipsomania in this era and alcoholism by the twentieth century, was classified within a subset of medical conditions related to insanity. The medicalization of heavy drinking within the context of the still-developing discipline of psychiatry shaped the ways in which such behavior was treated medically and assessed legally.

Isaac Ray was a thirty-one-year-old physician in rural Maine when his *A Treatise on the Medical Jurisprudence of Insanity* was published in 1838. This text filled an appreciable need for a comprehensive discussion of mental illness and the law in the United States, signaling an expanded presence and authority for medical men in ongoing debates concerning legal responsibility. The book was favorably reviewed and was relied on extensively by lawyers and judges for decades, going through five editions before Ray's death in 1881. Although Ray was young at the time of publication, with little direct experience dealing with legal issues, he was well versed in the latest medical and legal writings from Europe. Like most doctors of his time, Ray's initial education was an apprenticeship under a local physician and then, more atypically, under George Cheyne Shattuck, a member of the faculty of Harvard Medical School. He finished his studies in 1827 at Bowdoin College, where his medical school dissertation dealt with the pathology of disease and stressed the importance of authoritative autopsies to search for and confirm causes of death. Ray had little patience for what he saw as the lack of knowledge and professionalism among his peers, and he noted that the growing emphasis on medical testimony unfortunately too often highlighted these inadequacies.[2]

Through his work, Ray looked not only to establish a career in medicine but to gain a legal audience with the hope that scientific knowledge would influence the law. He published regularly in legal journals and maintained a spirited correspondence with a variety of jurists. Despite the still-inchoate state of the field of psychiatry, Ray contended that questions of responsibility should fall under the purview of both law and psychiatry and foresaw a significant role for medical experts in the courtroom.[3] Existing legal definitions of insanity were limited and imprecise but continued to thrive, Ray argued, only because of "that reverence which is naturally felt for the opinions and practices of our ancestors." He underscored his point with references to archaic and superstitious practices surrounding the diagnosis and treatment of the insane. Medical science, on the other hand, he felt represented "advancement," and the law would be better served "yielding to the improvements of the times and thankfully receiving the truth from whatever quarter it may come."[4]

Ray established his own professional reputation by firmly aligning himself with those who sought reform in the emerging field of psychiatry. Among these were Philippe Pinel, a French physician often called "the father of modern psychiatry," who promoted what would be known as "moral therapy," and Pinel's student, J. E. D. Esquirol, who also furthered the cause of psychiatric reform and advocated an expanded understanding of insanity through a focus on the "passions" as well as the intellect. English physician James Cowles Prichard, who dedicated his 1835 *Treatise on Insanity and Other Disorders Affecting the Mind* to "Monsieur Esquirol," similarly focused on the emotional and volitional aspects of a condition he termed "moral insanity."[5] Prichard described a mental state that deemphasized reason as the defining quality of human action by suggesting mental disease could be characterized by a variety of non-intellectual forms of madness, including "a morbid perversion of the natural feelings, affections, inclinations, temper, habits, moral dispositions and natural impulses." He explained that it might exist "without any remarkable disorder or defect of the intellect or knowing and reasoning faculties, and particularly without any insane illusion or hallucination." For Prichard, insanity was not restricted to the brain but was the result of various somatic disorders, and as such the "disposition to madness" was a natural part of the human condition. In other words, anyone could potentially become mad.[6]

Intemperance, as a form of disease, was not specifically addressed in the *Treatise,* and Prichard referenced alcohol only as a contributing factor to or a symptom of other types of insanity. Yet the loss of reason, significance of habit, and the inauspicious human potential to descend into madness found in his theories certainly echoed some of the early temperance warnings against drinking. Prichard's description of insane homicide as lacking motive, plan, concealment, or escape also suggests certain parallels with the drunk murderer, and the examples he provides are of men who kill their wives and children "to whom they were most tenderly attached."[7]

Influenced by these theorists, Ray embraced the expansive concept of moral insanity—a diagnosis that included a variety of emotional and volitional impairments. He vociferously rejected the "wild beast" test, which went so far as to require that those in whom even "the slightest vestige of rationality" remained were subject to the penalty of the law. Arguing for reform in the field of medical jurisprudence, Ray's conception rested on both his medical understanding that the physical effects of mental illness could be confined to just a part of the brain, such as the moral center, and a keen sense of precedent taken from civil law that exempted those suffering from partial or temporary mental impairment from entering into valid contracts. He cited the example of a man who met the threshold to be declared "too much impaired" to manage his own property would, under current law, remain fully responsible and likely be executed for a murder committed under the influence of this same disease.[8]

With the publication of Ray's influential *Treatise,* the definition of insanity in the United States began to morph into one that had significant implications for both the medical and legal fields. Medical jurisprudence, a field that had barely existed just ten years earlier, offered the possibility of progress not just to medicine but to the legal system. Ray viewed legal reform as essential within the context of the "moral therapy" advocated by his intellectual mentors. He contrasted the emerging state of medical science with a history of the "reckless and inhuman treatment" of the insane, including those who had been accused of criminal acts, that had long been common practice.[9] In fact, one historian characterized Ray's *Treatise* as "a virtual manifesto in behalf of the innocent insane, a category of defendants whom Ray considered all too often the victims rather than the beneficiaries of American legal procedure."[10] Ray's theories, while controversial, would be enormously influential in expanding the use of the insanity defense over the next two decades.

Ray's explication of insanity as one that included the possibility of the loss of moral sense, not just the loss of reason, meant that the consequences of drunkenness could more easily be defined as a form of insanity. An 1829 address Ray delivered on temperance attests to an early and established interest in and professional recognition of the subject of alcohol.[11] Under moral insanity, behavior previously attributed to immoral character was more easily categorized under a wide spectrum of mental disease and as such could potentially serve as a legal excuse. The recognition of new diseases including moral mania, temporary insanity, kleptomania, pyromania, and dipsomania provided a variety of medical diagnoses for seemingly immoral actions.

By the 1840s a more flexible definition of insanity was endorsed by a broad swath of medical and legal professionals. In particular, the inclusion of various forms of "temporary insanity," "irresistible impulse," as well as those conditions brought on by an uncontrollable compulsion to drink, specifically provided for an expanded understanding of heavy drinking as a mental disease that abrogated responsibility.[12] True to his role as a pioneer in the medical jurisprudence of insanity, Ray dedicated two of the twenty-five chapters in the first edition of his *Treatise* to drunkenness and its legal consequences. One reason physicians up to this point had resisted viewing drunkenness as a disease was because of its temporary and voluntary nature. Only when it manifested itself as a settled form of insanity or as an unintended state, such as delirium tremens, did a voluntary behavior transform into a medical condition.

Ray's work reaffirmed the connection between the habit of drinking and settled insanity, as he observed that "the long-continued use of alcoholic liquors affects the moral and intellectual powers" in which "the original delicacy and acuteness of the moral perceptions are invariably blunted." However, he also extended the diagnostic reach of the physician to include a greater variety of drinking behaviors under the concept of moral insanity. The effects of drinking combined with the irresistible craving to drink, Ray noted, "strongly remind us of some of the manifestations of moral mania," despite its sometimes "*periodical* character." He quoted Cox's observation that those suffering from moral mania often appeared as though they were under the influence of intoxicating liquors.[13]

Beyond noting these similar effects on the moral faculties, Ray further expanded considerations of drunkenness as a disease by accounting for its habitual nature. Psychiatrist and scholar Jacques Quen has suggested that Ray's use of the term "drunkenness" was "similar in meaning to chronic alcoholism," although Ray assumed that such cases reflected organic changes in the brain.[14] In the nineteenth century, it was taken as a matter of scientific principle that mental illness, however induced, could be confirmed by a somatic indication such as brain lesions. Repeated drinking, Ray argued, caused the brain to become "accustomed to artificial stimulus" and in turn became an "indispensable habit." While acknowledging the initial "voluntary" nature of drinking, he explained that "pathological changes" affecting the brain "in turn, become efficient causes and act powerfully in maintaining this habit, even in spite of the resistance of the will." Ray questioned the degree of volition behind the decision to drink and therefore the legal assumption of intent behind the condition of drunkenness that made it no excuse for crime. He concluded that, "The drunkenness being thus an accidental, involuntary consequence of a maniacal state of the mind, it cannot impart the character of criminality to any action to which it may give rise." As evidence for the irresistible nature of the habit caused by drinking, Ray noted that "there are few who have not seen the melancholy spectacle of the most powerful motives, the most solemn promises and resolutions, a constant sense of shame and danger, bodily pain and chastisements, the prayers and supplications of friendship of as little avail in reforming the drunkard as they would have in averting an attack of fever or consumption."[15] Ray's description of the habit of drinking echoed the descriptions found in the temperance tract, even as he asserted the true cause was disease.

The disease concept of intemperance moved easily across already blurred moral and medical discourses, and experiences of intoxication were presented as simultaneously physical and moral. Insanity, more generally, had often been understood by many in the medical profession to be a consequence of a variety of immoral behaviors, including intemperance, but for many physicians, the individual choice to drink was key. With few exceptions, they were generally reluctant to connect habitual drinking with insanity. Their conception of mental disease was more likely to be consistent with traditional religious beliefs and social norms.[16] Even Ray acknowledged, "But since drunkenness is itself a sin, it becomes a question how far a person's liability for the consequences of his acts in that state can be affected by a condition which is itself utterly inexcusable."[17] With moral insanity, the recognition that insanity could exist as a temporary or periodical state, as well as the suggestion that the decision to drink was not necessarily a voluntary one, further expanded the idea that intoxication abrogated responsibility. Ultimately this equation provided greater fodder to reject the validity of a moral insanity diagnosis than it did to strengthen a legal defense based on intoxication.

Despite some concerns, the initial response to Ray's *Treatise* was generally favorable, as it provided a definition of insanity that could potentially facilitate and promote cooperation between the law and medicine, provide for a more humane consideration of the insane, and contribute in general to the professionalization of the medical field. Moral insanity seemed to offer both a more nuanced interpretation of human behavior and a diagnostic analysis that rested on scientific explanation. Certainly the "wild beast" test of insanity formalized in the early eighteenth century was insufficient to account for the variety of criminal deeds and motives that jurors were required to appraise, and Ray's work could contribute to a new legal test of insanity.

In 1843 the influential M'Naghten rules were laid down in the English case, stating that "if the prisoner retain the power of distinguishing right from wrong, his responsibility for crime is unaffected." This "right or wrong" test of insanity soon became widely adopted throughout the United States, and most current definitions of legal insanity have been influenced by this rule, which recognizes cognitive rather than volitional insanity as an excuse for crime. Despite the fact that the judge in this case cited Ray's *Treatise* as scientific support for his interpretation, Ray was critical of this legal definition of insanity, arguing it excluded the "affective and volitional disorders." Insanity did not follow a set pattern, nor could it be proven through a simple test, Ray argued. The following year, Ray testified in the murder trial of Abner Rogers, arguing that while the defendant knew the difference between right and wrong, he was insane due to "irresistible impulse." Chief Justice Lemuel Shaw of Massachusetts issued a broad ruling in this case that echoed the precedent set forth in M'Naghten but recognized the volitional aspects of the defendant's mental state when he instructed the jury that the defendant should be acquitted if his actions were "the result of disease." Shaw's corollary generated considerable debate among both physicians and lawyers over the nature of insanity and legal responsibility. Despite the "right and wrong" test becoming a generally accepted principle of law, jurists variously interpreted and voiced disagreement with the M'Naghten test as a point of law.[18]

Proponents of moral insanity had hoped that a more expansive definition of insanity would allow the mentally ill to get the humane treatment they needed and be shielded from unfair prosecution for crimes for which they could not reasonably be held responsible. Its critics, however, feared that the inclusion of a broad spectrum of aberrant behavior created too nebulous a concept, one that viewed virtually all criminal behavior as a symptom of a diagnosable moral defect. The larger net cast by the diagnosis of moral insanity, it was argued, threatened to excuse true criminals alongside actual patients. And ironically, rather than increase the reputation and relevance of physicians in the courtroom, the controversy over moral insanity meant many medical professionals began to avoid testifying in criminal trials and even saw their relevance diminish in other areas of medical jurisprudence, such as the adjudication of wills.[19]

Alfred S. Taylor, a British toxicologist who published his own text, *Medical Jurisprudence*, in 1845, openly questioned the basis and implications of the moral insanity doctrine. While acknowledging that insanity could be characterized by either a defect in the intellect or an "aberration in the feelings, passions, and emotions," Taylor declared it "doubtful" that moral insanity could exist "without greater or less disturbance of the intellectual faculties." Like many physicians before him, he presumably saw the study of insanity as a question of medical jurisprudence to be of limited utility. In his text, he noted that his subjects were listed "in order of their importance," with insanity left to the last section of the text, and "criminal responsibility" the very last chapter. His opinion that drunkenness "is held to be no excuse for crime" appears in the last two pages of the text.[20] He did agree that the "right and wrong test" had its shortcomings, but he feared the repercussions of the acceptance of moral insanity within the canon of medical jurisprudence. He argued, "Some have looked upon such cases as instances of insanity of the moral feelings only,—'moral insanity' but an unrestricted admission of this doctrine would go far to do away with all punishment for crime, for it would then be impossible to draw a line between insanity and moral depravity, and the law will not at present excuse an act committed through moral depravity."[21]

Despite Ray's urging that the medical field should promote the most progressive scientific methods and professional standards, moral insanity would typify the problematic application of medical expertise to criminal culpability by midcentury. Ultimately, the association of psychiatrists with this theory helped to turn the study of insanity, as James Mohr describes, "from a professional asset to a public embarrassment."[22] Moral insanity by definition stressed the emotions and passions over the intellect, thus broadening categories of mental impairment. However, scientific theories do not arise in a vacuum; moral insanity was influenced not only by current social conditions but by legal expediency. Lawyers utilized various legal arguments, including "temporary insanity" and lack of intent, in a bid to gain sympathy from jurors, who might be persuaded to agree on a lesser charge, or even an acquittal, for their clients. The medical evidence, sometimes verging on "mumbo jumbo" as one legal historian has argued, was less important than the establishment of an argument upon which the jury could hang a verdict of "not guilty."[23]

The most well known of the temporary insanity defenses was the "unwritten law" that upheld the right of a husband to kill his wife's lover "in the heat of passion"—a premeditated murder did not fit the criteria. Hendrik Hartog, a legal historian, has studied the "unwritten law" and focused on a number of well-known cases to demonstrate how the excuse of insanity allowed for a "recognized exception within the law." One of the most famous, or infamous, cases of the use of a temporary insanity defense was the 1859 trial of Daniel Sickles, a New York congressman, who shot and killed his wife's lover, Philip Barton Key. Since it was suggested that the adultery created the conditions for Sickles's "temporary insanity," evidence of the affair was a crucial part of the trial, and Sickles was found not guilty.[24] An "unwritten" law, however, isn't really a law, which meant that creative strategies were often required to play sufficiently on the sympathy of a jury to get them to return a "not guilty" verdict. Rarely, Hendrick notes, were women granted the same "legal privilege"; the violent "frenzy" incited by a spouse's infidelity "was less a medical or psychological defect and more a legitimate and appropriate attribute of male identity."[25] It was not a stretch for defense attorneys to describe a state of intoxication as a similar form of "temporary insanity," even as the law consistently held that drunkenness was "no excuse," largely because of its voluntary nature. And similar to the "unwritten law," this exculpatory form of insanity was more likely to be accorded based on perceptions of intemperate behavior and a middle-class male identity. As physicians and jurists struggled with the implications of changing definitions of mental illness and the law, a plea of insanity offered a viable, if not always successful, defense for some who committed murder while under the influence of alcohol.

Moral insanity was an especially promising option as a defense strategy. It described a type of insanity that paralleled drunken behavior: it could be temporary in nature and was characterized by passion or emotion. When it led to violence, the crimes were often perpetrated on loved ones and lacked clear planning. An act committed in passion could arguably reflect a diagnosable state of mind, and as more jurisdictions instituted statutes that separated murder charges into various degrees, it had become increasingly crucial to determine the defendant's mental state during the commission of a crime. A number of cases had already established the relevance of intoxication to intent, and courts sometimes viewed this condition as a significant mitigating factor in limiting, if not excusing, guilt. Citing an 1837 English case, the *American Law Register* raised the question of the relation between drunkenness and a crime committed in passion: "Thus judges have charged that drunkenness may be taken into consideration, in cases where what the law deems sufficient provocation has been given; because the question is, in such cases, whether the fatal act is to be attributed to the passion of anger excited by the previous provocation, and that passion is more easily excited in a person when in a state of intoxication than when sober."[26]

The case of *United States v. McGlue* suggests a more complicated relationship between insanity and drunkenness than had existed two decades earlier. On May 1, 1851, James McGlue, the second officer of the bark *Lewis*, stabbed and killed the first officer, Charles Johnson. McGlue's defense was that he was suffering from the disease of delirium tremens, and evidence was presented "to prove his intemperate drinking of ardent spirits during several days before the time in question, and also certain effects of this intemperance." The prosecution looked to prove ordinary drunkenness and countered that the defendant had been drinking "down to a short time before the homicide; and that when he struck the blow it was in a fit of drunken madness." McGlue was ultimately acquitted of the charge of murder. The case has some interesting parallels to the 1827 case of Alexander Drew. The murder occurred on board ship, though there was some debate as to whether McGlue's vessel was on the high seas or at port in Muscat in North Africa; both men were found not guilty based on a defense of delirium tremens.[27]

Points of law related to the insanity defense, however, had proliferated since that earlier case. Questions ruled on during McGlue's trial related to the presumption of sanity, a consideration of the degree of insanity as it related to the nature of the act, degrees of murder, and the role of experts. A clear assertion was made that voluntary intoxication conferred responsibility but that acts committed while suffering from delirium tremens were "not punishable" under the law. The medical evidence was extensive with "physicians of great eminence" testifying on behalf of both the prosecution and the defense. Without clear medical consensus, the jury was cautioned by Judge Benjamin R. Curtis on how to weigh the respective opinions of the experts: "If you consider that any of these states of fact put to the physicians are proved, then the opinions thereon are admissible evidence, to be weighed by you. Otherwise, their opinions are not applicable to this case."[28] Physicians had counted on medical jurisprudence to contribute to an enhanced reputation for their field, and by the 1840s the presence of expert medical witnesses had become commonplace, but perhaps less consequential than was hoped.

Disagreement over diagnoses of insanity and their significance to responsibility led to quarrels within and between medical and legal fields. Instead of resolving questions of medical jurisprudence, the multiplicity of opinions often created greater confusion that led jurists and jurors alike to form their own conclusions apart from expert testimony. The final instructions to the jury in the McGlue case, which sought to outline the key distinction between voluntary intoxication and a state of insanity recognized by the law, suggested a very fine line between intoxication and insanity: "If the prisoner, while sane and responsible, made himself intoxicated, and while intoxicated committed a murder by reason of insanity, which was one of the consequences of that intoxication, and one of the attendants on that state, then he is responsible in point of law, and must be punished. This is as clearly the law of the land as the other rule, which exempts from punishment acts done under delirium tremens."[29] The jury was charged with determining the cause and nature of the defendant's mental state amid confusing legal rulings and disputed medical evidence. In this case, McGlue was found not guilty.

Newspapers reporting on the murder also pondered questions of intent and insanity, but in a way that may have more closely reflected current social concerns and prevailing cultural attitudes. One of the first reports of the murder appeared in a newspaper based in Boston, where the trial was held, on July 21. The *Boston Daily Atlas* reported that McGlue and Johnson "had been on the most friendly terms throughout the voyage, and no provocation or quarrel of any sort is known to have arisen between them." The accuracy of this statement is unclear, since the paper reported that its information was based on letters received from Zanzibar, and the *New York Daily Times* later contradicted this report, noting there had been a previous quarrel between the two men. Yet the Boston paper's assertion of camaraderie served to highlight what was viewed as a troubling trend in the next paragraph: "It is not a little remarkable, that two persons are already confined in our jail for murders committed without any known provocation." Thus, McGlue's actions allowed the writer, in his article titled "Another Murder," to more expansively address the nature of crime and society.[30]

The papers were poised to offer their own opinions of the defendant's mental state. It was reported that McGlue was "unwell" on the morning of the murder, and one article concluded, even before the trial began, "the circumstances would seem to justify a plea of insanity."[31] It is unclear to what extent the writer of a later article praising McGlue's acquittal accepted the medical testimony that the accused was "laboring under the influence of delirium tremens." Rather, he seemed to form his own judgment relying on reports of the defendant's behavior as evidence: "I don't see but the acquittal was right; McGlue was unquestionably—out of his mind; his jumping from a train of cars, some months before he went to sea caused a fracture of his skull; this fact seems to have given him a most unhappy brain for drinking, yet he got on a debauch at Zanzibar, became crazy in a temporary manner, and committed murder, thus furnishing the millionth case of the curse of rum drinking."[32] The writer's conclusion seems to be based on a patchwork of theories not easily parsed: a traditional medical interpretation that looked to physical signs of insanity, an acceptance of insanity as a temporary condition that echoed more recent medical thought, and an acknowledgment of temperance warnings on the dangers of drinking. Whether the jury used similar reasoning is unknown, but undoubtedly they decided, through some combination of their interpretation of medical evidence, their understanding of the law itself, and their own experiences and perspectives, that McGlue was suffering from some version of insanity.[33]

Intraprofessional conflict and the expansion of the definition of insanity to include the effects of intoxication undermined the relevance of expert medical testimony and allowed more room for the interpretation of ordinary citizens. Speaking to the jury, Justice Curtis acknowledged ongoing medico-legal debates over moral insanity as well as the difficult balancing act between creating a more humane system for the insane and excusing criminal behavior:

> Some observations have been made, by the counsel on each side, respecting the character of this defence. On the one side, it is urged upon you, that the defence of insanity has become of alarming frequency, and that there is reason to believe it is resorted to by great criminals, to shield them from the just consequences of their crimes, when all other defences are found desperate; that there exist in the community certain theories, concerning what is called moral insanity, held by ingenious

> and zealous persons, and brought forward on trials of this kind, tending to subvert the criminal law, and render crimes likely not to be punished, somewhat in proportion to their atrocity. On the other hand, the inhumanity, and the intrinsic injustice of holding him guilty of murder, who was not, at the time of the act, a reasonable being, have been brought before you in the most striking forms.[34]

Justice Curtis's instructions in the McGlue case deviated from those judges who in an earlier era forthrightly insisted that "drunkenness provided no excuse for crime." He also provided a much more tentative definition of insanity as compared to that of Judge Story, who in the Drew case left little of the decision making to the jury and practically directed a verdict from the bench.

The theory of moral insanity had expanded the definition of insanity, and thus the insanity defense, such that intoxication could be viewed as relevant to more than just degree of crime. Intoxication, it was argued, could create a condition of insanity that provided exculpatory evidence in a defense to murder. Yet few agreed on just how and where the line should be drawn. There also seemed to be little agreement on exactly what type of insanity led to the acquittal in this case. An 1854 article in the *Monthly Law Reporter* cited *United States v. McGlue* as an example of an accepted defense of delirium tremens; a discussion of the same case cited in a later 1870 trial noted "the evidence left it doubtful whether the furious madness exhibited by the prisoner was the result of present intoxication or of delirium supervening upon long habits of indulgence."[35] Society continued to seek to limit the exculpatory nature of intoxication; however, those limits appeared quite fungible by mid-nineteenth century.

Individuals under the influence of alcohol who murdered generally had little else to rely on in a court of law outside of a sympathetic jury. Defense attorneys attempted to portray their clients as ordinary citizens whose passions were exaggerated by drink, and they utilized the tools society offered them: the tragic temperance tale of the drunkard, a temporary insanity incited by passion, a diagnosis of moral insanity that afflicted emotional responses, and legal precedents that accepted intoxication as relevant to intent. These explanations, whatever their value, were not unrelated. Drunkenness was quite common, and it was the rare juror who could not relate, at least indirectly, to the experience of an intoxicated individual behaving poorly, though whether they viewed this behavior as a mitigating or aggravating factor varied. References to "common-sense" judgments on the meaning of drunkenness were prevalent in courtrooms, and the theory of moral insanity helped put the stamp of medical expertise on this point.

Despite some early skepticism, clear opposition to the doctrine of moral insanity did not emerge until the mid-1850s, when John P. Gray took over the *American Journal of Insanity* and mounted a sustained attack on Isaac Ray and the implications of his theories. Ray had been one of the founding members of the Association of Medical Superintendents of American Institutions for the Insane (AMSAII), later the American Psychiatric Foundation, but by the early 1860s, a key contingent of asylum superintendents within this group emerged in opposition to moral insanity. Their contact with large numbers of patients within the asylum system was utilized to provide evidence disproving the existence of the condition of moral insanity. Gray was a prominent psychiatrist and expert in forensics who served as the superintendent of the New York State Lunatic Asylum at Utica from 1854 to 1886, and he had even been called on to offer his opinion to President Abraham Lincoln on cases of homicide. He became a renowned expert witness whose testimony was used to dispute the concept of moral insanity.[36]

Disagreeing that a distinction could be made between the intellectual and moral faculties, Gray warned that moral insanity served only to excuse crime and undermine the social order. Using his status and access to patients as an asylum superintendent, Gray argued there was no "clinical" or "physical" evidence to support an argument for "irresistible impulse," "impulsive insanity," or moral mania as mental diseases that abrogated responsibility for criminal behavior. Other asylum superintendents joined Gray in taking a firmer stance against moral insanity. In the 1866 "Proceedings of the Association" of the AMSAII, W. S. Chipley, superintendent of the Eastern Kentucky Lunatic Asylum, observed that among the thousands of patients respectively under his care and the care of various other medical superintendents, there had not been a "single case of what is termed moral insanity."[37]

The "Gray-Ray debate," as it became known, heated up through the 1860s as the rift over moral insanity spilled out from the pages of medical journals and into courtrooms. The very public implications of this debate were repeatedly played out in the press fueled by the spectacle of criminal trials and the growing ubiquity of the insanity defense. High-profile trials such as those of Daniel Sickles and later Charles J. Guiteau, the assassin of President James A. Garfield, undermined the insanity defense and, it was feared, the professional status of physicians. The media attention and public impact of the Sickles case highlighted the troubling implications of the latest medical definitions of insanity when they were employed in a court of law. "The medico-legalists," observes historian James Mohr, "had created a monster; with enough nerve and the right lawyers, a citizen with clout could use the concept of temporary insanity to quite literally get away with murder."[38] Despite the promise of moral insanity to contribute to the professional status and legal relevance of physicians, contention among medical and legal authorities undermined these goals.

FIGURE 6. John P. Gray. Courtesy of the U.S. National Library of Medicine.
FIGURE 7. Isaac Ray. Courtesy of Prints and Photographs Division, Library of Congress.

The inclusion of intemperance in the nosology of insanity contributed to a growing public perception that moral insanity provided a means for criminals to escape the consequences of their actions. Asylum superintendents were especially concerned with their professional status and public perceptions of their role in society as they struggled with the place of excessive alcohol use within the framework of insanity. While some physicians worked to establish dedicated inebriety asylums, by the 1880s many medical professionals distanced themselves from the moral morass of diagnosing drunkenness and the inherent difficulties in treating patients who, once sober, resisted confinement in an asylum.[39] Amid debates over moral insanity, intoxication further problematized definitions of mental illness in both the legal and medical fields.

Andrew McFarland, superintendent of the Illinois Insane Asylum, felt strongly that the doctrine of moral insanity was too often utilized to protect the criminal class and was thereby undermining the best efforts of the profession to treat psychiatric illnesses. Accepting some of the "moral treatment" arguments that had helped birth the moral insanity doctrine, McFarland characterized the practice of sending "palpable insane men" to the penitentiary as a "blemish on our civilization." However, he rejected a diagnosis of moral insanity as nothing more than an excuse for criminal acts. "Already some pretenders to psychological science," he asserted, "have thrown reproach upon the entire plea of insanity in criminal cases, by substituting the captivating name of moral insanity for what is nothing else but sheer villany." He contended that the disease was so rare that he knew of only one "doubtful" case in more than 4,400 treated.[40] His attack highlighted concerns among many asylum physicians that the legal and social consequences of a general acceptance of moral insanity would not just allow criminals to escape punishment but would undermine recognition and treatment of the truly insane. McFarland's fears were not hypothetical, and the inclusion of disorders related to intemperance under the rubric of moral insanity proved especially problematic.

In an 1863 article titled "Insanity and Intemperance," that appeared in the *American Journal of Insanity*, McFarland discussed a case in which testimony regarding a defendant's history of drinking compromised what he viewed as a viable defense of insanity. He held faith, however, that medical knowledge would be able to sort out the truth: "It is not merely with the broad resemblances between insanity and drunkenness that we have to deal, in some of the cases which occur; not the question how far a fit of intoxication renders the individual irresponsible for what he does; but we sometimes have the two states conjoined in the same individual, each with its liabilities and immunities, making a skein of commingled guilt and irresponsibility, which science must disentangle." McFarland's assessment of the complicated connections between insanity and intemperance preceded a discussion of two Illinois court cases. The first, which involved a claim to property, he outlined only briefly; the second, "of much greater importance," concerned the trial and conviction of William Hopps for murdering his wife.[41]

Hopps, fifty-nine years of age, had arrived in the United States from England thirty years earlier and established himself as a successful farmer in Wheeling, Illinois, a town approximately twenty miles north of Chicago. In 1839 he married Martha, described as a "quiet, industrious Scotch woman," and they had thirteen children, ten of whom were still living at the time of the trial in December 1862. For a number of years, Hopps had apparently been physically abusing his wife and accusing her of various indiscretions, including giving birth to a child fathered by another man and even engaging in prostitution. At their home on the night of June 30, 1862, he fatally stabbed her in the abdomen and purportedly showed no remorse afterward, claiming his wife's behavior as justification for his murderous actions.[42] No testimony presented at trial suggested Hopps's wife had indeed been unfaithful, and McFarland assured his readers that "no woman could exist in whom such accusations could be more unfounded." The *New York Times* reported, somewhat less graciously, that "the only plea was that Hopps was laboring under a delusion in regard to his wife's chastity—a woman with grown-up children—at the time of the commission of the murder."[43]

The defense attempted to establish that Hopps was insane and thus not responsible for the murder, but their argument was complicated by the fact of his intoxication at the time of the crime. McFarland, who acted as a witness for the defense, recognized the challenges in proving insanity in this case, "of obtaining credence for the fact that a mental disease and a vicious habit may co-exist; and to create a doubt that where the habit of intemperance and insanity exist together, they are not in relation of cause and effect."[44] The defense employed a variety of tactics to convince the jury of Hopps's insanity. Physical signs were offered. McFarland described the incongruity between the defendant's expressions and his speech and the telling nature of his "fatuous laugh." The pupil of his eye, McFarland testified, appeared "immoveable, neither expanding or contracting with the admission or exclusion of light. I believed it has passed beyond the control of his intellect, and only responded to the play of his passion, and I thought I detected something fiendish in it."[45] He also attributed the onset of insanity to a precipitating physical condition, "an obstinate dumb ague" of twelve years earlier.[46] At least five other physicians testified as to Hopps's "nervous temperament," rapid pulse, "odor of the skin," and a temperature of the head higher than the rest of the body to provide physical, and seemingly empirical, evidence that Hopps was indeed insane.[47]

Somatic signs remained important to physicians' attempts to establish insanity and seemed to mesh with the public's understanding that true mental disturbance would be reflected in appearance. At least one reporter drew just such a conclusion: "After looking at the accused full in the face for several minutes we could not but feel that there may be some truth in the theory of the defense, to wit: that he was at the time of the murder, and has been for years past, insane." The defense also relied heavily on establishing a hereditary cause for Hopps's insanity. A significant part of the testimony concerned the defendant's brother, Ralph, deemed "incontestably insane" through prior legal proceedings; in fact, William had previously been appointed conservator of his brother.[48] Dr. Henry Wing, most likely reflecting the view of all the physicians for the defense, confirmed the significance of a strong hereditary disposition for insanity, stating, "I regard the fact of his brother's insanity as an important fact in forming my opinion of the prisoner's condition." Testimony also confirmed that one of Hopps's daughters suffered from Saint Vitus's dance.[49]

Establishing the nature of Hopps's delusions as *distinct* from his drunkenness perhaps proved the most intractable point. The fact of Martha Hopps's abuse may have resonated more squarely with the most vicious and immoral aspects of drinking than it did with the exculpatory implications of insanity. William Hopps's pattern of drinking was well established, as was his abuse of his wife while intoxicated. Both points were stressed repeatedly by witnesses, and it was reported that his wife had applied for divorce at one point. Eva Wydneir, who had lived with Martha Hopps, noted she was abused by her husband "frequently with words and blows," and when intoxicated, he would call her a "G—d d—d b—h." John Ermichell, who worked for Hopps, also attested to the use of epithets and physical abuse as well as Hopps's threats to kill his wife.[50] Accounts of wife abuse had been employed effectively by the temperance movement to demonstrate the pernicious, and sometimes unanticipated, effects of alcohol, but testimony of domestic violence in the Hopps household may also have had the effect of reinforcing the idea that the defendant was a common, and perhaps especially mean, drunkard.

Despite the fact that Hopps had "always used ardent spirits freely," McFarland offered an alternative explanation for the defendant's behavior, emphasizing testimony that indicated he was "not regarded as an intemperate man."[51] He assured the jury that "the justification for the act committed by Hopps existed in his mind years ago," and the "liquor had but a secondary place, if a place at all, in acting upon the disease." Hopps's insanity, he continued, was defined by the nature of his delusion, and this particular type of monomania could neither be simulated nor brought on by liquor.[52] Commenting on the case some months later, McFarland clarified that Hopps's drinking was aptly interpreted as a symptom of his insanity: "the vice and disease acted and reacted on each other. When the paroxysm was coming on, he ran to the bottle by that instinct of the disease which feeds a natural excitement with an artificial one." Diminishing the detrimental significance of Hopps's drinking even further, he argued it was also possible that intoxication had actually served to delay the murderous act, noting that "the fixed purpose of the lunatic was sometimes lost sight of in the windy brawl of the drunkard."[53]

By popular accounts, McFarland made a "dignified" and "impressive" witness, offering testimony "which was of a purely scientific character," and "devoid of the slightest ambiguity."[54] Medical evidence, however, did not convince the jurors in this case who proclaimed Hopps "guilty of wilful murder." The editors of the *Chicago Medical Examiner* attempted to explain the verdict, citing "the chief ground on which the jurors were induced to set aside the unanimous testimony of medical witnesses, was doubtless the belief that whatever mental impairment or derangement existed, had been the result of the long continued and inordinate use of intoxicating liquors."[55] This type of settled insanity, however, even if caused by excessive drinking, had been established as a legitimate defense since the previous century and should have supported a case of insanity. In this case it seems doubtful that the jurors made a medical or legal determination as much as they made a practical one.

Those who believed that the physician as expert witness would enlighten legal minds and influence jurors often found that a very different experience awaited them. McFarland complained about his treatment as a witness for William Hopps: "In the defence on a plea of insanity, the expert witnesses stand in the bad light of partisans. They are not allowed the privilege of neutrality. In most of our courts they are sworn in the same motley group with witnesses of fact, and it is a chance if they do not have to stand the same pettifogging fire on cross-examination, to which those luckless unfortunates are yet subject, notwithstanding the march of refinement everywhere else."[56] McFarland was especially dismayed at the guilty verdict that contradicted his medical assessment, blaming both judge and jury. He had assured the jury that Hopps's behavior was consistent with insanity rather than intoxication, that his actions were not characterized by "that diffusive character of insanity usually displayed by persons insane from the use of intoxicating liquors."[57] He faulted the instructions to the jury, which did "not recognize the disease and the vicious habit as two incidents, to be separately considered," and thus the "fatal idea that the prisoner was either insane or drunk, was that which a juryman, not much in the habit of thinking, would most likely entertain."[58] McFarland was further outraged that not only was Hopps supplied "intoxicating liquor, apparently without stint or limit," while in prison, but that the liquor account book was read in court.[59]

Yet it is possible that the jurors felt that McFarland and the other physicians were not the best qualified to evaluate Hopps's drinking habits. Toward the end of the trial, the prosecution introduced some "rebutting evidence" supplied by several neighbors of the defendant. While not providing extracts of this testimony, the newspaper reported, "The drift of the testimony was, that Hopps was in the habit of drinking, and had been for a number of years, and that he acted as though under the influence of liquor, though not drunk, at the time the homicide was committed."[60] Drunkenness was not a medical condition, and Hopps's peers who sat in judgment of him may have accepted the assessment of his neighbors over that of physicians brought in as experts for the defense. Hopps did, however, gain an acquittal on appeal, even as one paper called this result "a mockery upon justice, and a travestie upon law" and insisted, "no one outside the Jury believes he was insane, except with liquor and passion."[61]

Despite promoting what might be interpreted as a fairly progressive sense of the relationship between alcohol and mental disease in his defense of Hopps, McFarland drew a clear line between his medical views and moral insanity, blaming his inability to convince the jury of Hopps's insanity on the latter theory. "It should be explained," he concluded, "that during the trial, the usual passage-at-arms took place between the counsel for the prosecution and a witness expert, on the subject of *moral insanity*—wholly foreign to the points of the case, and intended for mere effect." He very much resented the fact that the popularity of the moral insanity defense meant that physicians were compelled to address ideas he characterized as "broad burlesque."[62] In one sense, the Hopps case did not differ substantially from that of McDonough in 1817, in which the defendant's drunkenness left the jury unconvinced of a state of insanity; the social baggage of drunkenness could complicate a finding of insanity. However, McFarland, who himself was born in 1817, was educated and practiced medicine in a very different professional context.

By midcentury the fields of psychiatry and medical jurisprudence had gained substantial recognition, and physicians had carved a niche for themselves in both the civil and criminal court system. From McFarland's perspective, the debates over moral insanity in the courtroom were undermining the authority and relevance of the medical profession. Physicians who were not willing, or perhaps not prepared, to wade publicly into current debates on medical theories in the combative atmosphere of a criminal trial often withdrew from the legal process and subsequently hampered the cooperation between doctors and lawyers.[63] Without clear agreement on just what constituted responsibility under the law, juries, as well as the press and the general public, came to their own varied, and often contentious, conclusions.

While in Hopps's case McFarland tried to convince the jurors of insanity where they saw only drunkenness, W. S. Chipley was outraged by the outcome of the trial of Robert Smith, in which he viewed the defendant's behavior as attributable to only drunkenness but which the court interpreted as insanity. Chipley feared that the expansion of the diagnosis of insanity allowed immoral men, often aided by their lawyers, to escape just punishment by claiming, and even feigning, insanity. The vital role of the "psychologist" in detecting "feigned insanity" was underscored in his 1865 paper read before the AMSAII. "In a certain sense," he held forth, "our positions make us ministers of justice and humanity; in so far, as we may be able to expose the subterfuges of the simulator and make apparent the irresponsibility of those who are really deprived of reason." He contrasted the efforts of knowledgeable, and seemingly incorruptible, physicians with those of lawyers, to whom "the claims of truth, justice and humanity, might subject them to the charge of failing to earn their fees."[64] In the Smith trial, Chipley was particularly dismayed that the courts accepted what he viewed as dubious theories of mental illness to excuse crime.

On the evening of April 23, 1864, a dispute broke out at the bar of the United States Hotel in Louisville, Kentucky, between a patron, Smith, and the barkeeper, Frederick Landauer, when the former attempted to get a drink on credit.[65] Words were exchanged between the two, culminating in Smith's challenging the barkeeper to take the conflict to the "street." Landauer agreed, and as he began to move out from behind the bar, Smith shot his victim in the abdomen with a Derringer pistol. Landauer died before morning, and Smith was arrested and charged with killing "wilfully, wickedly, feloniously, and of his malice aforethought."[66]

There was little room to dispute the basic facts of the case, that Smith had been drinking and got into an argument with Landauer over payment for a drink, which was corroborated by numerous witnesses present at the bar. The strategy in the initial trial seemed to be twofold, as the defense sought to gain an acquittal based on either self-defense *or* insanity. A great deal of the testimony elicited from witnesses who had been at the scene concerned the respective positions of the two men and the specific actions of Landauer before the shooting. The defense argued that Smith believed the barkeeper was reaching for a weapon behind the counter, emphasizing the confrontational language on the part of both men, as well as "the custom of barkeepers to keep pistols under the counter." Yet not only was there no clear evidence that Landauer actually had a weapon behind the bar, but Smith was described as having instigated the event and clearly had been drinking.[67] As drunkenness technically remained "no excuse" under the law, the defense needed to account for Smith's drinking in a way that did not aggravate his actions.

Additional testimony for the defense suggested that while Smith had not had very much to drink, he was atypically affected by alcohol because of a diseased mind attributable to a previous illness. Some physicians testified that a "morbid desire for intoxication" could be brought on through a disease of the brain structure such as a fever or blow to the head. Joseph Woodruff, who had been drinking with Smith that evening, stated "that he knew the accused well, and that when drunk he was wild and crazy—on this occasion he was somewhat under the influence of liquor." He insisted that the "accused could drink more intoxicating liquor than ordinary men and not become drunk." Both of Smith's parents testified that their son had been "attacked with brain fever" when he was a teen. His father testified, "that ever since then, the accused when taking a few glasses of liquor, was crazy and unmanageable—on such occasions he would not know what he was doing and would abuse or attack his father or other members of his family or his best friends—on one of these occasions he attempted to kill his father, the witness, with a dangerous knife—and witness exhibited a scar on his face made by him on that occasion."[68]

Despite this troubling portrait of the defendant, another witness, Mrs. Peters, assured the jury that "the accused when not under the influence of drink or excitement—is a kind hearted man—none better—when drinking he is not at himself but crazy from disease of the brain." Dr. Ryan explained that "brain fever, when sufficiently violent to produce delirium or derangement, frequently leaves the brain in a diseased condition so that the use of alcoholic liquor easily produced undue excitement and insanity." The brain could remain in this condition even after the fever had passed. Upon cross-examination, however, the doctor was forced to admit "that he never saw Smith drunk but once, last December, about, and that on that occasion he conducted himself like other drunken men."[69] It is not clear how the jury was expected to reconcile the argument that Smith rationally acted in self-defense even as he may have been made insane from the effects of alcohol on a diseased mind. Smith was found guilty of murder and promptly filed for an appeal.[70]

The appeal focused more squarely on proving that Smith suffered from insanity, moral insanity, in particular, and as such, the attorneys introduced new medical evidence related to Smith's mental condition. They also disputed the instructions to the jury, which, they argued, incorrectly characterized the relevance of Smith's intoxication. In his request for an appeal, Smith claimed to have "discovered important evidence in his favor," in particular, an affidavit submitted to the court by physician Henry M. Bullitt, who had concluded that Smith was correctly diagnosed with moral insanity most likely attributable to the "brain fever" he had suffered earlier in his life. The accused, Bullitt explained, "had been gentle and amiable till about the 16th or 18th year of his age, and then after an attack of brain fever, he became irascible, impulsive and violent." This "change of disposition," he concluded, indicated "the continued existence of a morbid or diseased state of the brain or its membranes," which could lead to a variety of aberrant behaviors including "an insane appetite for strong drinks, a form of insanity described by writers on the subject as oinomania." His state of mind directly affected the ability to adequately discriminate between right and wrong, causing the sufferer to "be subject to sudden and overpowering impulses, under the influence of which they lose completely the moral government of themselves." Bullitt further accounted for Smith's violent actions: "Such persons, with their dispositions thus changed will lay violent hands when under these fits of impulse upon Fathers, Mothers, Brothers or Sisters, or even Wifes—or their best friends, where such acts are of frequent occurrence, the provocation being fanciful or imaginary, there could scarcely remain room to doubt, that they were the result of true moral insanity, such as rendered the individual incapable when under excitement of controlling his impulses as the most confirmed lunatic." This evidence was particularly relevant to the argument that the jury instructions in the original case, which excluded the possibility of moral insanity, were both erroneous and insufficient. The verdict, guilty of murder, was set aside, and Smith was eventually found guilty of the lesser charge of manslaughter and sentenced to ten years in the penitentiary.[71]

The reversal of the original judgment not only was significant to Smith, who had been sentenced to hang, but became an oft-cited precedent defining intoxication as a mitigating factor to reduce the degree of crime and linking it to moral insanity.[72] Judge George Robertson, who delivered the opinion of the court in Smith's appeal, was quite critical of the actions of the court in the original trial, the record of which contained thirty-six instructions. He observed that not only was it unreasonable to expect the jury to "thread such a labyrinth" but also that the appeals court had been unclear on "what precise law was given to the jury." He questioned, "Shall a man's life be staked on such a confused, incongruous, and bewildering chaos of instruction?" The decision of the appeals court specifically cited four instructions that were in error. The first two dealt with the issue of self-defense, and the last two, on which the bulk of the decision focused, concerned the legal definition of insanity. Robertson observed that "enlightened jurists" had accepted moral insanity, and thus the judge's instructions were in error when he excluded the possibility that a man suffering from this disease "is no more a fit subject of punishment than an animal without a controlling will." He also disputed the instruction that the jury should "always find in favor of sanity," if there was a "rational doubt" as to mental state; rather, he ruled that if such a doubt existed, it should "favor the acquittal of the accused."[73]

In justifying his reversal of the verdict, Robertson relied on a definition of moral insanity that was already squarely under attack by a strong contingent of medical men, including Chipley. The judge demonstrated little awareness of this changing tide in the field as he optimistically stated, "Moral insanity is now as well understood by medico-jurists, and almost as well established by judicial recognition as the intellectual form." He also rejected the classical "right and wrong" test of insanity established in the M'Naghten case, viewing such a test as only applicable in cases of "intellectual" insanity and incompatible with moral insanity. He defined the latter state as one in which the sufferer's "will being paralyzed or subordinated, the uncontrollable appetite necessitates an act which he knows to be wrong" and turns the individual into "a helpless puppet in the hands of Briarean passions." The original judge's instructions informed the jury that "'in cases of homicide, without any provocation, the fact of drunkenness is entitled to no consideration;' and that 'temporary insanity which has followed as the immediate result of voluntary drinking to intoxication, is no excuse for crime.'" Robertson acknowledged the long-held fear that if drunkenness were considered an excuse, criminals would intentionally avail themselves of this advantage: "If a man designing a homicide, drink to intoxication either to incite his animal courage or prepare some excuse, the killing will be murder." Nevertheless, he insisted that intoxication could rightly act as a mitigating factor that reduced a crime to manslaughter if there was no malicious intent, merely "sensual gratification or social hilarity, without any premeditated crime," behind the act of drinking.[74]

Robertson did not seem troubled by the question of whether a state of intoxication was intentional or temporary, considerations that had more customarily excluded it as an exculpatory factor, acknowledging that "if transient insanity ensue, although it should not altogether excuse, yet it should mitigate the crime of the inevitable act." He questioned why the idea that drunkenness can provide "no excuse for crime" should "be still recognized as law in this improved age of a more enlightened and homogeneous jurisprudence." Robertson's view on the exculpatory significance of drunkenness, informed by his understanding of what he understood as accepted medical science and "true modern law," was quite expansive and bordered on accepting drunkenness itself as a form of insanity that abrogated responsibility.[75]

Chipley commented on the decision in the appeals case in a paper that was read before the Association of Medical Superintendents in April 1866 and subsequently published in the *American Journal of Insanity* along with a summary of the case. At this point, Gray had taken over as editor of the journal, which had resolutely taken an anti–moral insanity position under his leadership. Chipley began his remarks on the case by acknowledging the complicated questions accompanying medico-legal issues of intoxication. And even as he noted his respect for Robertson, he expressed his fear that the decision in this case was a "dangerous" one in which "drunkenness is distinctly recognized as 'an excuse for crime.'" Chipley affirmed that drunkenness is not insanity: "It is a voluntary state, not a calamity. It is simply temporary excitement, accompanied by more or less confusion of intellect, brought on by the voluntary act of the inebriate," and at best, it may mitigate crime in certain cases. If drunkenness exempts from punishment, he asked, then "what protection would the law give to society from the violence and vindictive passions of wicked, heartless, and desperate men, who are restrained by no higher motive than the fear of punishment?" He noted that it can be easily feigned and readily achieved and exists as a "transient" state.[76]

Yet Chipley painted a more nuanced picture of an appropriate response to drunkenness as he revealed some sympathy for the drunken offender, in whom "the law mercifully recognizes the weakness of human nature." He further conceded that drunkenness, defined neither as an excuse nor as insanity, can be used to "rebut the presumption of malice" in a case of "passion." There is a sense that Chipley's argument was informed by a practical sense as much as a scientific one, and he was at least intrigued by, if not entirely convinced of, an expanded definition of insanity that encompassed immoral behavior. "I will readily admit," he stated, "that all crimes are species of insanity; but I am not prepared to admit the plea of insanity as an excuse for violations of law" unless there is a true defect in the ability to know the difference between right and wrong. Similarly, he characterized the line between the habit of drinking, "one of the most powerful and controlling elements of our nature," and "insanity resulting from the abuse of ardent spirits" as blurred.[77]

Early attempts to medicalize the drinking habit generally fell under the rubric of moral insanity, a theory increasingly delegitimized by the medical profession, some of whose members viewed it as potentially excusing crime and undermining their professional status and relevance to society. Diagnosing diseases related to chronic or heavy drinking became a minefield for physicians as it raised larger questions of morality and social order. This was particularly true in a society in which the temperance movement preached that the choice to have the first drink is an immoral one; how then does one excuse the irresistible habit or uncontrollable passion that may be the result of that decision to drink?

Those physicians opposed to the acceptance of moral insanity found themselves in an awkward position. After Chipley's paper was read, a prolonged discussion among various and prominent members of the AMSAII on the "legal responsibility of inebriates" commenced. One member of the society characterized moral insanity as "a bug-bear in the meetings" and wished "that the Association would pass a resolution never to discuss this subject again." Gray was less concerned with the disagreement between his fellow members than he was with the way the subject was being handled in the courts: "It is by testimony, given by those who, though professional men, do not claim to be experts in such cases particularly, that discredit and odium are brought upon us."[78] Physicians recognized that their authority was being undermined by both the suggestion that all immoral behavior was diagnosable as well as the public squabbling between physicians in the courtroom and in medical journals. Even so, the doctrine of moral insanity was significantly shaping the way questions of responsibility were understood and decided.

Chapter 5

"They Are Simply Drunk"

Defenses based on intoxication exploded by the mid-nineteenth century as the causes and effects of chronic alcohol use more acutely became subjects of scientific study. Medico-legal doctrines were evolving within a changing United States, where the problems of an urbanizing and industrializing society increasingly seemed to require broader social attention and even institutional solutions. In this context, physicians expanded the etiology of mental illness as they promoted their own professional status, recognizing, for example, the particular circumstances of the mentally incompetent defendant by advocating for his exoneration based on an insanity defense, while simultaneously establishing asylums to address the social problem of the mentally ill as well as the inebriate. As the field of psychiatry expanded amid hopes for a cure for mental illness, some of its practitioners sought to medicalize the habit of heavy drinking itself.[1] However, the distinction between drunkard and patient remained elusive, and attempts to diagnose heavy drinking under the rubric of insanity created an added risk, in an already contentious field, that its proponents were merely providing an excuse for immoral behavior.

The lack of consensus in the ensuing years, as well as the influence of social and cultural variants, is only partially reflected in the wide variety of terms that emerged for "chronic drunkenness." Early in the nineteenth century, Benjamin Rush had characterized the compulsion to drink as a condition distinct from habit rather a "palsy of the will."[2] "Dipsomania," meaning "thirst frenzy," entered the language in 1819 to describe an uncontrollable desire for drink, though its use remained limited until midcentury. In the original 1838 publication of his *Treatise,* Isaac Ray included a discussion of the "imperious and irresistible" craving for alcohol noted by Esquirol but did not identify it as dipsomania until a later edition. "Oinomania" was used similarly, for a brief period, to describe a disease defined by the inability to resist alcohol, one in which individuals were "impelled by an overwhelming propensity to do that which they know to be wrong, and from which they derive no pleasure." In 1849 the term "alcoholism" was coined by Swedish physician Magnus Huss but was only used sporadically until the twentieth century. By the latter part of the nineteenth century, "inebriety" was employed to define a disease that affected the nervous system creating a morbid craving for alcohol. It was thought to especially affect the more advanced nervous systems of a better class of men to explain their inability to resist a craving for alcohol and other stimulants.[3]

The plasticity of terms for chronic alcohol use makes some sense for a condition that historically has been seen as a hybrid of free will and habit, of vice and disease. One historian advanced the idea that the disease concept of alcoholism was "consciously metaphoric" in order "to give a scientific framework within which a condition seen as sin, failure, and disorder can be made more manageable."[4] However, the combination of plausible medical authority and the imprecise definition behind dipsomania and its related diagnoses made it a potential defense strategy for those who had committed violent crimes while intoxicated. It was rare to see a successful defense that was based solely on dipsomania, but it did sometimes give the jury something to "hang their hat on" if they were inclined at all to be merciful in their verdict. The perceived character of the defendant as well as the context of the trial were also appreciable factors affecting the outcome.

Public debates over the legitimacy of the disease concept reveal a great deal more than just the complicated and incomplete process of medicalizing alcohol abuse. Judges, physicians, jurors, the public, and the press alike revealed their respective assumptions about society, crime, and responsibility as they argued over the relevance of intoxication as a defense. Many continued to believe that drunkenness provided no excuse for crime—if the decision to drink was voluntary in nature, the individual was therefore responsible for any resulting actions. However, if an individual were diagnosed with a disease that created an "irresistible compulsion" to drink, it undercut the rationale that a sound mind had exercised free will in making that decision in the first place. Physicians had expanded their purview over insanity and its relation to alcohol, and, like most everyone else, they recognized that some individuals did form what appeared to be an intractable drinking habit. Could this be the product of a diseased mind? And if it was, what were the implications for responsibility under the law?

In his commentary on the Hopps case, Andrew McFarland certainly saw a relationship between mental illness and chronic drinking but stopped short of diagnosing the drinking habit itself. Rather, he acknowledged that an insane man might turn to the bottle as he anticipated the "paroxysm" of insanity. In rejecting the existence of the disease of dipsomania, he offered an explanation for its proliferation: "So naturally does paroxysmal insanity ally itself with indulgence in intoxicating drinks, that some nosologists, under the title of *Dypsomania*, recognize their co-existence as a distinct disease."[5] Today, one suspects, McFarland would have used terms such as "self-medicating" or "dual diagnosis." Isaac Ray similarly remarked on the difficulties of separating insanity and the compulsion to drink, acknowledging "that insanity may sometimes be fairly attributed to drunkenness, cannot be doubted; but, considering the nature of maniacal impulses, and the abundant opportunities for gratifying the desire for drink, there is reason to suspect that the vice may be an effect rather than a cause; and farther inquiry often confirms the suspicion."[6] Even those who resisted defining the compulsion to drink as a separate disease were often left to wrestle with formulating an explanation for what seemed to be irrational behavior.

Asylum superintendents in particular observed the connection between heavy drinking and insanity, though their conclusions as to the significance of that link differed widely. Thomas Story Kirkbride, superintendent of the Pennsylvania Hospital for the Insane, attributed "intemperance" as a cause of insanity for 334 of 1,953 patients, with more than half listed as "unascertained." The Alabama Hospital listed intemperance as a cause of insanity for 12 of its 94 patients, and 16 of 375 cases at the Central Ohio Lunatic Asylum were thought to result from intemperance.[7] A petition to the legislature of New York to establish an inebriate asylum in 1857 claimed "that fifty-five per cent of all of our insanity, and sixty-eight per cent of all our idiocy, springs directly or indirectly from inebriety alone."[8] As these statistics attest, habitual drinking was broadly recognized as a significant social problem, yet its status as a medical or moral issue was unresolved.

In an 1862 article in the *American Journal of Insanity*, T. H. Tanner, physician to King's College Hospital in London, denounced the increasing popularity of the term dipsomania to describe "cravings for intoxicating liquors" as a form of insanity. The implications of this line of thought posed a "danger to society," he insisted, as heavy drinking is nothing more than a "degrading vice." Noting the absurdity of characterizing "every act of wickedness or folly" as a disease, he suggested such individuals could easily be "cured" by restricting their access to alcohol—via legal detention if necessary.[9] Providing a diagnosis for the bad behavior resulting from heavy drinking was criticized as being virtually synonymous with excusing immorality and crime. John Ordronaux, the New York state commissioner for lunacy, lambasted society's fascination with "astounding crime" and the tendency to place blame elsewhere so that "every vice, every crime is disease, nothing short." Ordronaux, who was both an attorney and a physician, had been a vocal critic of moral insanity, and now he identified one of the worst examples as the "present attempt to extenuate habitual drunkenness as a special disease, removing its subjects from the sphere of moral accountability."[10]

Even though the concept of the drinking habit as disease did not rest easily in the diagnostic manual, it could serve the practical purpose of recognizing the problem and legitimizing treatment.[11] Viewing alcoholism through a scientific prism grants primacy to medical concerns over moral judgment. However, those who rejected dipsomania and its related conditions in the second half of the nineteenth century feared just those implications and thereby consciously privileged moral concerns over medical diagnosis. Ascribing the alcohol craving and the habit of heavy drinking to a disease category meant removing some of the responsibility, and perhaps some of the stigma of drinking itself, from the actor. In an era of an influential temperance movement associated with middle-class morality, few were inclined to go that far. Society, it was believed, would benefit more from discouraging drinking in the first place, and perhaps the risk of a fixed habit or criminal punishment served a higher purpose than did a determination of disease. The challenge of meting out justice for the individual while protecting society continued to play out in the courtroom.

On October 17, 1857, James Rogers murdered John Swanston in New York City after a night of drinking with friends. He was ultimately found guilty of murder and executed, an outcome that was largely cast as in the best interests of society.[12] The crime occurred after an accidental and unfortunate encounter on Tenth Avenue. Swanston and his wife, Margaret, were returning from the market when Rogers, who was walking with two companions, reportedly bumped into Margaret Swanston. Words were exchanged, and Rogers fatally stabbed John Swanston with a dirk knife. The perpetrator fled the scene and was later apprehended at his mother's house in Woodbridge, New Jersey. The grim details of the crime were covered extensively by the New York papers in a manner intended to reach a popular audience. The picture of a married couple planning "happy schemes for the future" before the murder stood in stark contrast to the testimony of the widow "attired in black" and "bowed down by a tremendous grief." More significantly, accounts of the murder demonstrated a palpable concern over "the spirit of wanton rowdyism" that characterized midcentury New York, even as they evinced some sympathy for Rogers, a youth, who was intoxicated at the time of the murder.[13]

Rogers was described as either seventeen or eighteen years old, "a steady and industrious boy" who "although rowdyish in appearance, is not of desperate aspect." His two friends testified "that the prisoner had drunk beer with them twice during the evening, that he was intoxicated, and that they were trying to get him home." Once home, his family recounted that he "fell upon the floor, and that they had to undress him and put him to bed." There were multiple witnesses to the crime, including Rogers's companions, and the defendant himself admitted he had killed Swanston. The defense had little recourse but to argue that the crime was not premeditated. Rogers, his lawyers contended, "was mad with liquor, and did not know what he was doing," and at worst, he should be convicted of manslaughter. The jury disagreed and returned a verdict of guilty of murder in the first degree after less than an hour's deliberation.[14]

There were those who, right from the beginning, supported a harsh sentence for Rogers. In one account, he was depicted as a "rowdy" who "in the frenzy of intoxication, . . . drew his knife and plunged it into the heart of a man who had done him no wrong." Young men such as Rogers, without "the first rudiments of education," were thought to represent "that wanton brutality which seems to distinguish the ruffians that infest this city."[15] New York in 1857 was characterized by uncertainty and disorder. Just a few years before civil war broke out in the nation, the city faced mounting crime, gang warfare, a police riot between rival forces, and a financial panic. Given these circumstances, it is not surprising that the author of one editorial had written, "Public security demands that rigid justice should be dealt out to that very class of youths of which Rodgers is the type; and if it is earnestly intended to cleanse the Metropolis from the stain of crime with which it is disgraced, it is necessary that the work should be commenced at once." The verdict, it was urged, should serve as "a warning to other youths of similar instincts, to pause in their career before it is too late." For this writer, neither Rogers's youth nor his intoxication served as mitigating factors, describing Rogers as "old in sin."[16]

Others were more sympathetic but ultimately sided with the protection of society over individual mercy. An interview with Rogers after the verdict painted him in a "pitiable condition." He was described as "stunned" and "stupefied," with no memory of the event whatsoever, and his mother was "so prostrated with grief that she has been unable to leave her bed." Another article described him as possessing "none of the traits of a ruffian," exhibiting a "gentleness and almost girlishness of his demeanor." One reporter, however, also recognized the primacy of public safety, suggesting there would be no clemency for Rogers "when every day the records of fresh murders, one crowding on the heels of another, successively appal our citizens." Rogers's claim that he had no memory of the deed was used as further evidence to remind readers of the dangers of "the fearful corner groggeries . . . where the most maddening poison is sold."[17]

Initially, the execution had been set for January 15, but an appeal was filed that charged various errors were made during the trial. The jury had been instructed that the verdict should be manslaughter if the "mortal blow was struck in the heat of passion," but the court refused the defense counsel's request to further instruct that if "there was no intention or motive, by reason of drunkenness, to commit the crime of murder, that the jury should find a verdict of manslaughter." The appeal made some sense given the impreciseness of the law on issues of intoxication and intent, and courts in this era continued to struggle to definitively rule on the issue. Justice Hiram Denio, Chief Judge of the New York Court of Appeals, decried this lack of clarity in the law observing that, "The commission of crime is so often the attendant upon and the consequence of drunkenness, that we should naturally expect the law concerning it to be well defined." He then proceeded to offer roughly a dozen precedents dating back to the sixteenth century that limited drunkenness from being pled as an excuse for crime. Ultimately, the judge determined that

> in the forum of conscience there is no doubt considerable difference between a murder deliberately planned and executed by a person of unclouded intellect, and the reckless taking of life by one infuriated by intoxication; but human laws are based upon considerations of policy, and look rather to the maintenance of personal security and social order, than to an accurate discrimination as to the moral qualities of individual conduct. But there is, in truth, no injustice in holding a person responsible for his acts committed in a state of voluntary intoxication.[18]

Denio received praise in the *American Journal of Insanity* for his "principles" in holding individual responsibility and community needs above leniency for the intoxicated offender. Some physicians had feared that moral insanity, which they held as a controversial and unsupportable theory, and other related forms of mental disease were diluting the system of law and order. However, this was perhaps to be expected "when habitual drunkenness is elevated, by some high authorities, to the scientific distinction of a mania,—to wit, Dipsomania,—mere casual intoxication should be deemed a sufficient defense for so venal a crime as murder." Despite "strong sympathy" for Rogers, the journal agreed with most popular accounts that the case should serve as "an awful example, showing that neither boyhood, nor the freaks of intoxication, are to receive sympathy from legal tribunals, or to be indulged in violence and crimes under the favor of a loose and misguided construction of the acts committed under their impulses."[19]

A request for a commutation of Rogers's sentence was made to Governor John King. While the governor admitted that the "youth of the unhappy convict has pleaded strongly with me in his behalf," he based his ultimate refusal to intervene on prevailing arguments, a "consideration of public justice and of private security," and Rogers was hanged on November 12, 1858. Rogers had little standing or influence with which to make his case, and in the end, despite some sympathy for his youth, the execution was held up as a defense of morality and a bulwark against what was viewed as an "appalling increase of crime" in the city.[20] After the commission of a similar murder the following July by "beastly, drunken rabble," the *New York Times* referenced this case, asking if there was "Another Rodgers in the Field."[21]

A more forceful rejection of the idea of intemperance as a mental disease similarly led to a conviction in another murder case the next month. On December 31, 1858, in Atlanta, William A. Choice shot and killed Calvin Webb, a bailiff who had arrested Choice the day before on a charge of outstanding debt. It was reported that public outrage was such that Choice was almost lynched at the time, with a meeting of citizens crying out, "hang him! hang him!!" After his arrest, the prisoner remained under protection in Midgeville for fear of retribution by friends of the victim, a man described as a "respectable and peaceable citizen" who left behind a wife and several children. Choice's defense was not guilty by reason of insanity, and evidence was presented both of an earlier head injury and of intoxication at the time of the crime. Nevertheless, the defendant was found guilty and sentenced to hang. His attorney, who it was claimed "firmly believed in the insanity of Choice," subsequently filed an appeal to the Supreme Court of Georgia. The opinion on the case, written by Chief Justice Joseph Lumpkin, outright dismissed the general concept of moral insanity, which he argued "has no foundation in the law," and specifically questioned the disease of oinomania. Lumpkin's view reflected little patience for Choice's attorney B. H. Hill, whom he sarcastically called "the powerful and indefatigable champion of the accused" as he questioned both his arguments and expertise.[22]

The perilous division between North and South at this time, just months before Lincoln's election, provided a backdrop to the decision. Lumpkin described moral insanity as "an offshoot from that Bohon Upas of humanism, which has so pervaded and poisoned the Northern mind of this country, and which, I fear, will cause the glorious sun of our Union to sink soon in the sea of fratricidal blood!"[23] Lumpkin's interpretation of drunkenness and insanity forthrightly rejected the disease model in favor of what he most likely would have characterized as old-fashioned common sense, asserting, "As for myself I would rely as implicitly upon the opinions of practical men, who form their belief from their observation of the appearance, conduct and conversation of a person, as I would upon the opinions of physicians who testify from facts proven by others, or the opinions even of the keepers of insane hospitals." In fact, he welcomed evidence from "non-experts," and his decision upheld the admissibility of "opinions of persons not experts as to the sanity of the prisoner" and "opinions of witnesses that the prisoner appeared to be drinking." He further rejected testimony that the family's decision to limit Choice's access to weapons was a recognition of a diseased mind, concluding instead that it was a prudent choice given that the defendant was dangerous "while in his cups." Choice's earlier gripe with his victim was interpreted as evidence that spoke to a state of drunkenness rather than insanity: "A drunken man rarely if ever shoots or stabs another, unless he cherishes some resentment towards him. It is quite otherwise with the insane."[24]

The appeal alleged a number of errors in the original trial relating to the significance of Choice's intoxication to his culpability, including a failure to specifically instruct the jury on the disease of oinomania, by which the defendant "was irresistibly impelled by a will not his own, to drink; and being so impelled did drink, and thus became insane from drink, and while thus insane he committed homicide." Lumpkin refused to entertain either the existence or the implications of the disease of oinomania: "Whether any one is born with an irresistible desire to drink, or whether such thirst may be the result of accidental injury done to the brain, is a theory not yet satisfactorily established. For myself I capitally doubt whether it ever can be." Of course, as a man of the law, Lumpkin accepted the exculpatory nature of insanity, but he agreed with Judge O. A. Bull, the original judge on the case, that there were only two options for the jury to consider: "that the killing was murder, or excusable on account of the insanity of the accused." He thereby rejected the defense's objection that Choice's intoxication could serve as a mitigating factor and that instructions should have been given to the jury on lesser degrees of the crime. He asked, "what had the law of manslaughter to do with this case?" and suggested it would have been "a mockery and farce" to instruct on voluntary manslaughter. Lumpkin agreed wholeheartedly with Bull, who did not want to "confuse" the jury "by attempting to notice all these learned distinctions," and dismissed the significance of Choice's drunkenness to the question of sanity.[25]

The implications of recent psychiatric diagnoses related to drunkenness were interpreted as suggesting a far-reaching destruction of responsibility under the law, at odds with common sense. Despite what appeared to be widespread agreement on the decision in this case and the testimony of six physicians that the defendant was sane, Choice's attorney reportedly had some influence and made a successful application to the state legislature for a full pardon for his client. The effects of the social and historical context in this case were certainly palpable. The coverage of Choice's trial at times appeared alongside reports of the trial and execution of John Brown, the abolitionist who had raided Harper's Ferry hoping to incite a slave insurrection. Brown's lawyer had initially attempted to mount an insanity defense, but this was forthrightly rejected by his client, who sought no excuse for his actions.[26] After his pardon, Choice spent a brief time in an insane asylum and then became a sharpshooter for the Confederate army, serving with the Rome Light Guards. Accounts noted he "made a brave soldier."[27]

FIGURE 8. Memory Hill Cemetery, William A. Choice, Confederate Rome Light Guards. Mike Stroud, HMdb.org.

Courtroom debates and judicial decisions reflected broad cultural trends just as surely as they highlighted significant debates within the medical and legal fields. The trial and conviction of Ann Barry in 1866 not only touch on issues of drinking and insanity but also shed light on fundamental issues related to gender and alcohol, highlighted by the crime of infanticide and presumptions of class. Initial accounts of the drowning death of a child in Rochester, New York, in July 1865 did not identify Barry as the perpetrator. The local paper, reporting on a "most shocking case of infanticide," incautiously accused a young woman by the name of Cotter as a suspect, assuring its readers, "Cotter and crime are synonymous terms. WE never knew man or woman by the name that was not a thief or a prostitute." The next day, the paper sheepishly admitted its mistake and apologized, having "been informed that there are respectable people by the name." A week later it reported the arrest of Ann Barry, who was caught at the train station ready to head west. Returning to their derisive reporting style, the same paper described Barry as a woman "of stout build, a gross amorous female."[28]

At the time of her trial, Ann Barry was thirty-eight years old. Her marital status was unclear; she had married a man named Daniel Barry at some point in her twenties, but he was believed to be a deserter from the army, had not been seen for three years, and was possibly deceased. She reportedly had remarried a man named Frederick (also identified as Frank) Smith, but the legality of that marriage was in question, and she was not identified with his last name. The deceased child was purportedly the offspring of this latter relationship; Barry also had one other surviving child, who was twelve years old. She had been arrested numerous times for crimes, including petit larceny, and drunkenness and disorderly conduct, which caused her to be confined to the penitentiary on five different occasions. In early 1865 Barry was arrested for stealing clothes from a wash line and sentenced to six months, during which time she delivered a baby girl. Her daughter was approximately five weeks old at the time of her release on July 10.[29]

The fact of Barry's gender is essential to understanding the crime itself, infanticide, but it is also significant to perceptions of her drinking and questions related to her sanity. The crime of infanticide became highly publicized in the 1860s as a means of drawing attention to the plight of women in circumstances so dire that they would take the lives of their own children in a marked violation of women's most sacred duty. Sarah Barringer Gordon, in her study of a case that took place just three years after Barry's, noted this paradoxical view of the crime of infanticide. Despite the recognition of the circumstances that drove women to this state, sympathy had its limits, and support for women's criminal behavior, particularly the killing of babies, ultimately undermined the cause of social reform.[30]

Barry had not only committed infanticide; she had also reportedly been drunk at the time. Women's intemperance was not necessarily an uncommon problem. In 1849 New York City, for example, one reformer observed that 40 percent of those held in jails for public drunkenness were women. In his study of temperance and gender, Scott C. Martin points to the fact "that female drunkenness, as well as its recognition and discussion by reformers, occurred far more frequently than has been acknowledged by contemporary observers or modern scholars."[31] However, women drinkers did not fit easily into existing narratives of temperance, and middle-class reformers held even more pronounced strictures against women's drinking. Thomas Doner's 1877 autobiography, *Eleven Years a Drunkard*, notes, "Men can reform; society welcomes them back to the path of virtue. . . . But, alas, for poor women who have been tempted to sin by rum, for them there are no calls to come home, no sheltering arm, no acceptance of confessions and promises to amend."[32] Women's intemperance proved a much heftier social transgression.

One of the better-known temperance narratives to focus on a woman, *Confessions of a Female Inebriate*, was presented as the autobiography of a "lady," though it is widely believed to have been written by Isaac F. Shepard. The contravention of social norms of the main character's drinking was emphasized in the story through her "fraternization" with the servants as well as through neglect of her role as wife and mother. One night, while intoxicated, the protagonist mistakenly gave her sick daughter laudanum instead of the paregoric provided by the doctor. Her intemperance apparent to all, she blamed herself for the girl's death, which occurred a few days later.[33] The actual cause of death was left somewhat ambivalent, but the message is clear that, as in Barry's case, the victim of a woman's drunkenness was the child she should have protected and nurtured. These actions might have led to a powerful redemptive story for a man in a similar position, but here the author notes: "O how wide the difference with the heart of a woman! She may be forsaken, abused, trampled on, but amid all, the thought of separation does not enter her heart; if the whole world scorn and forsake him, it is the reason why she clings more closely to the wreck, but let the wife be scorned and forsaken of the world, and the husband will not bide the disgrace."[34] Temperance narratives generally reserved greater condemnation for women whose drinking led to the neglect, sometimes fatal, of their young children.[35]

Assumptions about gender and drinking accordingly provided the backdrop to Ann Barry's trial. Barry had confessed to the crime and was assigned counsel by the court due to her impoverished circumstances. At the trial's commencement, it was critical to establish that Barry was indeed the mother of the child that was found, and a great deal of testimony corroborated the fact that the defendant had given birth and left the penitentiary with a healthy child. This point of fact was essential not only to establish the facts of the crime but because, as Gordon has noted, jurors who were inclined to be sympathetic to a mother who killed her child looked for "a sense of plausible doubt about the cause of death (thus the exercise of compassion would not be based on an obvious ruse) and on the desperation of the accused (who presumably, therefore, acted out of panic and despair rather than as a calculating murderer.)" Given the extensive evidence provided by various employees and supervisors at the penitentiary, a witness who saw her at the canal, and Barry's own confession, there was little question as to the act itself.[36]

Other than some reference to Barry's challenging circumstances, there was little evidence of redemptive value presented at trial. Barry appeared as neither a good mother nor a good wife, and in fact, she was possibly a bigamist. The only acknowledgment that she might have had a sense of regret for her crime was her statement that, after seeing the child struggle in the water with a stone around her neck, "she felt sorry and would have rescued it if she could have done so at the moment" but was scared off by some approaching men.[37] The details of the crime are certainly grim, but male drunkards had employed defenses built on the idea that violence against a loved one was not only unintended but possibly evidence of a mind altered by the effects of alcohol.

It was at least possible that the horrific nature of the act, as well as a history of Barry's criminal and deviant behavior, could be used to justify a defense of insanity in this case. Both her drinking and the murder of her child might perhaps prove aberrant enough, particularly in light of typical gender conventions, to convince a jury that no sane woman could conduct herself in such a manner. A history of drinking might provide further support, as "delirium from habitual drunkeness would make her an irresponsible person," though simply being under the influence of liquor would not. The defense elicited testimony that was presumably intended to demonstrate that Barry's long history of drinking was somehow medically deranged in its nature. Initial questioning along this line was at first challenged by the prosecution who asked what the defense "expected to show by this testimony." Her attorney responded that "he was proposed to show that the defendant was insane continuously from the habitual use of intoxicating liquors, and they also proposed to show that from blows she received on the head at certain times she was at times insane." The defense was allowed to proceed with this line of questioning, but much of the testimony was unclear, especially whether Barry's husband had caused her injury, and a great deal was possibly detrimental to her character.[38]

The defense tried to argue that Barry was "a decent girl before her marriage," and the fault for her initial decision to drink, it was argued, was not Barry's but her husband's. Several witnesses testified that her first husband had "forced" her to drink on numerous occasions. It was not uncommon to portray women's drinking as yet another ill effect of men's intemperance on the domestic ideal; however, much of the testimony described Barry's behavior as decidedly less conventionally feminine. Witnesses recounted that Barry often "looked wild" and reportedly spoke out to her dead father. Even more transgressive, on one occasion she "took hold of her mother and threatened her," she laughed at her brother's funeral, and she kissed another woman who "could not get away from her." Despite objections, lay witnesses were allowed to speculate not only on Barry's behavior but on her medical condition, specifically the issue of whether or not she was actually insane. Several relatives and friends declared her to be of "unsound mind" as well as specifically suffering from delirium tremens.[39]

The testimony of four physicians for the defense lacked agreement on the concepts of insanity and legal responsibility. Elisha Preston, a local physician, threw in everything but the kitchen sink, stating an individual could be made insane by drunkenness, blows upon the head, repeated incidences of delirium tremens, or dipsomania, although he did admit that the act of infanticide was not in and of itself a sign of insanity. Another stated he did not see evidence of insanity but that he considered "every drunken person insane, temporarily."[40] Resolved that there was no evidence of "insanity proper," a writer for the *American Journal of Insanity* criticized these medical expert witnesses in an 1868 article titled "Drunkenness and Crime," maintaining that the testimony "showed that confused understanding of the limits of legal responsibility in such cases, which has tended to bring medical opinions on these subjects into disrepute." The significance of this statement in the journal is especially apparent as John P. Gray, superintendent at the State Lunatic Asylum at Utica and well-known opponent of the doctrine of moral insanity, had agreed to testify for the prosecution. While Gray acknowledged that habitual drunkenness could lead to dementia, mania, or a temporary state of delirium tremens, he absolutely rejected the argument that excessive drinking was in and of itself a disease. He stated in language likely to be well understood by the jury, "I do not recognize the disease called dipsomania; it is intemperance. I do not consider a person insane when intoxicated; they are simply drunk in my opinion."[41] Ann Barry thus was not a patient but an immoral criminal.

In the end, it is unclear what, if any, impact Gray's testimony had on the actual verdict rendered. Ann Barry was found guilty of murder in the second degree and sentenced to life at the state prison at Sing Sing. The local newspaper, which had been quite severe in its opinion of Barry, reported that, "The jurors, or the larger number of them, unhesitatingly stated that they were fully convinced that Ann Barry, with premeditation, took the life of her offspring, and that she was sane when she committed the deed." Yet, apart from the opprobrium associated with her drinking, Barry's gender likely had some mitigating effect on the final verdict and punishment. First-degree murder was a capital crime. The jury's decision to convict of murder in the second degree, rather than first degree as charged in the indictment, was reportedly based on an "abhorence to hanging a woman" on the part of two of the jurors, who were then able to convince the others. The question of capital punishment had been raised earlier, when it was reported that there was some difficulty in compiling a jury because so many potential jurors resisted rendering a verdict that would lead to the death penalty. It was observed that "the gallows is evidently growing very unpopular if the jurors are to be credited in their statements."[42] Degrees in the charge of murder had been instituted in part due to objections to the death penalty, and while intoxication was frequently cited as a relevant mitigating factor in making such a determination, in this case, it was likely reached in spite of Barry's drinking, which was presented as an aggravating factor. The reluctance to execute Barry seemed to stem more from her gender than from her defense.

Gray agreed with Barry's sentence, stating, "the woman received, I think, the punishment which she merited." Despite his unequivocal denial that Barry's actions were anything but criminal, Gray offered some recognition of the harsh social conditions she had faced:

> She was perfectly brutalized, and brutalized in the face of society. Society saw it, and yet took no particular pains to prevent it; no pains to reclaim her. She had just served out a period of several months in the workhouse, and was turned out with twenty cents and an illegitimate child a few months old. She took this small amount and bought enough whiskey to get partially drunk, tied a string around the child's neck, took off its clothes, which she subsequently pawned, and threw the child into the canal.

Yet he emphasized that no member of Association of Medical Superintendents would support the defense of moral insanity in this case, forthrightly rejecting an expansion of the diagnostic criteria of insanity to excuse what he described here as "simply a case of murder."[43]

Parsing the influence of medical ideas versus prevailing social biases on verdict and sentencing is both challenging and variable. While the legitimacy of moral insanity continued to be debated within the medical field, the diagnosis also offered new possibilities for understanding mental illness that did not sit comfortably within the legal rubric established in the M'Naghten case. The M'Naghten rule had been an attempt to create greater consistency in how the insanity defense was employed in criminal cases by defining insanity as a question of law relevant to establishing guilt, a legal rather than medical determination. The result was a more rigid definition of criminal responsibility than that suggested by the theory of moral insanity, which was much more open-ended—not only as it separated the intellectual and emotional aspects of behavior but as it included temporary conditions and newer definitions of mental disease. The M'Naghten rule had engendered controversy from the beginning with its proponents lauding the workability of a clear legal test and its critics arguing that this test failed to capture the complexity of the behavioral consequences of mental disease. Despite the considerable influence granted to the law in this rule, a number of judges considered this definition of insanity too rigid and the determination of insanity as a question of law misplaced.

Some U.S. courts reached an uneasy compromise by adding the "irresistible impulse" test to legal definitions of responsibility.[44] A well-regarded justice of the New Hampshire Supreme Court, Charles Doe, drew heavily on Isaac Ray's theory of moral insanity when he introduced, in 1866, what became known as the "New Hampshire rule." In formulating this interpretation of legal insanity, Doe believed that the M'Naghten case had erroneously characterized mental disease as a question of law rather than a question of fact to be decided by the jury. Doe was greatly influenced by Ray's theories of moral insanity, as evidenced by a substantial record of correspondence in these years and had largely based his 1868 dissent in the testamentary case of *Boardman v. Woodman* on his suggestions. However, Doe shied away from referencing Ray too extensively for fear of courting additional controversy. Consistent with his interpretation of the law, Doe did not seek to enshrine moral insanity within the law but rather to create a place in which changing understandings of insanity could be debated, by medical experts and lay witnesses alike, as matters of fact for the jury to determine.[45]

Doe therefore argued for a much more malleable definition of insanity that could simultaneously adapt to the latest medical theories and incorporate the experiences of non-experts. At the same time, he questioned the special status mental illness held under the law: "Why should the law say that delusion is a test of any form of mental disease, when the law will not say that certain other symptoms are the tests of gout or small pox?"[46] He feared that legal rules, such as the test of right and wrong, were too inflexible and potentially mired in outdated theories, citing the pronouncements of seventeenth-century legal scholar Sir Matthew Hale on witchcraft to make his point. Such precedents, once established, remained products of past history and social practices that were often no longer relevant. His approach, he argued, was one that "takes off the shackles of precedent and authority,—opens the subject to be decided in each case as an entirely new subject. Juries may make mistakes, but they cannot do worse than courts have done in this business." Some critics had insisted that complicated points of law and confusing judicial instructions meant that juries were already making decisions based on "horse sense" rather than the law.[47] This was particularly true in cases involving intoxication, in which unsettled medical debates, entrenched cultural assumptions, and weighty social consequences made for a slippery medical and legal argument determining legal responsibility. Given Doe's insistence on an evolving definition of insanity and his contention that jurors were best suited to decide a defendant's mental condition, it is not surprising that the case most significant to establishing the New Hampshire doctrine, *State v. Pike,* was based on a defense of a fairly recent and decidedly controversial diagnosis—dipsomania.

On May 7, 1868, in Hampton Falls, New Hampshire, Josiah L. Pike assaulted Thomas Brown and his wife, both in their seventies, with an ax in the course of a robbery. The crime, described as "one of the most revolting, cold blooded crimes ever recorded," shocked the community. The couple was still alive when a farmhand reporting for work the next morning was greeted by Mr. Brown, "covered with blood," and his wife, barely conscious and shielded with rugs by her husband. Both succumbed to their injuries soon afterward. Six or seven hundred dollars was reportedly stolen, and Pike, a former employee of the victim, was arrested shortly thereafter with "part of the plunder upon him," including new clothes and a watch. It was reported that Pike had confessed his guilt to the sheriff, though he later denied it.[48]

Pike's trial was at the end of October before Chief Justice Ira Perley and Justice Doe. The defense hoped to prove that Pike was insane, specifically that he "was a victim of dipsomania (an insane thirst for intoxicating liquor)."[49] The challenge for the defense was not only to establish that Pike was not guilty by reason of insanity when he committed the crime of murder and robbery but to first convince the jury that his drunkenness should be characterized as dipsomania, a mental disease that excused from responsibility. The evidence against Pike was strong, and his defense made little attempt to refute the facts of the case. The newspaper reported that the testimony of a "score" of witnesses for the state "tended to fasten beyond doubt the murderous act upon the accused, which fact was evidently accepted by counsel for the defence, as there was little attempt by cross-examination to invalidate the testimony." Rather, Pike's defense to this "shocking act" was that he was suffering from what was described as "insanity caused by drunkenness—a disease called dipsomania by physicians which rendered the party irresponsible for his acts."[50]

As was often true in these cases, witnesses for the defense painted a picture of a man who was "dangerous" only when intoxicated. Two of Pike's brothers "testified to his uncontrollable appetite for liquor and his apparent necessary want of the same" to the extent that they had to lock him up to keep him from drinking. A successful insanity defense required that the jury be convinced that Pike's behavior met the level of mental disease rather than the type of drunken behavior that was likely familiar to most of them. As such, defense witnesses further testified to the unique character of Pike's intoxication, noting "that liquor did not effect his body to enfeeble it, but strengthened and stimulated, for he was never known to stagger or reel like other men under the influence of liquor." When drunk Pike was described as "unconscious of what he was doing, acting with all the cunning and madness of an insane man." His brothers further noted their father had exhibited similar behavior, perhaps alluding to early theories on the hereditary character of insanity, and one newspaper suggested that Pike had "inherited his father's weakness."[51]

Intemperance, as an inherited trait, could provide support for a diagnosis of dipsomania; however, the transmittal of undesirable traits was in this period defined less precisely and portrayed more ominously as a threat to the community. Speaking on the "dangerous classes," in an article published just the year before Pike's crime, T. Edwards Clark, professor of chemistry, noted that "habits" often "find permanent record in our descendents," and "children are found following in the footsteps of dissipated parents" with profound consequences to society. "Drunkenness," in particular, he continued, "often descends in some other form, and shows itself in crime and vice."[52] Temperance supporters often employed inexact language that spoke to the transmission of bad habits and tendencies to children, thus the history of Pike's father likely would have also spoken more broadly to the impact of drinking on families. The senior Pike was known to drink heavily and was purportedly "particularly violent," causing his wife to be "afraid of her life" and in a "continual state of fear." Eventually she left with the children, and her husband "died a drunkard."[53]

It is unclear where a jury, or the general public for that matter, drew the line between the violent and immoral behavior associated with drunkenness as a vice and the violent and immoral behavior associated with drunkenness as a disease. Pike's defense was well-buttressed by medical testimony that assured the jury that the defendant was not legally responsible for his actions, that the disease of dipsomania was an accepted medical finding, and that science identified the "morbid desire for intoxication" as a physical and mental disorder. Utilizing the term "methomania" in an 1869 article, Stephen Rogers cataloged a variety of symptoms that indicated a diagnosis of this form of insanity including an "irresistible desire" to drink, concealment of drinking, drinking alone, and drinking without regard to taste or quality. He recounted some of the horrific effects of this loss of "self-control," brought on by "insane hallucination, or by the frenzy of tormenting desire." The story of a methomaniac who was unable to obtain alcohol after being placed in an almshouse illustrated the depth of the desire for intoxicating drinks:

> He went into the wood-yard, seized an axe, and, placing his hand upon a block, cut it from the arm at a single blow. With the bleeding stump raised, he ran into the house crying, "My hand is off! Get some rum! get some rum!"
>
> In the confusion of the moment, a bowl of rum was brought, and, plunging the bleeding member of his body into the fluid, he raised the bowl to his mouth, drank freely, and then exultingly exclaimed, "Now I am satisfied!"

The intense craving for alcohol and resulting loss of control formed the crux of the diagnosis and raised the question of whether such an individual could be legally responsible for his actions.[54]

The question of vice versus mental illness was rampant in medical debates on the existence of diseases, such as dipsomania, that explained habitual drinking. A consideration of the consequences to society as well as to the medical profession were never far removed from the discussion.

Dr. Yorick G. Hurd of the Insane Hospital at Ipswich was convinced that Pike was "a victim of dipsomania, as much as any patient he ever attended for insanity." Dr. E. A. Perkins of the Inebriate Asylum in Boston, presumably concerned with establishing the legitimacy of the diagnosis, spoke hypothetically on the case, concluding that "the presumptions were strongly in favor of the prisoner's mind being diseased with dipsomania, and that he was morally unaccountable for what he did when in a state of intoxication brought on by this unnatural, uncontrollable and insane appetite for liquor." Other physicians concurred. The state similarly used medical experts to challenge this testimony, but their strongest controverting evidence may have been non-expert witnesses who testified that Pike "acted like other drunken men."[55]

Despite the general ubiquity of the insanity defense, Justice Perley's instruction to the jury that he had never known a defendant to put in a plea of dipsomania suggests the newness of the diagnosis and the untried nature of the defense. Dipsomania was not only controversial; it was unfamiliar to many. Newspaper accounts included definitions for the term ranging from "an insane thirst for intoxicating liquor" to "in a word a crazy drunkard." The jury remained unconvinced of the defense argument, and Pike was found guilty of murder in the first degree and sentenced to be hanged. Upon Pike's conviction, it was reported that "dipsomania [was] not a sufficient plea for homicide" and that "the Judge did not consider it a good excuse."[56]

Several points related to establishing a successful insanity defense were contested in the appeal, highlighting ongoing debates over the rules for determining insanity as well as a still-tenuous acceptance of intoxication as a form of mental illness that could excuse crime. Justice Perley had instructed the jury that the symptoms and tests of mental disease, and even the existence of the disease of dipsomania itself, were to be decided as a matter of fact, rather than as a matter of law as had been interpreted under the M'Naghten rules. Reflecting Doe's interpretation of the law and establishing what would be known as the New Hampshire doctrine, the court ruled that "whether there is such a disease as dipsomania, and whether a respondent had that disease, and whether an act done by him was the product of such disease, are questions of fact for the jury."[57]

Indeed, it appeared that the relatively recent nature of research on the subject was a key factor in upholding this point, as the court noted, "if there are any diseases whose existence is so much a matter of history and general knowledge that the court may properly assume it in charging a jury, dipsomania certainly does not fall within that class." Thus the existence of the disease itself, let alone whether or not it was a factor in Pike's guilt, was left to the jury to decide.[58]

Yet the judges disagreed on the type of evidence the jury could consider in making such a determination, seemingly divided over the extent to which intoxication could be viewed as a medical condition. During the trial, non-expert witnesses testified for the state, describing various incidents concerning Pike's behavior and state of intoxication, but the defense was not permitted to call non-expert witnesses to testify as to Pike's insanity. The appeals court upheld procedure, stating that "any witness may testify, that a person was intoxicated, or under the influence of intoxicating liquor." However, "the opinion of a witness, who is not an expert, as to the sanity of a respondent, is incompetent, although formed from observation of the respondent's appearance and conduct." Doe dissented on the latter point, arguing that the testimony of non-experts should be given consideration. Of course, as the distinction between intoxication and sanity was, by definition, unclear in the case of dipsomania, a witness's testimony on intoxication likely blurred into a judgment of Pike's sanity.[59]

The consideration of dipsomania as a defense in this case led to the formulation of the New Hampshire doctrine, which expanded the test of insanity created in the M'Naghten rule.[60] Yet the legal significance of the case was irrelevant to Pike, who was executed on November 9, 1869, in Concord, New Hampshire, for the murder of the Browns. Pike's last words belied the defense that he was not responsible for his actions due to disease, as he warned others from a similar fate: "But I wish to leave a warning in my last words to those who are inclined toward intemperance. It has decided my fate and ruined my soul. I entreat those who deal in intoxicating drink to stop that dreadful work; and O, I implore their victims to stop before it is too late."[61] In focusing on the compulsion to drink rather than just the effects of intoxication, diseases such as dipsomania shaped medical, legal, and even popular understandings of the alcohol habit, but their potential to excuse crime and subsequently inflict harm on society remained troubling.

In 1873 the third edition of Wharton and Stillé's *Medical Jurisprudence* appeared in print. Despite the fact that physician Moreton Stillé had died before publication of the original 1855 edition, his name continued to appear next to that of attorney Francis Wharton as a testament to the collaboration between the medical and legal fields that had been lacking in other similar works. The text had quickly become required reading in medical and law schools with both its popularity and numerous revisions providing a sense of the changes in medical jurisprudence in the second half of the nineteenth century. Questions of responsibility as they related to insanity and drunkenness were substantially addressed in the first volume of the text, dedicated to "mental unsoundness." Not surprisingly, the first edition had presented an optimistic vision of the elucidating impact of medical testimony in the courts. The use of competing medical witnesses had not yet become standard in such cases, and "moral insanity" was not yet under significant attack.[62]

Eighteen years later a more expansive, and potentially exculpatory, definition of drunkenness as a disease was perceived by a broad contingent of jurists, physicians, and reformers to be at odds with the greater good of society. Wharton noted that before the 1860s "there had been no positive and final repudiation by psychological science of the theory of criminal monomanias"—a fact he quickly sought to remedy in his third edition. He criticized the growing "toleration of the idea of irresponsibility" and noted there had since emerged "almost an unbroken denunciation of a scheme of psychological romanticism which sober-minded men have learned to feel is as repugnant to science as it is hostile to society" He praised some of the judicial reform affecting the adjudication of the truly insane, but he warned of the "enlargement of irresponsibility" that "enfranchised a dangerous class of outlaws, too insane to be punished for crime, and yet too sane to be restrained." Using "drunkenness" as an example, Wharton advocated for an interpretation of law that avoided the "extremes" of execution or acquittal, as exemplified in the German system of "diminished responsibility" and in the American system, which weighed intent and degree of crime.[63]

Questions of responsibility by and large were malleable under the law, yet in weighing the cost to society, the courts remained reluctant to extend the exculpatory potential of intemperate behavior too far. In 1873, the same year Wharton published the third edition of his *Treatise*, the case of *State v. Johnson* was heard in Connecticut. The defense had failed to convince a jury that Johnson was not guilty of murder because he was suffering from the disease of dipsomania, which "had affected his nervous organization, and which rendered him more easily affected by intoxicating liquor." A verdict of guilty of murder in the first degree was reached. In a subsequent appeal, the jury's decision was overturned because it was decided that the original judge did not sufficiently mediate the implications of that charge. The appeals judge was concerned that when the jury "was told that 'drunkenness does not excuse a party from the consequences of a criminal act,' it is probable that they did not distinguish between excusing a crime and showing that the specific crime charged had not been committed," specifically murder in the first degree. "The danger," he continued, "is that the jury, while making up their verdict, excluded from their minds the subject of intoxication altogether." The jury rightly should have considered evidence of the defendant's intoxication to decide whether the prisoner "was incapable of deliberation."[64]

A new trial was ordered, and Johnson was this time convicted of murder in the second degree. The defense again appealed asserting the instructions to the jury should have specifically stated that Johnson's intoxication may have caused him to be "unable to form a deliberate and premeditated purpose to kill any person." The reduced sentence, however, was apparently as far as the courts were willing to go. The verdict was upheld on appeal, with the court noting the "implied malice" in the charge and the view that intoxication combined with killing is "a crime against society."[65] The trial and multiple appeals in Johnson's defense reflect both the impact and limits of a consideration of intoxication on criminal responsibility as the courts sought to balance justice for the offender alongside protection of the social order.

Chapter 6

"An Apology for Sin and for Crime"

In the anniversary address of the first issue of the *Quarterly Journal of Inebriety* in 1876, Theodore L. Mason, president of the American Association for the Cure of Inebriates (AACI), congratulated his organization on its advancement of the disease concept of inebriety. He recalled how the association's members had been attacked as "not only utopian but immoral" for daring to consider inebriety a disease, and he strove to distinguish their goals from those of moral reformers who felt that "to speak about inebriety as a disease was represented as framing an apology for sin and for crime."[1] Formed in 1870, the AACI consisted of a small group of inebriety specialists, physicians who believed that the habitual use of alcohol was a specific disease that could be cured through treatment in a specialized hospital. This centerpiece publication of the AACI, which appeared six years later, continued to further the growing interest in and treatment of inebriety. That same year, the American Medical Association included a session on alcohol and drug inebriety at its annual meeting, and by 1891 a large number of medical libraries and asylums and more than two thousand individual doctors subscribed to the journal.[2]

Belying Mason's optimism, however, assessments of habitual drunkenness continued to occupy a space somewhere between vice and disease. The concept of inebriety was not revolutionary, having significant historical precedent in the rhetoric of both physicians and clergymen. Members of the AACI were not the first to call the alcohol habit a disease, nor were they the first to point out the seemingly addictive nature of various stimulants. In some ways, the early writings of the inebriety specialists did not differ significantly from those of reformers in their emphasis on the social costs of the abuse of alcohol. For decades temperance advocates had described chronic alcohol use as a disease, citing the addictive nature as well as the physical and mental health consequences of drinking, even as they warned the public from the vice of "demon rum." The inebriety specialists were similarly concerned with the "habitual use of alcohol potations" and the broader effects of "drunkenness" on society.[3] Mason acknowledged the association of disease with vice in attempting to counter some of the criticism against inebriety, asserting that "*sin* was no less *sin* because it was followed by *disease* as its direct consequence, so *disease* was no less truly *disease* because it was caused by a *sin* or a *vice* or both."[4]

Joseph Parrish, former superintendent of the Pennsylvania Sanitarium and the Maryland Inebriate Asylum and one of the founders of the AACI, similarly viewed inebriety as a disease distinguishable from the ordinary vice of drinking. In his study of "alcoholic inebriety," he utilized numerous clinical cases to draw the line between the "vice aspect" and the "crime view" of inebriety. "Professional criminals," he noted, are "too shrewd to become intoxicated," whereas the inebriate exhibits characteristics such as "timidity, incautiousness and inefficiency" that tend to limit the commission of crime.[5] Unlike the moral reformers, inebriety specialists' bailiwick was in treating the repeated or habitual user of alcohol, and their focus was on the resulting propensity to disease rather than on the initial decision to drink. Through presumably observable and quantifiable symptoms, inebriates were defined as patients rather than as sinners or common criminals. and their actions were viewed as the result of disease.

Inebriety specialists advanced a view of excessive drinking that was not diagnosed as a form of insanity per se but rather as a dysfunction of the higher nerve centers. In this they were influenced by George M. Beard's theories on nervousness and neurasthenia. Beard's *Stimulants and Narcotics* was first published in 1871, predating his better-known works on "neurasthenia" and "American nervousness." Drawing a correlation between American civilization and nervousness, Beard suggested that nervous disease, a "deficiency or lack of nerve force," was a product of modern times. "The chief and primary cause of this development and very rapid increase of nervousness," he observed, "is *modern civilization,* which is distinguished from the ancient by these five characteristics: steam-power, the periodical press, the telegraph, the sciences, and the mental activity of women." Among the various symptoms of nervousness, Beard noted a "susceptibility to stimulants and narcotics and various drugs, and consequent necessity of temperance; increase of the nervous diseases inebriety and neurasthenia (nervous exhaustion)."[6] Beard furthermore insisted that different causes could apply to different classes of men: "Drunkenness as a vice, among the better classes of civilized lands, is then decreasing, while drunkenness as a disease, inebriety, is increasing," though "among the lower grades of social life, the *vice* of drunkenness abounds in its most revolting aspects."[7] The prevailing if unresolved distinctions between drinking as a vice and drinking as a disease frequently rested on an overt sense of class distinction. As one physician proclaimed, "There are many such men who are inebriates—men of learning, integrity and piety—which is only another proof that inebriety is a disease."[8]

Ultimately, however, the association with Beard was doubly unfortunate for the inebriety movement. While neurasthenia made a significant impact upon its introduction, the diagnosis became vague and diffuse before the end of the century.[9] Additionally Beard lacked credibility among the next generation of neurologists emerging in the 1870s and 1880s. He was often perceived as arrogant, and his scientific theories were viewed as unsophisticated by his peers; one even referred to him as the "Barnum of American medicine." His involvement in the defense, based on insanity, of Charles J. Guiteau for assassinating President James A. Garfield certainly did not endear him to much of the public who saw in that trial some of their worst fears of physicians providing an excuse for violent crime realized.[10]

Inebriety, like dipsomania, suffered an uneasy relationship with medico-legal interpretations of insanity. By the 1880s, debates within the medical field over responsibility and intoxication may be best represented by two individuals: Thomas D. Crothers, an acknowledged leader of the inebriety movement, and Edward Charles Spitzka, a prominent neurologist. Crothers served as the superintendent of the Walnut Hill Asylum (later the Walnut Lodge Hospital) in Connecticut, professor of nervous and mental diseases at the New York School of Clinical Medicine, and editor of the *Quarterly Journal of Inebriety*. A staunch advocate of promoting a disease model of addiction and treatment for alcoholism, he remained well aware of the difficulties in applying a medical model to excessive drinking.[11] "Although fanatically devoted to the cause of medicalizing drunkards," observed one historian, Crothers "admitted that the prospects for medicalizing drinking through an analogy with lunacy were not good, given the state of public opinion."[12]

Yet this project was challenged by more than public opinion. The next generation of physicians who came of age professionally in the wake of the debates over moral insanity had to navigate the promise of medical professionalization alongside the simultaneous decline of optimism over providing viable treatment and achieving an effective cure for what was often viewed as ordinary vice.[13] While unfailingly advocating for treatment and expressing faith in a cure, Crothers reminded his readers that the inebriate presented a difficult case, as he often appeared "to be in possession of his mind," though he rightly existed "on the other side of that mysterious border-line of mental health."[14] The temporary nature of drunkenness proved challenging to physicians who had admitted intoxicated patients into asylums only to face a sober and seemingly sane individual after only a few days. In one example reported in the *New York Times* in 1869, Hermann Albert challenged his detention at Blackwell's Island on the grounds that he "was not a lunatic in any proper sense of the word." Although his father testified that Albert "had no control over himself after he had taken a couple of glasses" and had on prior occasions "beaten him while in a condition of inebriety," the patient was discharged. Judge Daniel P. Ingraham stated he did "not put much confidence" in the medical testimony and instead encouraged Albert to reform his habits. Once sober, there was little evidence that the defendant's behavior was indicative of insanity rather than ordinary unruly drunkenness, and the judge concluded, "if this man could be held, under the evidence, in the Lunatic Asylum, on Blackwell's Island, then a large portion of the citizens of this City should be there also."[15]

Representing a new class of neurologists, Edward C. Spitzka, described as "brilliant, acerbic and highly controversial," possessed a sophisticated European education in medicine and an expanded faith in the influence of hereditary factors on insanity. A graduate of the Medical Department of the University of the City of New York, Spitzka became a rising star in the field of neurology. He practiced as a surgeon at Mount Sinai Hospital and was a consulting neurologist at numerous other institutions. He variously served as president of the New York Neurological Society and the American Neurological Society and acted as editor to the *American Journal of Neurology and Psychiatry*. To the general public, Spitzka was most well known for his participation in the defense of Guiteau at his murder trial. However, while convinced of Guiteau's mental incompetence, Spitzka vigorously opposed any attempt to expand the definition of insanity to include what was termed "moral insanity." He agreed with physicians such as John P. Gray who had vociferously rejected moral insanity, but he often found himself at odds with asylum superintendents as he embraced heredity factors and downplayed the significance of organic changes as causes of insanity.[16]

Spitzka was also quite cautious about the connection between mental illness and heavy drinking. He argued for a clear and lengthy etiology of "chronic alcoholic insanity" to be differentiated from the state of intoxication that resulted from voluntary drinking. He recognized the existence of "certain mental disturbances of a character peculiar to alcoholism," but he cautioned that "not all forms of mental disorder found in such subjects properly belong to the group of dementia or insanity 'from organic disease.'" Spitzka recognized the insidious nature of the alcohol habit that was characterized by "a marked enfeeblement of the will" that at first manifests itself in "the inability of the inebriate to resist the temptation to drink." However, it was only with "continuance of the vice," leading to the emergence of "positive signs of the disorder of a somatic character" and "deterioration of a neurotic character," that a "well-characterized psychosis can be confirmed."[17] Crothers's description of the symptoms of inebriety, which included "moral prostration" or "paralysis of the will," was suggestive of what Spitzka would have viewed as out-of-date and discredited formulations.[18]

Attempts to reconcile psychiatry and the law, a relationship historian Janet A. Tighe has compared to a troubled marriage, were increasingly apparent in the proliferation of professional organizations by mid-nineteenth century. Disputes arose not only between but often within the medical and legal fields. One of the earliest and most influential of the medico-legal societies in this period was the New York Medico-Legal Society, formed in 1867 under the guidance of attorney Clark Bell. Focusing on calls to reform the insanity defense as a means to expand its influence and attract membership, the New York Medico-Legal Society found itself mired in debate by the 1880s.[19] A good number of the papers and talks presented by the organization focused on the relationship of inebriety to insanity and criminal responsibility. Already a hot-button issue in society and a legal morass, the subject became a specific point of contention between Crothers and Spitzka after the former presented a paper on "The Trance State in Inebriety" at the November 2, 1881, meeting.

Crothers described a trance state following inebriety that resulted in "impaired judgement, and lessened responsibility." The condition was characterized by a "loss of memory or consciousness" and provided "clear evidence of profound disturbance of the higher brain centers." The implications for medical jurisprudence were potentially significant as Crothers noted, contrary to earlier assumptions, that the condition was "very common" and "present in a greater or less degree" in "all chronic states of inebriety." Accordingly, Crothers made a renewed plea for the recognition of inebriety as a disease that requires diagnosis and treatment by qualified medical professionals rather than punishment: "looking back at the monstrous injustice and legal crime that is daily committed in this punishment of inebriates, who are practically insane, I am convinced that the time has come for a revolution of sentiment and practice, in which both the inebriate and the community must be held responsible, not alone for his acts, or the consequences of them, but the causes and conditions which have developed in this way; then the victim will be forced to avail himself of every means for prevention, restoration and recovery."[20]

His study of the "trance state," which he viewed as "of the greatest practical importance to medico-legal relations" rested on a series of cases, including those "in which the criminal impulse was prominent." A telling observation highlighting the nature of the trance, according to Crothers, was the "lack of recollection" by the perpetrator and "purposeless character" of the crimes. His analysis of some of the cases, however, appears a bit naive, such as his acceptance of a horse thief's claim that he had forgotten his crime based on the fact that he helped the owner look for the missing horse or the assertion that a bank teller must have been in a trance state when he forged a note because he claimed to have been later "amazed" at the presence of money in his pocket. While promoting the need for professional diagnosis, Crothers further contributed to the nebulous sense of this type of insanity when he cautioned that the condition of the trance state might not be "distinct enough to be recognized by court or jury."[21]

After his talk, Crothers was directly challenged by Spitzka, who criticized the third-party nature of the evidence and the lack of expected physical symptoms accompanying the mental state of the patients. He concluded that Crothers's evidence of "trance-like states" was merely the "ordinary everyday and characteristic symptoms of chronic alcoholism." It is unclear how seriously Crothers's views were considered by anyone other than Beard, who took the floor to defend the validity of "unconscious states." Reporting on the meeting, the author of an article in *Science* offhandedly dismissed Beard, stating he was unable to follow Beard's remarks, which "wander off to the fall of a Swiss mountain and to Astronomy." The author further derided the "alcoholic trance" as a condition in which inebriates "were supposed to commit all sorts of ridiculous, or injurious, or even criminal actions, without a subsequent recollection of what they had done." Crothers's paper presented a challenge to both science and the law on the relevance of intoxication to crime. Defending the state of the field, Spitzka remarked "that, instead of science being behind in its views on the question of alcoholism, it was the paper which was far from being up to the science of the day." Another physician also disagreed with Crothers's conclusion "that alcoholism, aside from its effect in producing chronic insanity, should constitute an excuse for crime." At least one attorney was supportive in acknowledging the need for a clearer legal definition of the "habitual drunkard," and the article concluded with Crothers's statement "that our knowledge of alcoholism was not at all perfect" and maintained "that his views were an addition to science, notwithstanding what had been alleged that evening."[22]

While there was general agreement that inebriety constituted a disease, the more practical aspects of its relationship to legal responsibility remained unresolved. In 1888 the Medico-Legal Society of New York published a volume of papers, dating back twenty years, related to the "medical jurisprudence of inebriety" that revealed a continuing debate over the medical versus moral interpretation of heavy drinking. Not surprisingly, physicians associated with asylums continued to be the strongest advocates of a disease model, and they presented themselves as the torchbearers of medical knowledge regarding the disposition and treatment of the inebriate. Edward C. Mann, superintendent of the Sunnyside Medical Retreat in New York, saw little inconsistency between existing law and the current state of medical knowledge: "The present law holds drunkenness to be no excuse for crime. The disease of dipsomania is not drunkenness. The state of intoxication is merely one of many symptoms of the disease." He urged that the "law should respect and accept the teachings of science," which offered evidence that the dipsomaniac was not responsible for his actions "because he is not master of his desire to drink." The mind, he noted, was accurately understood through the workings of the brain, arguing that this type of patient "is perverted in the exercise of his psychic powers by abnormal conditions of his brain and centric nervous system." Emphasizing the hereditary causes of inebriety, Mann's theories bordered on biological determinism as he called for laws forbidding inebriates to marry so as to "stamp out the hereditary descent of organically defective persons." In the meantime, however, he saw no reason that "sick men should be punished," viewing such patients as wholly irresponsible for their crimes.[23]

Physician T. L. Wright also argued that inebriates should not be legally responsible for their crimes. Utilizing language reminiscent of the temperance advocates, he declared that "the drunken man is not his own master." However, this statement was less a warning than a medical conclusion, as Wright continued to recount how the "redundant fibrous substance in the drunkard's brain shrinks" and causes the nerve cells to perish and the nerve fibers to be torn apart. This "physical degeneration," he argued, accounted "misconduct as the child of disease, rather than of criminal will."[24] Reverend William Tucker, however, adamantly refused to allow biology to detract from moral obligation, arguing that "the brain is the instrument, not the cause, of mind." Despite "limitations caused by heredity," he implied that a higher law governing human action must be followed. "While man is not under obligation to do that which he has no ability to," Tucker insisted that "he is under obligation to try or make the effort to that which he has not the ability to do."[25]

More often than not, it was the moral rather than the medical conclusions of the inebriety specialists that subjected them to both professional and public skepticism. The contentious status of the insanity defense, and especially the backlash against moral insanity, by this time created an even greater hurdle to arguing for chronic alcohol use as a disease that mitigated criminal responsibility, and the concept of inebriety was quite vulnerable to attack. The medical field had failed to establish any broadly accepted sense of the relationship of chronic alcohol use to insanity, with the exceptions of permanent insanity and delirium tremens. And drinking was still considered a vice, perhaps even more than at any time in the past.

By the 1880s the Woman's Christian Temperance Union had grown in influence and contributed to the established premise that men's drinking was a threat to home and family. Viewing the problem as intractable, the temperance movement, in the last few decades of the century, began to more fully embrace legal prohibition, focusing on the saloon and exploiting its connection to societal fears of immigration, urban crime, and degeneration.[26] Furthermore, the insanity defense, under which the various diseases of drunkenness were subsumed, was increasingly viewed with skepticism. The dispute between Crothers and Spitzka on the responsibility of the inebriate transpired in the same year Guiteau assassinated President Garfield and pled insanity as a defense. The details of that crime and subsequent trial provoked a sensational public conversation on the causes and consequences of insanity as debates between psychiatrists and lawyers were reported extensively in the papers. Despite some notable support for the idea that Guiteau was indeed insane, there were greater fears that the public would be "cheated" out of vengeance and that the "vile assassin" would escape responsibility if he were declared legally insane.[27] An examination of two murder cases, whose crimes also occurred in 1881, provides some additional insight into the context in which defenses based on drunkenness, as well as insanity more broadly, faced backlash.

On a clear and cold morning just three days into the new year of 1884, two men were hanged in the courtyard of the county jail in Newark, New Jersey. On the front page of the January 4 edition of the *Newark Morning Register*, images of the two men were displayed prominently. A quick glance at their pictures sitting side by side might lead one to believe that they had been accomplices in a single crime. In truth, their crimes occurred six months apart, and no indication exists that the two men knew each other before their trials. Reading the text under their pictures provides very different first impressions of the men. Of Robert Martin, the first to die, the caption reads, "He meets death firmly," whereas James Graves, we are told, was "carried to the gallows." Graves's picture is also less detailed, less flattering than Martin's, and the first line of the article states, "Graves was always an avowed infidel."[28]

The trials of the two men were covered extensively in the local press. Martin shot and killed his wife and baby daughter in June 1881; Graves used his pistol to mortally wound a neighborhood boy in December that year. Both men attempted an insanity defense at trial and failed. Neither succeeded at appeal, nor was either successful in obtaining a last-minute reprieve. In one sense, these executions represent the reluctance of the legal system and the general public to accept what was often by that time referred to as the "insanity dodge." Yet behind this confluence of events, the two men were separated by class and circumstance. Martin, a well-off Englishman, had been drinking heavily at the time of his crime. Graves, who had not, presented a more classical insanity defense and drew the attention of Edward Spitzka, who supported his case.

In a manner typical of the sensationalism that had come to characterize the press in this period, Martin's crime was reported as "one of the most appalling murders known in the annals of crime in this city."[29] Martin had returned home on the evening of June 15, at the end of a day in which he "drank about seven glasses of beer, two glasses of gin and four glasses of brandy."[30] After arguing with his wife over the whereabouts

Newark Morning Register

THREE CENTS.

NEWARK, N. J., FRIDAY, JANUARY 4, 1884.

EXECUTED!

Martin Dies First.

HE MEETS DEATH FIRMLY.

The Drop Falls at 10:27.

JAS. B. GRAVES

CARRIED TO THE GALLOWS

He Departs This Life at 11:05 A. M.

FIGURE 9. *Newark Morning Register*, January 4, 1884. Courtesy of the Charles F. Cummings New Jersey Information Center, Newark Public Library.

of his son Edward, Martin followed her down the stairs and shot at her three times as she held their eighteen-month old baby. Sarah Martin died almost immediately; the baby, Nellie, suffering from "two ghastly wounds in the abdomen," died several hours later. Their eleven-year-old son, Charles, was also home at the time. It was reported that Martin, taken into police custody almost immediately, declared, "O, I am going to be hung; I have shot my wife."[31]

Characterizations of the intemperate "family man" revealed a familiar narrative of seemingly idyllic domestic life destroyed by alcohol. The crime was described as taking place "in a comfortable, and what had been a happy home." Robert Martin was a widower with three sons when he married Sarah Jane Jackson, and they eventually had three more children together. The couple had led "a happy life until within a short time, when he became adicted to strong drink. She, being a temperate woman, was, of course, opposed to his drunken excesses. Usually, it was reported, he was a kind man and he was very fond of the murdered child, who was his pet."[32] Early accounts of the crime noted that Martin most likely had not intended to kill his young daughter, who was hit by a bullet that "flew wide of its mark."[33] One editorial used the opportunity to condemn the influence of alcohol, a "maddening stimulant," and contrasted the case of Martin with those in which "a deliberate plan for murder was carried out." They expressed pity for "the man who allows himself to become such a slave to intoxicating drink that he loses all love for wife and child of any comfortable home with its humanizing influences all love of God and fear of man, and becomes a fiend incarnate ready to bear the assassin's knife or pistol against those that ought to be dearest to him of all in earth."[34]

Despite the fact that the Martins' domestic life was typically portrayed as happy, there were indications that the reality was more complicated, and the family had been previously affected by Robert Martin's intemperate habits. It was reported that he had beat his wife some years earlier when they lived in Cuba and that he became "irritable" when drinking. Sarah Martin's mother and sister recounted that he had "treated his wife badly and beat her" until she had returned home to her mother.[35] Even as familial violence and loss continued to serve as a warning of the misery and degradation to which an intemperate man could sink, by the 1880s reformers, women especially, were just as likely to use these stories to condemn men's drinking. As temperance advocates lost faith in the powers of moral suasion, women turned increasingly to alternative solutions in their advocacy for increased legal rights and easier access to divorce. One study of divorce records in this period concludes that "intemperance was a deciding factor in over one-quarter of American divorces between 1887 and 1906," indicating an increasing "impatience" with men's drinking.[36] In this case, Sarah Martin was persuaded to return to her husband after a year. Hours after his arrest, Martin recounted how his wife had "upbraided me for squandering my time and money which she said belonged to the family," and proclaimed that she "deserved to die."[37]

At the opening of the trial, Martin's counsel, ex-judge Caleb S. Titsworth, suggested there was an exculpatory lack of intent because Martin was not conscious of his actions. He admitted his client had "his faults; he used intoxicating drinks in large quantities; sometimes he got more than he ought to have, and it made a madman of him so that he would not be conscious of what he did, but among all who knew him he was known as generous, clever, gentlemanly, never hurting or wronging any one."[38] He attributed Martin's condition to a recent bout with malaria as much as to intoxication and suggested an alternative version of events, unsupported by testimony, that there was no intent because the shooting was accidental:

> When he got home he has no recollection of seeing his wife; went up to his room and was getting ready to go to bed; while he was thus preparing himself for bed, and was putting some money in an iron box behind the door, he heard his wife in the hall, and not meaning any harm, pointed the revolver around the door, and said: "See here," and the pistol was discharged. The report filled him with terror, and what happened after that he did not know. When he took up the pistol he had no idea it was loaded, and did not know that it was cocked. He had no intention to shoot anybody. After that he was a wild man not responsible for what he did.

Martin purportedly possessed no memory of his actions and had to be told afterwards that he had shot his wife and child, and he remained unaware of his environment or circumstances at the police station. "It would appear," counsel argued, "that he had no motive to commit a murder, that he had no feelings of revenge against his wife to gratify. He had suffered beyond what we can imagine. This was more an accident than a crime."[39] The description echoes the cases of "alcoholic trance" presented by Crothers.

While Martin's defense was insanity, the definition of just what that meant in relation to the use of alcohol remained unsettled, and medical experts on both sides presented multiple interpretations of the effects of intoxication. It was unclear if the physicians for the defense were testifying that Martin suffered from a permanent state of insanity brought on by years of alcohol use or was affected by a temporary altered state of mind, albeit one that went beyond the anticipated results of intoxication. Dr. H. C. Hendry, who had known the defendant for several years, "came to the conclusion that he was suffering from chronic alcoholism; I mean by that that he was in the condition of a man who had been indulging in intoxicants for some time." He believed his intellect had been affected by a condition that "was not the direct effect of immediate drinking." County Physician Peter V. P. Hewlett, who spoke to Martin shortly after the crime, testified that the prisoner had identified himself as "Champagne Charlie" and "began to sing." In his opinion, "Martin did show to me signs of aberration of mind; I mean he acted differently than other men would under the circumstances; he acted like a crazy man." The prosecution, on the other hand, countered the idea that Martin's behavior was due to anything more than the foreseeable intoxication resulting from his decision to drink. In his opening arguments, the prosecutor characterized Martin as returning home "after being out drinking, but not drunk." Police Surgeon Joshua Ware Read assured the jury that this was nothing more than drunkenness. He "was not in doubt as to his [Martin's] sanity that night; I was on the alert to detect any signs of aberration of mind, and did not detect any signs of insanity; there were no doubts in my mind that he was sane, except that aberration which might originate from the continuous intemperate use of alcoholic stimulants."[40]

Along with efforts to prove Martin was insane and thus irresponsible under the law, the defense tried to paint a picture of their client as a good and upstanding man. Such assurances made sense in light of the possibility of acquittal, and subsequent release, if the defense were successful. A sympathetic portrayal also potentially could be enough to convince the jury to find for second-degree rather than first-degree murder, thus sparing Martin's life. In closing arguments, the defense reiterated that Martin's behavior under the influence of alcohol in this case was out of the ordinary, emphasizing Martin's "weakness" due to recent ill health, his lack of intent, and a history of "affection" for his family. His decision to drink was portrayed as a normal and perhaps even admirable quality reflecting his social nature. "Now, gentlemen," his attorney asked the jury, "who are the men who become victims of drink. Are they the mean men who grasp pennies? No, they are the kind, generous men. Martin was one of those. He could not go out in the street without meeting a friend and hence the difficulty of keeping sober."[41] Drinking served an important cultural function for men in this period, and despite the influence of the temperance movement, many men of the jury may not have necessarily viewed drinking, especially social drinking, as a vice.[42]

One can get some sense of the mixed reactions to Martin on the part of the jury and the public by looking at both the verdict and the events after the close of the trial. In his instructions to the jury, Judge David A. Depue allowed that while intoxication did not excuse crime, it could "reduce the grade of crime." However, he reminded the jury that this doctrine "should be applied with caution, that no undue and dangerous immunity or license be given to crime by persons whose passions are inflamed by drink."[43] According to the *Newark Morning Register*, the jury originally stood at seven for murder in the first degree and five for murder in the second degree before unanimously agreeing that Martin should be convicted of the more serious charge which carried a penalty of death.[44] Within months, however, supportive public sentiment swirled around Martin. His pastor characterized him as "another case of a real good fellow doomed by drink," and a petition requesting a commutation of sentence was reported as being "signed by many of the Grand Jury that indicted Martin, all the jury that tried the case, almost every prominent lawyer in Essex county, many clergymen and a host of our best citizens."[45]

Martin's class status most likely played a significant role in contributing to his depiction as someone deserving of mercy for his crime. Descriptions of Martin's home suggest a middle-class lifestyle. He was also reported to have been a machinist but had made enough money when he worked in Cuba that he no longer had to work. Outrage at the nature of the crime was tempered by a recognition of alcohol's insidious effects on what appeared to be an otherwise decent man, though those who supported the commutation likely still expected that Martin would serve a life sentence.[46] Some may also have considered the fact that Martin was receiving a legacy of one hundred dollars a month that would be denied his children upon his death.[47] It would not have been too surprising if Martin's verdict had been set aside. The decision to convict Martin certainly reflected growing suspicion of the insanity defense, but the verdict of first-degree murder was perhaps less expected considering precedent and the mens rea requirements of proving murder in the first degree. Just a year earlier, Judge Depue had presided over the trial of Edward Kissam, who killed his wife Mary after a night of heavy drinking on Christmas Day, claiming little memory of the event. Kissam, identified as a "negro waiter," presented a very different domestic life and claimed that his wife, who was also drunk, injured herself by falling. He was convicted of murder in the second degree.[48] Martin's verdict and the subsequent campaign for a pardon perhaps demonstrate the tensions between the effectiveness of women's temperance activism in publicizing domestic abuse and continuing faith in the reclamation of the drunkard, at least among the middle class.

An application for a writ of error was filed in March 1882 because the word "deliberate" did not appear in the indictment; thus, Titsworth argued, the only verdict that could have been rendered was murder in the second degree. He further took issue with the testimony of Read, who recounted a conversation with Martin from his notes, making it appear Martin "was in a frame of mind a short time after the murder to give a clear, connected, and cool statement of the crime."[49] Public opinion seemed to be on his side. Martin's life had already been spared by a reprieve from Governor George C. Ludlow just days before his scheduled hanging. Upon receiving that news, it was reported that "on the streets general satisfaction at the result was expressed on all hands, and many persons who never saw Robert Martin in their lives, shook hands warmly and expressed hopes that the month of life granted to the poor man by the Governor may be indefinitely extended."[50] It was not. The *New Jersey Law Journal*, which had indicated its support for Martin on several occasions, reported that it was "surprised and pained at the determination of the Governor not to commute the sentence. It seems to us plainly a case in which the verdict ought to have been murder in the second degree."[51]

While not addressing Martin's case specifically, Crothers argued against capital punishment for what the *New York Times* characterized as "drunkard murderers," calling it "a legal fiction to suppose that a crime committed while under the influence of alcohol was the voluntary act of a sane man."[52] Citing a number of recent cases in which judges refused to recognize drunkenness "as any possible excuse for crime," he suggested these were "dying theories" that would soon be modified by scientific knowledge. "The plea of irresponsibility by reason of intoxication," he argued, "should be accepted not as an excuse for crime, but as a fact showing the incapacity of the accused to control himself or enjoy the liberty of a man in sound mind."[53] Crothers was particularly disturbed at the system of punishment rather than treatment for inebriates who committed crimes. He argued, that in the case of inebriates, it was not unusual to find a series of past crimes, ranging from theft to assault and "finally murder," committed by such men, for whom the "fear of the law and the consequences of acts make little impression." Despite noting that only 10 percent of inebriates were convicted of crime each year, his portrait of the inebriate more likely undermined his argument, as he described one individual who, "under the influence of alcohol, commits assault to-day, will do so to-morrow, and next year, and so on, as long as his inebriety continues. No legal punishment of fines and imprisonment can stop him." Rather, Crothers viewed treatment by medical professionals as the only effective means of preventing further misdeeds. Punishment, furthermore, did not provide an answer since the resulting degradation and impoverishment of the inebriate and his family, Crothers argued, further perpetuated crime. In fact, one of the arguments against executing Martin was to save his sons from the "disgrace" of their father's sentence.[54]

Crothers assured his readers that inebriety was an involuntary condition resulting from the excessive use of alcohol, which "numbs and paralyzes the higher operations of the brain." Under the influence of alcohol, the "brain is incapable of accurately comprehending the nature of acts and the relation of surroundings," and rational action is impossible. In such cases, the insanity is clear, and the idea of punishment is both cruel and often contradictory to its stated purpose: "The death penalty to such cases has no horrors. It is rather welcomed. The struggle for life is the attractive publicity that makes a hero of the man, and the mystery of the end of life intensifies the interest to the last moment." Crothers, rather, called for a "change of public sentiment and law" affecting criminal inebriates and challenged the value of current policy, asking, "does the State bring to life the murdered family by simply going through the accustomed forms of judicial procedure?" Calling court proceedings "a mere mockery of justice," he argued that the "only true and enlightened policy for the State is to provide asylums for this class of insane." He disagreed with public trials "where the details of the trial are made prominent, or the farcical questions of sanity are publicly tested." Rather, he urged, the best course of action was lifelong care in an appropriate facility.[55]

Despite the efforts to obtain a commutation of sentence for Martin, his execution was scheduled for January 1884 and would coincide with that of James Graves. As Graves's attorneys mounted a last-chance bid to obtain a pardon just days before his scheduled hanging, they called on Spitzka to examine the defendant. Contrasting the two cases, Spitzka derided the public support for Martin in the wake of the denial of a pardon for Graves:

> It may be well to state, as a unit to enable the formation of an estimate of the Court of Pardons, that while the application in the case of Graves was unanimously denied, the vote to grant a like commutation to a man who had brutally murdered his wife and child was evenly divided, the distinguished chancellor and three judges voting to grant it, while the governor and three other judges voted against it. However, it may be said in their behalf that they correctly represented the popular sentiment, which was indifferent regarding Graves, while the sentimental part of the community made itself heard in numerous petitions on behalf of Martin and visits of morbidly inclined females to the jail.[56]

For Spitzka, Graves represented a case of legitimate insanity; Martin, who was drunk, did not.

The *Newark Morning Register* described Graves's crime as "one of the most cold-blooded, deliberate and cruel murders that has occurred for some time." On the night of December 20, 1881, Eddie Soden, aged thirteen, was on his regular route lighting lamps with his friend, Willie

Hawthorne.[57] The boys were familiar with Graves and spotted him in front of a cork store in the course of their duties. When Soden reached Market Street, near Lawrence, to light a lamp, Graves moved toward the boy and shot him in the back with a pistol. Soden was brought to a nearby pharmacy and then to his home, where he died one and a half hours later. Graves, aged sixty-three, had a history of conflict with the Soden family, who lived upstairs from where he had once boarded and continued to take his meals. The children sometimes obstructed the stairs to his door and were heard to have called him "Monkey Graves." Graves had been arrested previously for waving a revolver and threatening to shoot members of the Soden family. According to the local paper, Eddie's mother said to her dying son, "the villain has killed you at last, my darling; he said he would two years ago and he has kept his word."[58]

Graves, described as "a low sized man with very sharp features," confessed immediately. His counsel, Abner Kalisch, who had represented Edward Kissam in his murder trial the year before, presented a defense of insanity but recognized the "prejudice" against the defense. His client, he argued, was incapable of distinguishing right and wrong and was nothing more than "a wreck moved by instinct and passion like a brute." Evidence of a long history meant to indicate mental illness included testimony that Graves sometimes wore a mask in public, talked to himself, and had a habit of chewing his tongue.[59] Dr. A. N. Dougherty, the only physician to testify for the defense, described him as "an emaciated, weakly, pale, man" who had a "constant habit of licking his lips, showing a great deal of nervous excitement."[60] One of the key pieces of evidence in the case for insanity was a journal kept by Graves that documented his practice of "self-pollution" that dated back forty years.[61] Dougherty affirmed to the court that such habits make men "debased and degraded." Another physician, while recognizing "traces of this habit" and acknowledging that Graves possessed "a nervous temperament" and "weakness of mind," resisted declaring him insane, stating, "I do not believe in the insanity that comes when you put your finger on the trigger, and ceases when you kill your victim."[62] At the end of arguments, the jury deliberated on the case for a little over two hours before returning a verdict of guilty of murder in the first degree. One paper congratulated the jury, assuring the public that "there was no room left for honest minds to doubt, and, although public opinion is not always a safe expression of what is right, there was no room left for cavil in the case of Graves."[63]

Throughout the trial, there had been ample comparison to the Guiteau case, whose proceedings sometimes overlapped with those of Graves. One newspaper remarking on Graves's indictment suggested that, "the insanity plea will not probably be pressed as far as in the case of Guiteau. But it is the ready and convenient excuse framed for a city officer who has betrayed his trust, and why should it not be made available in the case of Graves?" The writer cast further aspersions on the medical witnesses in such cases, declaring, "there is not certainty that half the so-called 'experts' are not themselves the victims of some delusion of their own."[64] Spitzka, described as "the gentleman who got such a world-wide though unenviable, celebrity through his testimony in the Guiteau case," observed that the American public was in a state of reaction against the present era in which the "mere assertion of insanity in the case of a criminal was sufficient to diminish, if not to abolish, his penalty." Highlighting Graves's mental condition, he remarked that the references to Guiteau during the trial were understood by all except the prisoner himself.[65]

Speaking before the New York Neurological Society a few months after the execution, Spitzka further expressed his fear that the pendulum had swung too far in the opposite direction:

> That, however, it is not impossible to render a person deeply sunken in dementia a proper subject for the gallows, it was left for the Governor and the Court of Pardons of a neighboring state to demonstrate within the past month. The features attending the denial of a reprieve, and the execution of James Graves, recently hung in Newark, are so startling and constitute such a significant commentary on the fallacy of certain attempted reforms in our expert system that I may be permitted to occupy your time this evening with a history and commentary of them.

He provided evidence to his audience that Graves demonstrated clear signs of long-established dementia that were supported by his physical appearance, his past and present behavior, hereditary factors, and the results of postmortem examination. For Spitzka, insanity was confirmed by the specialized knowledge, such as an autopsy, that a trained physician like himself could provide, not by questionable medical experts and public opinion.[66]

Disagreeing with Spitzka's assessment, Sanford B. Hunt, in his dual role as editor of the *Newark Daily Advertiser* and physician who testified as to Graves's sanity, praised the actions of his state in the Graves case. He compared what he viewed as a just result in this case to the goings-on in Washington: "Juries in New Jersey take their law from the Judge. A requisition from Governor Ludlow would perhaps, bring Guiteau to Monmouth county for trial and there would then be none of this long delay which has occurred in Washington." He appealed to the public fear that insanity that provided an excuse for crime could be easily feigned, "each assassin proclaiming himself insane at the moment and sane in his previous and subsequent action. The only difference, morally, is that in Guiteau the meanness was guided by an educated mind. In Graves it was only ignorant and grovelling. Both chose a public place with the same purpose—the show of recklessness which might be considered evidence of insanity."[67] Spitzka expressed nothing short of contempt for Hunt and his claims to medical knowledge, referring to Hunt as "this expert editor, or editorial expert." He assured his audience that his examination ruled out the possibility of simulation. He established what he saw as strong medical proof of insanity, providing details of a postmortem conducted on Graves that "were more than usually startling and confirmatory of the theory of dementia."[68] For Spitzka, Graves's diagnosis was supported by verifiable medical evidence in a way that Martin's intoxication could not be.

If the association with vice had not already doomed drunkenness as a defense, the increasing influence of the prohibition movement and greater skepticism toward the insanity defense provided the final nails in the coffin. Ultimately, despite some recognition of addiction and problems of establishing intent under intoxication, juries in subsequent years limited the significance of intoxication. By the end of the nineteenth century, it was no longer accurate to say that "drunkenness" could provide no defense to crime, but it was a last-ditch, poor excuse.

Epilogue

In a paper read before the Medico-Legal Society of New York in 1887, its founder, Clark Bell, addressed the "present legal status" of inebriety and the significant differences between civil and criminal law in their respective assessments of the intoxicated individual. Civil law, he noted, considers "habitual drunkenness" as "*prima facie* evidence of the subject's incapacity to manage his affairs" and thus provides a "protecting arm and shield" around those who are "so addicted to drink as to seriously interfere with the care of his estate . . . for their presumed good." The legal philosophy of the civil courts was one under which "the law has always regarded and treated intoxication as a species of mental derangement, and has considered, and treated the habitual or other drunkard, as entitled to the special care and protection of courts of equity in all matters relating to his civil rights." However, when it came to criminal relations, he observed that the law was "harsh" in its treatment of the inebriate. Here Bell noted that the courts ascribed to a different set of priorities when determining responsibility under civil versus criminal statutes. In the case of civil law, the goal is to protect the drunkard from himself; however, in criminal relations, "it is the weal of society which is to be conserved and protected." A staunch advocate of the view that inebriety is a disease, Bell urged for a modification of the present law so as to protect both society and the inebriate, expressing optimism that this would be achieved at some point in the future through the cooperation of the medical and legal fields.[1] Bell likely would be disappointed, as modern society continues to grapple with many of these same issues.

An interesting question to consider is not why a defense based on intoxication was only sporadically successful but rather why such a defense was ever considered in the first place. The key distinction between civil and criminal law, as Bell noted, is whether an injury resulting from the actions of an intoxicated person was harmful to that individual or to someone else. Society, more or less, is willing to protect the alcohol abuser from self-harm but draws the line when others are in harm's way. In fact, a strong argument could be made that there should be zero tolerance for crimes committed by those under the influence because the need to protect society is paramount. Before the nineteenth century, courts refused to entertain evidence of intoxication if the decision to drink was made voluntarily. Early precedent follows this application of a strict liability interpretation of the law, one that viewed mens rea as irrelevant, and could have continued to be applied to crimes committed while under the influence of alcohol. In fact, such a model exists today for drunk driving.[2]

Instead, a number of factors, medical, legal, and social, have contributed to a messier history of the use of intoxication as a defense. American courts by the early nineteenth century accorded an expanded exculpatory value to intoxication as a defense to crime, but these changes were never meant to excuse crime. Rather they were a reaction against the severity of the death penalty and a desire to mete out a punishment more suited to the particular circumstances of an individual act. Additionally, the medicalization of heavy drinking, from delirium tremens to dipsomania to inebriety, created categories of mental illness from which to argue for limited or even absent responsibility under the law, but here the primary goal was treatment of the patient rather than defense of the drunkard. By the 1880s few medical professionals were willing to risk their status by promoting controversial theories that seemed at odds with the best interests of society.

Similarly, the cautionary temperance tale of a good man ruined by the effects of alcohol provided some explanation for the violent actions of a drunkard, but the main objective was to curb the pernicious effects of drinking in a nation rife with alcohol. Temperance women utilized decidedly less sympathetic accounts of violence and abuse to emphasize the threat of men's drinking to women and families. Additionally, organized opposition to the saloon, the association of drinking with immigrants and the lower classes, and the growth of hereditary theories on race and ethnicity contributed further to an atmosphere in which drinking became more closely associated with vice, crime, and hereditary degeneration.

The viability of intoxication as a defense continues to occupy a nebulous place in the law. In 1996 the U.S. Supreme Court, in *Montana v. Egelhoff*, upheld Montana's legal code, which significantly limited the exculpatory value of voluntary intoxication. The crime in this case was a typically horrific one in which James Allen Egelhoff, after a night of drinking with two friends, was discovered in the rear of a car "yelling obscenities" as his two companions lay dead in the front seat, each of a single gunshot wound to the head. Egelhoff's blood alcohol content later measured at 0.36 percent, a fact that Montana statute held as irrelevant "in determining the existence of a mental state which is an element of the offense." Egelhoff was found guilty at trial and sentenced to eighty-four years' imprisonment. The Supreme Court of Montana then reversed that decision on appeal, finding that the "that evidence of his voluntary intoxication was 'clearly relevant' to the issue whether he acted knowingly and purposely."[3] The case was then appealed to the Supreme Court of the United States, which limited the scope of its decision to Montana's statute: "The people of Montana have decided to resurrect the rule of an earlier era, disallowing consideration of voluntary intoxication when a defendant's state of mind is at issue. Nothing in the Due Process Clause prevents them from doing so, and the judgment of the Supreme Court of Montana to the contrary must be reversed."[4] In so ruling, they chose not to address the broader relevance of intoxication to the law.

The rulings of these various courts reflect a lack of consensus over the question of if and to what extent intoxication should act as an exculpatory factor for the perpetrator of violent crime. The general ambivalence on the issue is further reflected in the five-to-four Supreme Court decision, and the opinion, written by Justice Antonin Scalia and joined by Chief Justice William Rehnquist, Justice Anthony Kennedy, and Justice Clarence Thomas, who represented a plurality of the court, with Justice Ruth Bader Ginsburg filing a separate concurring opinion. While the ruling fails to provide a satisfactory sense of resolution, the arguments within the decision further demonstrate what little headway we have made on this question. Scalia cites "historical practice" as his guide, starting with a 1992 case and moving back through Hale, Blackstone, and Coke, eventually citing the sixteenth-century *Reniger v. Fogossa* decision, which states, "If a person that is drunk kills another, this shall be Felony, and he shall be hanged for it, and yet he did it through ignorance, for when he was drunk he had no Understanding nor Memory; but inasmuch as that Ignorance was occasioned by his own Act and Folly, and he might have avoided it, he shall not be privileged thereby."[5] The reference is remarkable not just for its age but for its historical context. One legal scholar expressed "astonishment" at any substantial consideration of "the views of Coke, Hale, and Blackstone on peneological policy." He reminds his readers that "these are the same gentlemen who believed, among many other quaint beliefs, that an age of majority (and thus criminal responsibility) ranging upward from seven years old is acceptable," and who operated within a legal system that included more than "200 capital offenses and under which individuals as young as ten were executed for stealing necessities."[6]

The Supreme Court opinion acknowledged not just tangled and far-reaching legal precedent but the complicated historical background of the relationship between intoxication and responsibility in stating, "The doctrines of *actus reus, mens rea,* insanity, mistake, justification, and duress have historically provided the tools for a constantly shifting adjustment of the tension between the evolving aims of the criminal law and changing religious, moral, philosophical, and medical views of the nature of man."[7] The Supreme Court's decision in this case is just one example of a trend, begun in the 1980s, toward stricter limitations on the exculpatory significance of alcohol. While the context is one in which society accords victims greater recognition and rights, it is an approach based on the precedent of "common law."[8]

Today we recognize the need for treatment for alcoholics and those suffering from a variety of other addictions. But once violence is introduced into the equation, concern for the good of the individual tips to concern for the common good. To consider the drunkard's defense today, one would look to diminished capacity, a defense that allows evidence of intoxication but only to prove someone did not possess the sufficient mental capacity to form intent, as required in certain charges. There are attorneys out there still willing to argue the drunkard's defense, but concern for society continues to take precedence, and the law remains tethered still by the maxim that "drunkenness is no excuse for crime."

NOTES

Introduction

1. "State v. James R. Bennett," June 19, 1826, Box MT 184, Tennessee State Library and Archives.
2. "Bennett v. State (Mart. & Yerg. 133) in the Supreme Court of Tennessee, 1827," in *The Adjudged Cases on Insanity as a Defence to Crime*, ed. John Davison Lawson (Saint Louis, MO: F. H. Thomas, 1884), 571.
3. "Bennett v. State," 571–72.
4. For a discussion of the historical origins of addiction, see Harry Gene Levine, "The Discovery of Addiction: Changing Conceptions of Habitual Drunkenness in American History," *Journal of Studies on Alcohol* 39 (1978): 143–74; Jessica Warner, "'Resolv'd to Drink No More': Addiction as a Preindustrial Construct," *Journal of Studies on Alcohol* 55 (November 1994): 685–91; Mariana Valverde, *Diseases of the Will: Alcohol and the Dilemmas of Freedom* (Cambridge: University of Cambridge Press, 1998).
5. Quoted in Mitchell Keiter, "Just Say No Excuse: The Rise and Fall of the Intoxication Defense," *Journal of Criminal Law and Criminology* 87 (1997): 484. Note that the law did make a distinction between voluntary drunkenness and involuntary drunkenness—even as the latter condition was considered to be rare.
6. See James C. Mohr, *Doctors and the Law: Medical Jurisprudence in Nineteenth-Century America* (New York: Oxford University Press, 1993); Janet Ann Tighe, "A Question of Responsibility: The Development of American Forensic Psychiatry, 1838–1930" (PhD diss., University of Pennsylvania, 1983); Charles E. Rosenberg, *The Trial of the Assassin Guiteau: Psychiatry and the Law in the Gilded Age* (Chicago: University of Chicago Press, 1968).
7. See William L. White, "Addiction as a Disease: Birth of a Concept," *Counselor* 1 (2000): 46–51, 73. Timothy Hickman views narcotic addiction as "much more emphatically a product of its historical moment than was heavy drinking," in Timothy A. Hickman, "'Mania Americana': Narcotic Addiction and Modernity in the United States, 1870–1920," *Journal of American History* 90 (March 2004): 1269–94. For an expanded list of key works and developments, see William White, Ernest Kurtz, and Caroline Acker, "The Combined Addiction Disease Chronologies," Selected Papers of William L. White, http://www.williamwhitepapers.com/pr/2001AddictionasDiseaseChronology.pdf.
8. Valverde, *Diseases of the Will*, 51.
9. Sarah Tracy's work examines how the classification of alcoholism as a disease provides a means for social negotiation among patients, families, doctors, government, and reform groups: Sarah W. Tracy, *Alcoholism in America: From Reconstruction to Prohibition* (Baltimore: Johns Hopkins University Press, 2005). See also Michelle L. McClellan, *Lady Lushes: Gender, Alcoholism, and Medicine in Modern America* (New Brunswick, NJ: Rutgers University Press, 2017).

10. See Madelon Powers, *Faces along the Bar: Lore and Order in the Workingman's Saloon, 1870–1920* (Chicago: University of Chicago Press, 1998); Catherine Gilbert Murdock, *Domesticating Drink: Women, Men and Alcohol in America, 1870–1940* (Baltimore: Johns Hopkins University Press, 1998); Nicholas O. Warner, *Spirits of America: Intoxication in Nineteenth-Century American Literature* (Norman: University of Oklahoma Press, 1997); Andrew Barr, *Drink: A Social History of America* (New York: Caroll and Graf, 1999). For an early history of drinking in America, see W. J. Rorabaugh, *The Alcoholic Republic: An American Tradition* (New York: Oxford University Press, 1979).
11. For an anthropological perspective, see Robert B. Edgerton and Craig MacAndrew, *Drunken Comportment: A Social Explanation* (Clinton Corners, NY: Percheron Press, 2003). See also Linda A. Bennett and Genevieve M. Ames, eds., *The American Experience with Alcohol: Contrasting Cultural Perspectives* (New York: Plenum Press, 1985).
12. Karen Halttunen, "Early American Murder Narratives: The Birth of Horror," in *The Power of Culture: Critical Essays in American History*, eds. Richard Wightman Fox and T. J. Jackson Lears (Chicago: University of Chicago Press, 1993), 67. A number of other works have used murder cases to study nineteenth-century society including Rosenberg, *Trial of the Assassin Guiteau*; Patricia Cline Cohen, *The Murder of Helen Jewett: The Life and Death of a Prostitute in Nineteenth-Century New York* (New York: Vintage, 1999); Joan Jacobs Brumberg, *Kansas Charley: The Story of a 19th-Century Boy Murderer* (New York: Viking, 2003).
13. Halttunen, "Early American Murder Narratives," 78.
14. Holly Berkley Fletcher, *Gender and the American Temperance Movement of the Nineteenth Century* (New York: Routledge, 2008); Jed Dannenbaum, *Drink and Disorder: Temperance Reform in Cincinnati from the Washingtonian Revival to the WCTU* (Chicago: University of Illinois Press, 1984); Scott A. Sandage, "Deadbeats, Drunkards, and Dreamers: A Cultural History of Failure in the United States, 1819–1893" (PhD diss., Rutgers University, 1995).
15. A notable exception is the murder pamphlet *The Manheim Tragedy*, which recounts a story of the murder and rape of two white women by two Black men. While the "work of rum" is said to have contributed to the criminal character of the men, their defense was minimal at best with one of the defense attorneys apologizing for performing his "sworn duty" and the other refusing to submit a closing statement. *The Manheim Tragedy: A Complete History of the Double Murder of Mrs. Garber and Mrs. Ream* (Lancaster, PA: H.A. Rockafield, 1858). For additional discussion of stereotypes and anti-alcohol attitudes in African American culture, see Denise Herd, "Ambiguity in Black Drinking Norms," in *The American Experience with Alcohol: Contrasting Cultural Perspectives*, ed. Linda A. Bennett and Genevieve M. Ames (New York: Plenum Press, 1985), 149–70. See also David M. Fahey, *Temperance and Racism: John Bull, Johnny Reb, and the Good Templars* (Lexington: University Press of Kentucky, 1996).
16. Lee Jolliffe, "'Black Fiends' and 'Atrocious Murders': Redefining 'Sensationalism' through Coverage of Interracial Crime in the Nineteenth-Century Press," in *After the War: The Press in a Changing America, 1865–1900*, ed. David B. Sachsman (New York: Routledge, 2017), 235–46. For juries, see James Forman, Jr., "Juries and Race

in the Nineteenth Century," *Yale Law Journal* 113 (2004): 895–938; Elizabeth Dale, "Not Simply Black and White: Jury Power and the Law in Late Nineteenth Century Chicago," *Social Science History* 25 (Spring 2001): 7–27. The context of the Civil War and Reconstruction was even more significant in the South; see Christopher Waldrep, *Roots of Disorder: Race and Criminal Justice in the American South, 1817–1880* (Chicago: University of Illinois Press, 1998).

17. Scott C. Martin, *Devil of the Domestic Sphere: Temperance, Gender, and Middle-class Ideology, 1800–1860* (DeKalb: Northern Illinois University Press, 2010), 7–20.
18. Mohr, *Doctors and the Law*, 52.
19. Chet Mitchell, "Intoxication, Criminality, and Responsibility," *International Journal of Law and Psychiatry* 13 (1990), 1. For more on the recent history of intoxication and the law, see the remainder of this issue dedicated to "Intoxication and Criminal Responsibility."

Chapter 1: "Not the Intended Result of Drink"

1. Benjamin Rush, *An Enquiry into the Effects of Spiritous Liquors upon the Human Body, and Their Influence upon the Happiness of Society* (Philadelphia: Thomas Bradford, 1784), 3. In subsequent editions, revisions include changing the title to "An Inquiry . . ." and replacing "spiritous liquors" with "ardent spirits."
2. Rush, *An Enquiry* (1784), 6; Stephen Fried, *Rush: Revolution, Madness, and the Visionary Doctor Who Became a Founding Father* (New York: Broadway, 2018), 266.
3. Rush, *An Enquiry* (1784), 3–4.
4. Eric T. Carlson, Jeffrey L. Wollock, and Patricia S. Noel, eds., "Biography," in *Benjamin Rush's Lectures on the Mind* (Philadelphia: American Philosophical Society, 1981): 1–43; Lisbeth Haakonssen, *Medicine and Morals in the Enlightenment: John Gregory, Thomas Percival and Benjamin Rush* (Amsterdam: Rodopi, 1997). Other important biographies of Rush include Donald J. D'Elia, *Benjamin Rush: Philosopher of the American Revolution* (Philadelphia: American Philosophical Society, 1974); Alyn Brodsky, *Benjamin Rush: Patriot and Physician* (New York: Truman Talley, 2004); Brian S. Katcher, "Benjamin Rush's Education Campaign against Hard Drinking," *American Journal of Public Health* 83 (1993): 273–81.
5. Paul Starr, *The Social Transformation of American Medicine: The Rise of a Sovereign Profession and the Making of a Vast Industry* (New York: Basic Books, 1984); Ronald L. Numbers, "The Fall and Rise of the American Medical Profession," in *Sickness and Health in America: Readings in the History of Medicine and Public Health*, ed. Judith Walzer Leavitt and Ronald L. Numbers (Madison: University of Wisconsin Press, 1997): 225–36; Fried, *Rush*.
6. James C. Mohr, *Doctors and the Law: Medical Jurisprudence in Nineteenth-Century America* (New York: Oxford University Press, 1993), 7–8; Benjamin Rush, "On the Study of Medical Jurisprudence," in Benjamin Rush, *Sixteen Introductory Lectures to Courses of Lectures upon the Institutes and Practice of Medicine* (Philadelphia: Bradford and Innskeep, 1811), 363–95.
7. Benjamin Rush, *An Inquiry into the Effects of Ardent Spirits upon the Human Body and the Mind* (Boston: James Loring, 1823), 26–28. For more on the medical and political connections in Rush's writing, see Jacquelyn C. Miller, "Passions and Politics: The

Multiple Meaning of Benjamin Rush's Treatment of Yellow Fever," in *A Melancholy Scene of Devastation: The Public Response to the 1793 Philadelphia Yellow Fever Epidemic*, ed. J. Worth Estes and Billy G. Smith (Canton, MA: Science History, 1997) 79–95.

8. Fried, *Rush*, 318–20.
9. Benjamin Rush, *An Inquiry into the Effects of Spiritous Liquors on the Human Body and the Mind* (Boston: Thomas and Andrews, 1790), frontispiece.
10. Benjamin Rush, *An Inquiry into the Effects of Ardent Spirits upon the Human Body and Mind* (New York: Cornelius Davis, 1811), 28.
11. See table of contents for Theodric Romeyn Beck, *Elements of Medical Jurisprudence*, vol. 1 (Albany: Websters and Skinners, 1823).
12. Mohr, *Doctors and the Law*, 57–60.
13. Mohr, *Doctors and the Law*, 14–17.
14. Mohr, *Doctors and the Law*, 26.
15. "Insanity Produced by Intemperance," *American Jurist and Law Magazine* 3 (January 1830): 5–6.
16. Beck, *Elements of Medical Jurisprudence*, xii, 372–76.
17. Beck, *Elements of Medical Jurisprudence*, 375.
18. I have used Beck's spelling of "McDonough" here. Other records used the spelling "M'Donnough."
19. Beck, *Elements of Medical Jurisprudence*, 375–76.
20. *Trial of William M'Donnough on an Indictment for Murder of His Wife* (Boston: Thomas G. Bangs, 1817): 4–5. Some witnesses also called into question the conduct of his wife, Elizabeth, and suggested she may have been intoxicated. See also Karen Halttunen, *Murder Most Foul: The Killer and the American Gothic Imagination* (Cambridge, MA: Harvard University Press, 1998), 161–2.
21. *Trial of William M'Donnough*, 5.
22. *Trial of William M'Donnough*, 10–11.
23. *Trial of William M'Donnough*, 15–16.
24. *Trial of William M'Donnough*, 16–20, 29–31.
25. William Cranch, *Reports of Cases Civil and Criminal in the United States Circuit Court of the District of Columbia*, vol. 2 (Boston: Little, Brown, 1852, 1951), 158.
26. Cranch, *Reports of Cases*, 158. This references the second trial, which took place in December 1818. The first occurred in June 1818, but a new trial was granted due to a procedural issue. See 152.
27. See "Treatment Advocacy Center Brief," Psychlaws.org, which references United States v. Clarke, www.psychlaws.org/PressRoom/TACfinalbrief.pdf. For a review of cases, both English and American, on "insanity produced by intoxication," see John Davison Lawson, ed., *The Adjudged Cases on Insanity as a Defence to Crime* (Saint Louis, MO: F. H. Thomas, 1884), 747–54. I have used what appears to be the common spelling of M'Naghten's name in the literature, though disagreement persists; see Bernard Diamond, "On the Spelling of Daniel M'Naghten's Name," *Ohio Law Review* 25 (1964): 84–88; J. Thomas Dalby, "The Case of Daniel McNaughton: Let's Get the Story Straight," *American Journal of Forensic Psychiatry* 27 (2006): 17–18.

28. Lawrence P. Tiffany, "The Drunk, the Insane, and the Criminal Courts: Deciding What to Make of Self-Induced Insanity," *Washington University Law Quarterly* 69 (January 1991): 222–23.
29. Harry Gene Levine, "The Discovery of Addiction: Changing Conceptions of Habitual Drunkenness in America," *Journal of Studies on Alcohol* 39 (1978): 143.
30. William L. White, "Addiction as a Disease: Birth of a Concept," *Counselor* 1 (2000): 46–51, 73.
31. Thomas Trotter, *An Essay, Medical, Philosophical, and Chemical, on Drunkenness and Its Effects on the Human Body*, ed. Roy Porter (1804; repr., London: Routledge, 1988), xiv–xv, 3–5.
32. Trotter, *An Essay*, 8–10.
33. Benjamin Rush, *Medical Inquiries and Observations upon the Diseases of the Mind*, 5th ed. (Philadelphia: Grigg and Elliott, J. Conrad, 1835), 264.
34. Stephen Brown, "Observations on Delirium Tremens," *American Medical Recorder* 5 (April 1822): 193–215.
35. Joseph Klapp, "On Temulent Diseases," *American Medical Recorder* 1 (1818): 462–78.
36. Klapp, "On Temulent Diseases," 464–65.
37. Matthew Warner Osborn, *Rum Maniacs: Alcoholic Insanity in the Early American Republic* (Chicago: University of Chicago Press, 2014), 49.
38. Klapp, "On Temulent Diseases," 462–63.
39. The cases of Clarke and McDonough are later referenced in medical literature as early cases of delirium tremens, but a contemporary diagnosis seems unlikely based on the descriptions of cases and early dates. Thank you to Matthew Warner Osborn for clarification on this point.
40. "Insanity Produced by Intemperance," 5–20.
41. "Insanity Produced by Intemperance," 6.
42. "Insanity Produced by Intemperance," 7–8.
43. "Insanity Produced by Intemperance," 7–8.
44. United States v. Drew, 25 F. Cas. 913 (Circuit Court, D. Massachusetts 1828).
45. "Insanity Produced by Intemperance," 7–9; "Capital Trial," *Boston Courier*, June 12, 1828.
46. United States v. Drew.
47. United States v. Cornell, 25 F. Cas. 650 (Circuit Court, D. Rhode Island 1820).
48. United States v. Drew; "Insanity Produced by Intemperance," 9–10; "Capital Trial"; "Notes to Leading Criminal Cases," *Monthly Law Reporter* 6 (February 1854): 553–54.
49. A full transcript of the original trial could not be located, but there is no indication of medical testimony being given based on a direct excerpt of the judge's opinion in United States v. Drew or in the description in the *America Jurist* article, which states that the judge came to his decision after hearing two witnesses.
50. "Insanity Produced by Intemperance"; "General Intelligence—Capital Trial," *Christian Watchman*, June 13, 1828, 95; Isaac Ray, *A Treatise on the Medical Jurisprudence of Insanity* (1871; repr., New York: Arno Press, 1976), 572.
51. "General Intelligence," 95.

52. Henry St. Clair, *The United States Criminal Calendar, or an Awful Warning to the Youth of America* (Boston: Charles Gaylor, 1833): 229–33.
53. Daniel Drake, "Observations on Temulent Diseases," *American Medical Recorder* 2 (1819): 59–65.
54. Henry D. Shapiro and Zane L. Miller, eds., *Physician to the West: Selected Writings of Daniel Drake on Science and Society* (Lexington: University of Kentucky Press, 1970).
55. Emmet Field Horine, *Daniel Drake (1785–1852): Pioneer Physician of the Midwest* (Philadelphia: University of Pennsylvania Press, 1961).
56. Conevery Bolton Valencius, *The Health of the Country: How American Settlers Understood Themselves and Their Land* (New York: Basic Books, 2002). See also Michael Leverett Dorn, "Climate, Alcohol and the American Body Politic: The Medical and Moral Geographies of Daniel Drake (1785–1852)," (PhD diss., University of Kentucky, 2002).
57. Michael L. Dorn, "(In)temperate Zones: Daniel Drake's Medico-Moral Geographies of Urban Life in the Trans-Appalachian American West," *Journal of the History of Medicine* 55 (July 2000): 256–91.
58. Daniel Drake, "Oration on the Causes, Evils, and Preventives of Intemperance (1831)," in *Physician to the West: Selected Writings of Daniel Drake on Science and Society*, eds. Henry D. Shapiro and Zane L. Miller (Lexington: University Press of Kentucky, 1970), 204.
59. Drake, "Oration," 205.
60. Drake, "Oration," 206.
61. Drake, "Oration," 213.
62. Drake, "Oration," 213–14.
63. Daniel Drake, "Medical Jurisprudence—Report of a Trial for Murder," *Western Journal of the Medical and Physical Sciences* 1 (1830): 44–65. An "Erratum" appears at the end of Drake's article on this case stating that Birdsell is actually named John, rather than James.
64. Drake, "Medical Jurisprudence—Report of a Trial," 44–46.
65. Drake, "Medical Jurisprudence—Report of a Trial," 44–47; "Conviction for Murder," *Raleigh Register and North-Carolina Gazette*, July 2, 1829, 359. For an account of this case through an historical study of jealousy, see Dawn Keetley, "A Husband's Jealousy: Antebellum Murder Trials and Caroline Lee Hentz's *Ernest Linwood*," *Legacy* 19 (2002): 26–34.
66. Drake, "Medical Jurisprudence—Report of a Trial," 46–47.
67. Drake, "Medical Jurisprudence—Report of a Trial," 44–65; "Delirium Tremens—Medical Jurisprudence," *Boston Medical and Surgical Journal* 2 (October 20, 1829): 567–72; See also Stanley L. Block, "Daniel Drake and the Insanity Plea," *Bulletin of the History of Medicine* 65 (Fall 1991): 326–39, which places the Birdsell case within the history of the insanity defense.
68. Drake, "Medical Jurisprudence—Report of a Trial," 47, 55–56.
69. "Insanity Produced by Intemperance," 10.
70. "Conviction for Murder," 359.

71. Drake, "Medical Jurisprudence—Report of a Trial," 48; Daniel Drake, "Medical Jurisprudence: Sequel of the Case of John Birdsell," *Western Journal of the Medical and Physical Science* (July–September 1829): 219.
72. Drake, "Medical Jurisprudence—Report of a Trial," 48, 55–56.
73. Drake, "Medical Jurisprudence—Report of a Trial," 51–61.
74. Drake, "Medical Jurisprudence—Report of a Trial," 53.
75. Drake, "Medical Jurisprudence—Report of a Trial," 50.
76. Drake, "Medical Jurisprudence—Report of a Trial," 63.
77. Drake, "Medical Jurisprudence—Report of a Trial," 50–52.
78. Drake, "Medical Jurisprudence—Report of a Trial," 47.
79. "Delirium Tremens—Medical Jurisprudence," 571–72.
80. Drake, "Medical Jurisprudence: Sequel," 215–16; "Disappointment," *New-York Spectator*, August 11, 1829; "Execution of John Birdsell," *Scioto Gazette*, August 5, 1829.
81. "Disappointment."
82. Drake, "Medical Jurisprudence—Report of a Trial," 54.
83. "Medical Jurisprudence," *North American Medical and Surgical Journal* 8 (October 1829): 421.
84. Daniel H. Kitchen, "Delirium Tremens," *American Journal of Insanity* 31 (January 1875): 346.
85. Drake, "Medical Jurisprudence—Report of a Trial," 65. For more on this case exemplifying Drake's contribution to medical jurisprudence, see Block, "Daniel Drake."
86. Drake, "Medical Jurisprudence: Sequel," 218–21. For more on the significance of somatic signs of mental illness, see Gerald N. Grob, "Psychiatry's Holy Grail: The Search for the Mechanisms of Mental Disease," *Bulletin of the History of Medicine* 72 (Summer 1998): 189–219; and John Harley Warner, *The Therapeutic Perspective: Medical Practice, Knowledge and Identity in America, 1820–1885* (Princeton, NJ: Princeton University Press, 1997).
87. Isaac Ray, *A Treatise on the Medical Jurisprudence of Insanity*, ed. Winfred Overholser (1838 repr., Cambridge, MA: Belknap Press of Harvard University Press, 1962), 316–20.
88. Ray, *A Treatise* (1838), 320.
89. Ray, *A Treatise* (1871), 572–91.
90. Kitchen, "Delirium Tremens," 346.
91. Ray, *A Treatise* (1871), 569n.

Chapter 2: "A Victim of Intemperance"

1. Daniel Drake, "Oration on the Causes, Evils, and Preventives of Intemperance (1831)" in *Physician to the West: Selected Writings of Daniel Drake on Science and Society*, eds. Henry D. Shapiro and Zane L. Miller (Lexington: University Press of Kentucky, 1970), 213–14.
2. W. J. Rorabaugh, *The Alcoholic Republic: An American Tradition* (New York: Oxford University Press, 1979), 7–10.

3. Rorabaugh, *Alcoholic Republic*, 35–36. See also Mark Edward Lender and James Kirby Martin, *Drinking in America: A History* (New York: The Free Press, 1982).
4. "Lyman Beecher and the Cosmic Theater," in Robert Abzug, *Cosmos Crumbling: American Reform and the Religious Imagination* (New York: Oxford University Press, 1994), 30–56; Ian Tyrell, *Sobering Up: From Temperance to Prohibition in Antebellum America, 1800–1860* (Westport, CT: Greenwood Press, 1979).
5. For a discussion of earlier "total abstinence," see Jessica Warner, "'Resolv'd to Drink No More': Addiction as a Preindustrial Construct," *Journal of Studies on Alcohol* 55 (November 1994): 689.
6. Lyman Beecher, "Six Sermons on the Nature, Occasions, Signs, Evils and Remedy of Intemperance," in David F. Musto, *Drugs in America: A Documentary History* (New York: New York University Press, 2002), 58. See also "Diseases which Arise from the Use of Intoxicating Liquors," in Ralph Barnes Grindrod, *Bacchus: An Essay on the Nature, Causes, Effects, and Cure of Intemperance* (London: J. Pasco, 1839), 335–55.
7. Beecher, "Six Sermons," 44–86; Katherine A. Chavigny, "Reforming Drunkards in Nineteenth-Century America: Religion, Medicine, Therapy," in *Altering American Consciousness: The History of Alcohol and Drug Use in the United States, 1800–2000*, ed. Sarah W. Tracy and Caroline Jean Acker (Boston: University of Massachusetts Press, 2004), 108–23.
8. Beecher, "Six Sermons," 49.
9. Harry Gene Levine, "The Discovery of Addiction: Changing Conceptions of Habitual Drunkenness in America," *Journal of Studies on Alcohol* 39 (1978): 148–49. For more on free will and alcohol in this period, see chapter 2, "Repairing Diseased Wills," in Mariana Valverde, *Diseases of the Will: Alcohol and the Dilemmas of Freedom* (Cambridge: University of Cambridge Press, 1998), 43–67.
10. Warner, "Resolv'd," 685–91; Levine, "Discovery of Addiction," 150–51.
11. Jerome Nadelhaft, "Alcohol and Wife Abuse in Antebellum Male Temperance Literature," *Canadian Review of American Studies* 25 (March 1995): 15–16; Karen Halttunen, *Murder Most Foul: The Killer and the American Gothic Imagination* (Cambridge, MA: Harvard University Press, 1998), 135–71.
12. State v. Wilson, April 1836, Maine State Archives (Augusta, ME); "Rum and Murder," *Connecticut Courant*, June 22, 1835, 3; Isaac Ray, *A Treatise on the Medical Jurisprudence of Insanity*, ed. Winfred Overholser (1838 repr., Cambridge, MA: Belknap Press of Harvard University Press, 1962), 314–16; "Rum and Murder," *Ohio Observer*, July 9, 1835; "Horrid Murder," *Vermont Patriot and State Gazette*, June 22, 1835.
13. State v. Wilson, 151.
14. "Report of Murder," *New-York Spectator*, June 22, 1835; "Horrid Murder"; "Rum and Murder," *Connecticut Courant*.
15. "Horrid Murder"; "Domestic Items," *Zion's Herald*, July 22, 1835, 115.
16. Ray, *A Treatise*, 314.
17. "Horrid Murder."
18. Ray, *A Treatise*, 316.
19. State v. Wilson, 152.
20. "Rum and Murder," *Connecticut Courant*.

21. "Chapter of News," *Zion's Herald*, June 24, 1835, 99.
22. "Horrid Murder."
23. Andie Tucher, *Froth and Scum: Truth, Beauty, Goodness, and the Ax Murder in America's First Mass Medium* (Chapel Hill: University of North Carolina Press, 1994), 88.
24. Tucher, *Froth and Scum*, 89–90, 10–12; Aurora Wallace, *Newspapers and the Making of Modern America: A History* (Westport, CT: Greenwood Press, 2005).
25. John T. Cunningham, ed., *Murder Did Pay: 19th Century New Jersey Murders* (Newark: New Jersey History Society, 1981), 1–6.
26. Thomas Augst, "Temperance, Mass Culture, and the Romance of Experience," *American Literary History* 19 (Summer 2007): 298.
27. "Intelligence—Domestic," *Christian Register*, June 22, 1835.
28. "Report of Murder"; "Letter to the Editor," *Boston Investigator*, June 19, 1835.
29. "Rum and Murder," *Connecticut Courant;* "Rum and Murder," *Ohio Observer.*
30. The *Ohio Observer* seems to have adopted its story from the *Connecticut Courant* almost word for word. The other stories I have found on the murder do not include these utterances from Wilson, and while Ray also suggests that Wilson expressed no remorse, he states that he "continued furious, talking wildly and incoherently" for several days after his arrest. Ray, *A Treatise*, 315.
31. "Report of Murder."
32. Nadelhaft, "Alcohol and Wife Abuse," 24; Scott A. Sandage, *Born Losers: A History of Failure in America* (Cambridge, MA.: Harvard University Press, 2005), 47–150; Holly Berkley Fletcher, *Gender and the American Temperance Movement of the Nineteenth Century* (New York: Routledge, 2008): 7–14.
33. Iain Gately, *Drink: A Cultural History of Alcohol* (New York: Gotham, 2008), 259.
34. Chavigny, "Reforming Drunkards," 109–13; Jed Dannenbaum, *Drink and Disorder: Temperance Reform in Cincinnati from the Washingtonian Revival to the WCTU* (Chicago: University of Illinois Press, 1984); John W. Crowley, "Introduction", in *Drunkard's Progress: Narratives of Addiction, Despair, and Recovery*, ed. John W. Crowley (Baltimore: Johns Hopkins University Press, 1999), 12–18.
35. John B. Gough, *An Autobiography of John B. Gough (1845)* in *Drunkard's Progress: Narratives of Addiction, Despair, and Recovery*, ed. John W. Crowley (Baltimore: Johns Hopkins University Press, 1999), 111–72; Elaine Frantz Parsons, *Manhood Lost: Fallen Drunkards and Redeeming Women in the Nineteenth-Century United States* (Baltimore: Johns Hopkins University Press, 2003), 21–26.
36. Crowley, "Introduction," 12–13.
37. "Welcome to John B. Gough," *New York Times*, October 9, 1855.
38. Gough, *An Autobiography*, 111–12. John B. Gough, *Platform Echoes; or, Living Truths for Head and Heart* (Hartford, CT: A. D. Worthington, 1887); David S. Reynolds, "Black Cats and Delirium Tremens: Temperance and the American Renaissance," in *The Serpent in the Cup: Temperance in American Literature*, ed. David S. Reynolds and Debra J. Rosenthal (Amherst: University of Massachusetts Press, 1997), 26–27; Dannenbaum, *Drink and Disorder*, 28–29.
39. Crowley, *Drunkard's Progress*, 29–30; Tim Ruppel, "Gender Training: Male Ambitions, Domestic Duties, and Failure in the Magazine Fiction of T. S. Arthur," *Prospects* 24 (1999): 311–37.

40. T. S. Arthur, "'The Experience Meeting,' from *Six Nights with the Washingtonians* (1842)," in *Drunkard's Progress: Narratives of Addiction, Despair, and Recovery*, ed. John W. Crowley (Baltimore: Johns Hopkins University Press, 1999), 30.
41. Arthur, "The Experience Meeting," 38.
42. Arthur, "The Experience Meeting," 33–45.
43. Arthur, "The Experience Meeting," 30, 33.
44. Chavigny, "Reforming Drunkards," 111–12.
45. William S. Damrell, "Publisher's Preface," in Lucius M. Sargent, *Temperance Tales* (Boston: John P. Jewett, and Wm. S. Damrell, 1853), 3.
46. Reynolds, "Black Cats and Delirium Tremens," 22.
47. Reynolds, "Black Cats and Delirium Tremens," 25.
48. Mark Canada, *Literature and Journalism in Antebellum America: Thoreau, Stowe, and Their Contemporaries Respond to the Rise of the Commercial Press* (New York: Palgrave, Macmillan, 2011), 2–5.
49. Reynolds, "Black Cats and Delirium Tremens, 22.
50. Mark G. Vásquez, *Authority and Reform: Religious and Educational Discourses in Nineteenth-Century New England Literature* (Knoxville: University of Tennessee Press, 2003), 79.
51. Halttunen, *Murder Most Foul*, 37–40.
52. Tucher, *Froth and Scum*, 10–11; Karen Halttunen, "Early American Murder Narratives: The Birth of Horror," in *The Power of Culture: Critical Essays in American History*, eds. Richard Wightman Fox and T. J. Jackson Lears (Chicago: University of Chicago Press, 1993), 92.
53. Halttunen, *Murder Most Foul*, 136.
54. Reynolds, "Black Cats and Delirium Tremens, 25–26.
55. Halttunen, *Murder Most Foul*, 191–92.
56. Matthew Warner Osborn, "Diseased Imaginations: Constructing Delirium Tremens in Philadelphia, 1813–1832," *Journal of Social History* 19 (August 2006): 191, 200, 203.
57. Edgar Allan Poe, "The Black Cat," in *The Works of Edgar Allan Poe in One Volume* (New York: Walter J. Black, 1927), 209–16.
58. Reynolds, "Black Cats and Delirium Tremens," 34–36. For more on these tales and temperance literature more generally, see additional chapters in David S. Reynolds and Debra J. Rosenthal, eds., *The Serpent in the Cup: Temperance in American Literature* (Amherst: University of Massachusetts Press, 1997); Nicholas O. Warner, *Spirits of America: Intoxication in Nineteenth-Century American Literature* (Norman: University of Oklahoma Press, 1997).
59. Crowley, *Drunkard's Progress*, 2.
60. Crowley, *Drunkard's Progress*, frontispiece.
61. Halttunen, *Murder Most Foul*, 135; Barbara Welter, "The Cult of True Womanhood, 1820–1860," *American Quarterly* 18 (Summer 1966): 151–74.
62. Jeanne Boydston, "The Woman Who Wasn't There: Women's Market Labor and the Transition to Capitalism in the United States," *Journal of the Early Republic* 16, Special Issue on Capitalism in the Early Republic (Summer 1996): 199; Linda Kerber, "The Republican Mother; Women and the Enlightenment—An American Perspective," *American Quarterly* 28 (Summer 1976): 187–205.

63. Halttunen, *Murder Most Foul*, 37–40.
64. Augst, "Temperance," 298.
65. Crowley, *Drunkard's Progress*, 10–11; Dannenbaum, *Drink and Disorder*, 33–34; Ruth M. Alexander, "'We Are Engaged as a Band of Sisters': Class and Domesticity in the Washingtonian Temperance Movement, 1840–1850," *Journal of American History* 75 (December 1988): 763–85.
66. Scott C. Martin, *Devil of the Domestic Sphere: Temperance, Gender, and Middle-Class Ideology, 1800–1860* (DeKalb: Northern Illinois University Press, 2010), 49. Karen Sanchez-Eppler has also studied the way images of children as the victims of a father's intemperance were used in temperance tales in Karen Sanchez-Eppler, "Temperance in the Bed of a Child: Incest and Social Order in Nineteenth-Century America," in *The Serpent in the Cup: Temperance in American Literature*, ed. David S. Reynolds and Debra J. Rosenthal (Amherst: University of Massachusetts Press, 1997), 60–92.
67. Carol Mattingly, *Well-Tempered Women: Nineteenth-Century Temperance Rhetoric* (Carbondale: Southern Illinois University Press, 1998), 13–14, 34–35.
68. "The Trial of Joel Clough for the Murder of Mary W. Hamilton," in *American State Trials*, vol. 1, ed. John Lawson (Saint Louis, MO: F. H. Thomas Law, 1914), 724–25; "The Authentic Confession of Joel Clough" (originally published "by Order of the Sheriff of Burlington County," 1833; repr., Hainesport, NJ: Heidelberg Press, 2005); Halttunen, *Murder Most Foul*, 71, 85–86, 218.
69. Jack D. Marietta and G. S. Rowe, *Troubled Experiment: Crime and Justice in Pennsylvania, 1682–1800* (Philadelphia: University of Pennsylvania Press, 2006), 109–12.
70. See chapter 6, "Strong Drink," in Ronald G. Walters, *American Reformers, 1815–1860* (New York: Hill and Wang, 1978), 125–46.
71. Thomas R. Pegram, *Battling Demon Rum: The Struggle for a Dry America, 1800–1933* (Chicago: Ivan R. Dee, 1998).
72. "Effects of Intemperance," *Christian Secretary*, November 22, 1828.
73. "Awful Effects of Intemperance," *Christian Watchman*, October 17, 1828.
74. "Mr. Sprague's Speech," *Journal of the American Temperance Union* 3 (April 1839): 50–51.
75. "A High Fence," *Journal of the American Temperance Union* 3 (June 1839): 81.
76. "Murder and Suicide," *Journal of the American Temperance Union* 4 (November 1840): 165.
77. John Marsh, *Temperance Recollections: Labors, Defeats, Triumphs: An Autobiography* (New York: Charles Scribner, 1866), 133–34.
78. "The Sixth Commandment," *Journal of the American Temperance Union* 2 (August 1838): 123; "Murder—Most Foul," *Journal of the American Temperance Union* 4 (May 1840): 69.
79. Marsh, *Temperance Recollections*, 261.
80. "The Traffic, the Traffic," *Journal of the American Temperance Union* 2 (October 1839): 160.
81. "Temperance Zeal Commendable," *Journal of the American Temperance Union* 2 (February 1838): 23.

82. Justin Edwards, *Temperance Manual* (New York: American Tract Society, 1847): 64–75.
83. Edwards, *Temperance Manual*, 79–80.

Chapter 3: "Not Capable of Entertaining This Specific Intent"

1. Frances Sayre, "Mens Rea," *Harvard Law Review* 45 (1932): 974–1026; Herbert Fingarette, *The Meaning of Criminal Insanity* (Berkeley: University of California Press, 1972), 128–37; Daniel N. Robinson, *Wild Beasts and Idle Humours: The Insanity Defense from Antiquity to the Present* (Cambridge, MA: Harvard University Press, 1996), 221–27.
2. Stephen J. Morse and Morris B. Hoffman, "The Uneasy Entente between Legal Insanity and *Mens Rea:* Beyond *Clark v. Arizona*," *Journal of Criminal Law and Criminology* 97 (2007): 1071–1150.
3. William Blackstone, *Commentaries on the Laws of England in Four Books* (Philadelphia: J. B. Lippincott, 1893), 21; Greg Bailey, "Blackstone in America: Lectures by an English Lawyer Become the Blueprint for a New Nation's Laws and Leaders," *Early America Review* 1 (Spring 1997). For additional discussion of the concept of mens rea, see Lawrence M. Friedman, *A History of American Law* (New York: Simon and Schuster, 2005), 59–60, 449–53; Janet Ann Tighe, "A Question of Responsibility: The Development of American Forensic Psychiatry, 1838–1930" (PhD diss. University of Pennsylvania, 1983): 4–10.
4. Gerald Leonard, "Towards a Legal History of American Criminal Theory: Culture and Doctrine from Blackstone to the Modern Penal Code," *Buffalo Criminal Law Review* 6 (2003): 713–15.
5. Tighe, "A Question of Responsibility," 3–6; Mitchell Keiter, "Just Say No Excuse: The Rise and Fall of the Intoxication Defense," *Journal of Criminal Law and Criminology* 87 (1997): 484–85.
6. Tighe, "A Question of Responsibility," 5.
7. Joel Prentiss Bishop, *Commentaries on the Criminal Law, Volume 1* (Boston: Little, Brown, 1858), 226–29.
8. Stephen A. Siegel, "Joel Bishop's Orthodoxy," *Law and History Review* 13 (Fall 1995): 215–59.
9. Cited in "State v. Johnson (41 Conn. 585), in the Supreme Court of Errors of Connecticut, November Term, 1874," in *The Adjudged Cases on Insanity as a Defence to Crime*, ed. John Davison Lawson (Saint Louis: F. H. Thomas, 1884), 610. This statement on accidental or unintended intoxication was commonly included when an argument against drunkenness as an excuse to crime was employed.
10. Statutory rape remains a strict liability offense in most states.
11. Leonard, "Towards a Legal History," 693–95, 705.
12. Friedman, *A History of American Law*, 207–12; Samuel Walker, *Popular Justice: A History of American Criminal Justice* (New York: Oxford University Press, 1980), 47–50. For more on the Pennsylvania statute, see Edwin R. Keedy, "History of the Pennsylvania Statute Creating Degrees of Murder," *University of Pennsylvania Law Review* 97 (May 1949): 759–77.
13. Alan Rogers, *Murder and the Death Penalty in Massachusetts* (Amherst: University of Massachusetts Press, 2008), 112–13. Thanks to Alan Rogers for providing clarification on this point.

14. Bishop, *Commentaries*, 298–302.
15. Lawrence M. Friedman, *Crime and Punishment in American History* (New York: Basic Books, 1993), 147. See also Robert Weinstock, "Drug and Alcohol Intoxication: *Mens Rea* Defenses," *AAPL Newsletter: American Academy of Psychiatry and the Law* 24 (January 1999).
16. Isaac Ray, *A Treatise on the Medical Jurisprudence of Insanity* (1871; repr., New York: Arno Press, 1976), 566.
17. Lawson, *The Adjudged Cases*, 757–58. The judge disagreed with the ruling in Rex v. Grindley in Rex v. Carroll.
18. John Phelps Putnam, ed., *United States Digest: Digest of the Decisions of the Courts of Common Law and Admiralty in the United States*, vol. 5 (Boston: Little, Brown, 1851), 112.
19. "Cornwell v. State (Mart. & Yerg. 147.) in the Supreme Court of Tennessee, 1827," in *The Adjudged Cases on Insanity as a Defence to Crime*, ed. John Davison Lawson (Saint Louis, MO: F. H. Thomas, 1884), 583–88. For citations, see p. xii.
20. "Cornwell v. State," 588.
21. "Notes to Leading Criminal Cases," *Monthly Law Reporter* 6 (February 1854): 556.
22. "Notes to Leading Criminal Cases," 556–59.
23. United States v. Cornell, 25 F. Cas. 650 (Circuit Court, D. Rhode Island 1820); "Cornwell v. State," 583–87; "Notes to Leading Criminal Cases," 558–59.
24. J. H. Lind, "Drunkenness as an Extenuation in Cases of Murder," *American Law Register* 24 (September 1876): 505–11.
25. "Medical Jurisprudence—Effects of Intoxication," *American Law Journal* 7 (October 1848): 149–50.
26. Elizabeth Dale, *The Rule of Justice: The People of Chicago versus Zephyr Davis* (Columbus: Ohio State University Press, 2001).
27. James W. Diehm, "Impeachment of Jury Verdicts: *Tanner v. United States* and Beyond," *St. John's Law Review* 65 (Spring 1991): 391–439.
28. Ray, *A Treatise*, 312.
29. C. J. Mittermaier, trans., "On the Effect of Drunkenness on Criminal Responsibility and the Application of Punishment," *American Jurist* 22 (July 1840): 290–316; Lind, "Drunkenness as an Extenuation," 510; Ray, *A Treatise*, 298–99.
30. Mittermaier, "On the Effect of Drunkenness," 312.
31. Lind, "Drunkenness as an Extenuation," 510.
32. Mittermaier, "On the Effect of Drunkenness," 312–13.
33. Lind, "Drunkenness as an Extenuation," 510.
34. Lind, "Drunkenness as an Extenuation," 510–11.
35. Mittermaier, "On the Effect of Drunkenness," 312.
36. Swan v. the State, 4 Hum. 136 (WL 1800 Tenn., 1843); "Swan v. State (4 Humph. 186.) in the Supreme Court of Tennessee, July 1843," in *The Adjudged Cases on Insanity as a Defence to Crime*, ed. John Davison Lawson (Saint Louis, MO: F. H. Thomas, 1884); "Notes to Leading Criminal Cases."
37. Swan v. the State, 4 Hum. 136; "Swan v. State (4 Humph. 186.)" 574; "Notes to Leading Criminal Cases," 563.
38. "Notes to Leading Criminal Cases," 557.
39. The State v. Bullock, 13 Ala. 413 (Supreme Court of Alabama, 1848); Lawson, *The Adjudged Cases*, 730–31.

40. "Pirtle v. State (9 Humph. 663.), in the Supreme Court of Tennessee, April Term, 1849," in *The Adjudged Cases on Insanity as a Defence to Crime*, ed. John Davison Lawson (Saint Louis, MO: F. H. Thomas, 1884), 645–52; Bishop, 302–4.
41. "Haile v. State (11 Humph. 154.), in the Supreme Court of Tennessee, December, 1850," in *The Adjudged Cases on Insanity as a Defence to Crime*, ed. John Davison Lawson (Saint Louis, MO: F. H. Thomas, 1884), 573–76.
42. James C. Mohr, *Doctors and the Law: Medical Jurisprudence in Nineteenth-Century America* (New York: Oxford University Press, 1993), 72–74.
43. Lind, "Drunkenness as an Extenuation," 508.
44. Andie Tucher, *Froth and Scum: Truth, Beauty, Goodness, and the Ax Murder in America's First Mass Medium* (Chapel Hill: University of North Carolina Press, 1994), 15.
45. *A Full Report of the Trial of Orrin Woodford for the Murder of his Wife, Diana Woodford* (Hartford: CT: Elihu Greer, 1846), 41–51.
46. *Full Report*, 9.
47. *Full Report*, 9–10.
48. *Full Report*, 10–11.
49. *Full Report*, 31.
50. *Full Report*, 24–26.
51. *Full Report*, 24–26.
52. "Horrid Murder from the Use of Rum and Cider," *Journal of the American Temperance Union* 9 (September 1845): 135.
53. *Full Report*, 10.
54. *Full Report*, 15–17.
55. Carol Mattingly, *Well-Tempered Women: Nineteenth-Century Temperance Rhetoric* (Carbondale and Edwardsville: Southern Illinois University Press, 1998), 1–2.
56. *Full Report*, 17.
57. Mattingly, *Well-Tempered Women*, 28.
58. *Full Report*, 68–69.
59. "Murder of a Wife by Her Husband," *New York Daily Times*, January 3, 1855, 3. This article misidentified Terence Hammill as "Thos. Hammond." Later newspaper accounts listed this name as an alias, and his name was spelled variously as "Hamill" or "Hammill." I have used "Hammill" here for the sake of consistency and as reflected in legal accounts. "Robbery," *New York Daily Times*, January 3, 1855, 3; "Probable Murder and Suicide," *New York Daily Times*, Jan 3, 1855, 3; "Trial of Terence Hamill for the Murder of His Wife," *New York Daily Times*, April 10, 1855, 2.
60. "Examination of Hammill, the Murderer," *New York Daily Times*, January 5, 1855, 8; "Hammill, the United States Bonded Warehouse Employe," *New York Daily Times*, March 29, 1855, 1.
61. "Trial of Terence Hamill for the Murder of His Wife," April 10, 1855; "Trial of Terence Hamill for the Murder of His Wife," *New York Daily Times*, April 11, 1855.
62. "Trial of Terence Hamill for the Murder of His Wife," April 10, 1855; "Trial of Terence Hamill for the Murder of His Wife," April 11, 1855.
63. "Notes," in *The Adjudged Cases on Insanity as a Defence to Crime*, ed. John Davison Lawson, 760; "Trial of Terence Hamill," April 11, 1855.

64. "Notes," 760; Friedman, *Crime and Punishment*, 147–48.
65. "Trial of Terence Hamill," April 11, 1855.
66. "Notes," 760–63; "Trial of Terence Hamill," April 11, 1855.
67. "Sentence of Terence Hamill," *New York Daily Times*, April 14, 1855.

Chapter 4: "The Broad Resemblances between Insanity and Drunkenness"

1. Norman Dain, *Concepts of Insanity in the United States, 1789–1865* (New Brunswick: Rutgers University Press, 1964); Charles E. Rosenberg, *The Trial of the Assassin Guiteau: Psychiatry and the Law in the Gilded Age* (Chicago: University of Chicago Press, 1968); Janet Ann Tighe, "A Question of Responsibility: The Development of American Forensic Psychiatry, 1838–1930" (PhD diss., University of Pennsylvania, 1983); James C. Mohr, *Doctors and the Law: Medical Jurisprudence in Nineteenth-Century America* (New York: Oxford University Press, 1993); Daniel N. Robinson, *Wild Beasts and Idle Humours: The Insanity Defense from Antiquity to Present* (Cambridge, MA: Harvard University Press, 1996).
2. Jacques Quen, "Isaac Ray on Drunkenness," *Bulletin of the History of Medicine* 41 (July/August 1967): 342–47; Tighe, "A Question of Responsibility," 2–3; See also Winfred Overholser, "Editor's Introduction," to Isaac Ray, *A Treatise on the Medical Jurisprudence of Insanity* (1838; repr., Cambridge, MA; Belknap Press of Harvard University Press, 1962), vii–xvi.
3. Mohr, *Doctors and the Law*, 145–46; Tighe, "A Question of Responsibility," 31–32; Winfred Overholser, "Pioneers in Criminology: III. Isaac Ray (1807–1881)," *Journal of Criminal Law, Criminology, and Police Science* 45 (September–October 1954): 249–63.
4. Ray, *A Treatise*, 13.
5. John Starrett Hughes, *In the Law's Darkness: Isaac Ray and the Medical Jurisprudence of Insanity in Nineteenth-Century America* (New York: Oceana, 1986), 3–15; Tighe, "A Question of Responsibility," 25–76, 141–57.
6. James Cowles Prichard, *On the Different Forms of Insanity* (London: Hippolyte Ballière, 1842), 19–20; James Cowles Prichard, *A Treatise on Insanity and Other Disorders Affecting the Mind* (London: Sherwood, Gilbert and Piper, 1835), 4–7; Hannah Franziska Augstein, "J. C. Prichard's Concept of Moral Insanity—a Medical Theory of the Corruption of Human Nature," *Medical History* 40 (1996): 311–43.
7. Prichard, *A Treatise on Insanity*, 384–99; Prichard, *On the Different Forms*, 58, 126–27.
8. Ray, *A Treatise*, 18–25.
9. Ray, *A Treatise*, 10–13.
10. Mohr, *Doctors and the Law*, 146.
11. Quen, "Isaac Ray on Drunkenness," 342.
12. Mohr, *Doctors and the Law*, 146–47; Overholser, "Editor's Introduction," xiii–xv.
13. Ray, *A Treatise*, 299, 304, 130.
14. Quen, "Isaac Ray on Drunkenness," 343.
15. Ray, *A Treatise*, 300–303, 324.
16. Gerald N. Grob, "Psychiatry's Holy Grail: The Search for the Mechanisms of Mental Disease," *Bulletin of the History of Medicine* 72 (Summer 1998): 192.

17. Ray, *A Treatise*, 310.
18. Tighe, "A Question of Responsibility," 82–86; Robinson, *Wild Beasts*, 163–76; J. Thomas Dalby, "The Case of Daniel McNaughton: Let's Get the Story Straight," *American Journal of Forensic Psychiatry* 27 (2006): 25–26, 28–29; Leonard W. Levy, *The Law of the Commonwealth and Chief Justice Shaw* (Cambridge, MA: Harvard University Press, 1957), 211–18; Alan Rogers, *Murder and the Death Penalty in Massachusetts* (Amherst, MA: University of Massachusetts Press, 2008), 208–11. See also "Trial of Rogers," in Isaac Ray, *Contributions to Mental Pathology: A facsimile reproduction with an introduction by Jacques M. Quen, MD* (1873; repr., Delmar, NY: Scholars, 1973), 210–28.
19. Tighe, "A Question of Responsibility," 12–13; Mohr, *Doctors and the Law*, 100–104, 148–50.
20. Alfred S. Taylor, *Medical Jurisprudence* (Philadelphia: Lea and Blanchard, 1845), iii, 498–523.
21. David W. Jones, "Moral Insanity and Psychological Disorder: The Hybrid Roots of Psychology," *History of Psychiatry* 28:3 (September 2017): 263–79; Taylor, *Medical Jurisprudence*, 513, 522.
22. Isaac Ray, "Medical Evidence," *American Jurist and Law Magazine* 24 (January 1841): 294–306; Mohr, *Doctors and the Law*, 140–41.
23. Lawrence M. Friedman, *Crime and Punishment in American History* (New York: Basic Books, 1993), 146–47.
24. Hendrik Hartog, "Lawyering, Husbands' Rights, and 'the Unwritten Law' in Nineteenth-Century America," *Journal of American History* 84 (June 1997): 67, 83–84; Friedman, *Crime and Punishment*, 146–47.
25. Hendrik Hartog, *Man and Wife in America: A History* (Cambridge, MA: Harvard University Press, 2000), 230.
26. J. H. Lind, "Drunkenness as an Extenuation in Cases of Murder," *American Law Register* 24 (September 1876): 506.
27. United States v. McGlue, 26 F Cas. 1093 (Circuit Court D. Massachusetts; 1851).
28. "United States v. McGlue (1 Curt. 1.), in the United States Circuit Court, District of Massachusetts, October Term, 1851," in *The Adjudged Cases on Insanity as a Defence to Crime*, ed. John Davison Lawson (Saint Louis, MO: F. H. Thomas, 1884), 54–55, 60.
29. United States v. McGlue, 26 F. Cas. Instructions to the jury were reprinted in "Law Cases Bearing upon Insanity," *American Journal of Insanity* (July 1856): 74–80. On juries and medical experts, see Mohr, *Doctors and the Law*, xiv–xv, 96–100.
30. "Another Murder," *Boston Daily Atlas*, July 21, 1851; "Murder on the High Seas," *New York Daily Times*, October 2, 1851.
31. "Examination on a Charge of Murder," *Boston Daily Atlas*, October 3, 1851; "Murder on Shipboard," *New York Daily Times*, October 4, 1851.
32. "Court Calendar," *Boston Courier Semi-Weekly*, October 30, 1851, 2; "Another Gale and Loss of Life—Sorrows of the Cape Cod Gals—Acquittal of McGlue," *New York Daily Times*, November 5, 1851, 4.
33. For more on the composition of juries in the nineteenth century including a discussion of the impact of judges in influencing jury decision, see Albert W. Alschuler

and Andrew G. Deiss, "A Brief History of the Criminal Jury in the United States," *University of Chicago Law Review* 61 (1994): 867–928.

34. United States v. McGlue, 26 F. Cas.

35. "Notes to Leading Criminal Cases," *Monthly Law Reporter* 6 (February 1854): 560–61; "State v. Hundley (46 Mo. 414.), in the Supreme Court of Missouri, August Term, 1870," in *The Adjudged Cases on Insanity as a Defence to Crime*, ed. John Davison Lawson (Saint Louis, MO: F. H. Thomas, 1884), 421.

36. Robert J. Waldinger, "Sleep of Reason: John P. Gray and the Challenge of Moral Insanity," *Journal of the History of Medicine and Allied Sciences* 34 (April 1979): 163–79; Gary S. Belkin, "Moral Insanity, Science and Religion in Nineteenth-Century America: The Gray-Ray Debate," *History of Psychiatry* 7 (1996): 591–613.

37. John P. Gray, "Homicide in Insanity," *American Journal of Insanity* 14 (October 1857): 119–45; John P. Gray, "Moral Insanity," *American Journal of Insanity* 14 (April 1858): 311–22; John P. Gray, "Responsibility of the Insane—Homicide in Insanity," *American Journal of Insanity* 32 (July 1875): 1–183; "Proceedings of the Association," *American Journal of Insanity* 23 (July 1866): 93–96; Tighe, "A Question of Responsibility," 49–68.

38. Mohr, *Doctors and the Law*, 150–53; Tighe, "A Question of Responsibility," 51–68; Waldinger, "Sleep of Reason," 163–79; Belkin, "Moral Insanity," 591–613.

39. For more on the general history of asylums, see David J. Rothman, *The Discovery of the Asylum: Social Order and Disorder in the New Republic* (Boston: Little, Brown, 1971); Gerald N. Grob, *The Mad among Us: A History of the Care of America's Mentally Ill* (New York: The Free Press, 1994). For the history of inebriety asylums specifically, see Sarah Whitney Tracy, "The Foxborough Experiment: Medicalizing Inebriety at the Massachusetts Hospital for Dipsomaniacs and Inebriates, 1833–1919" (PhD diss., University of Pennsylvania, 1992).

40. Andrew McFarland, "Minor Mental Maladies," *Chicago Medical Examiner* 4 (August 1863): 353–69.

41. Andrew McFarland, "Insanity and Intemperance," *American Journal of Insanity* 19 (April 1863): 448. The last name of the defendant is variously spelled as "Hopp" or "Hopps." I have used "Hopps" as that is what is reflected in the official case record.

42. McFarland, "Insanity and Intemperance," 451–53; "Trial of William Hopp for the Murder of His Wife," *Chicago Daily Tribune*, December 19, 1862.

43. "From the West," *New York Times*, May 13, 1866; McFarland, "Insanity and Intemperance, 452.

44. Andrew McFarland, "Editorial: Trial of Wm. Hopps for Murder," *Chicago Medical Examiner* 3 (December 1862): 766.

45. "Wm. Hopps on Trial for Murder," *Chicago Medical Examiner* 3 (November 1862): 701.

46. McFarland, "Insanity and Intemperance," 451.

47. "Trial of Wm. Hopp for the Murder of His Wife—Fifth Day," *Chicago Daily Tribune*, December 24, 1862.

48. McFarland, "Insanity and Intemperance," 451; "Trial of William Hopp for the Murder of His Wife—Second Day," *Chicago Daily Tribune*, December 20, 1862; "Trial of William Hopp for the Murder of His Wife—Third Day," *Chicago Daily Tribune*, December 21, 1862.

49. "Trial of Wm. Hopp for the Murder of His Wife—Fifth Day."
50. "Trial of William Hopp for the Murder of His Wife—Second Day"; "Trial of Wm. Hopp for the Murder of His Wife—Fifth Day."
51. McFarland, "Insanity and Intemperance," 451.
52. "Trial of William Hopp for the Murder of His Wife—Sixth Day," *Chicago Daily Tribune*, December 25, 1862.
53. McFarland, "Editorial," 767; McFarland, "Insanity and Intemperance," 456.
54. "Trial of William Hopp for the Murder of His Wife—Sixth Day."
55. "Wm. Hopps on Trial for Murder," 703.
56. McFarland, "Editorial," 769.
57. "From the West."
58. McFarland, "Insanity and Intemperance," 469. McFarland did praise the judge for allowing the privilege of the "benefit of a doubt" normally given in criminal cases to be given to insanity.
59. McFarland, "Editorial," 769.
60. "Trial of William Hopp for the Murder of His Wife—Sixth Day."
61. "From the West"; Hopps v. the People of the State of Illinois 31 Ill. 385 (WL 3121 1863).
62. McFarland, "Insanity and Intemperance, 461.
63. Mohr, *Doctors and the Law*, xiv.
64. W. S. Chipley, "Feigned Insanity—Motives—Special Tests," *American Journal of Insanity* 22 (July 1865): 3.
65. The last name of Smith's victim is variously spelled as "Landaw," "Landaur," and "Landauer." I have used the spelling from the official indictment.
66. "Commonwealth vs. Robert Smith (1864)," Jefferson County Circuit Court, Kentucky Department for Libraries and Archives, Frankfort, Kentucky. My thanks to archivist James Prichard for his assistance in locating, copying, and mailing these records. "Excitement at the United States Hotel," *Louisville Daily Democrat*, April 24, 1864; "In Court of Appeals, State of Kentucky, Smith v. Commonwealth with Remarks by W. S. Chipley," *American Journal of Insanity* 23 (July 1866), 1–2.
67. "Commonwealth vs. Robert Smith."
68. "Commonwealth vs. Robert Smith."
69. "Commonwealth vs. Robert Smith."
70. "Jefferson Circuit Court: Sixth Day's Proceedings," *Louisville Daily Democrat*, May 8, 1864; "Jefferson Circuit Court: Eighth Day's Proceedings, *Louisville Daily Democrat*, May 11, 1864.
71. "Commonwealth vs. Robert Smith"; "Removal of a United States Commissioner in Kentucky—A Murderer Sentenced," *New York Times*, April 9, 1867, 4.
72. "Smith v. Commonwealth (1 Duv. 224), in the Court of Appeals of Kentucky, Summer Term, 1864," in *The Adjudged Cases on Insanity as a Defence to Crime*, ed. John Davison Lawson (Saint Louis, MO: F. H. Thomas, 1884), 669–74. A list of subsequent cases that cite Smith are identified on p. xxix.
73. Smith v. Commonwealth 1 Duv. 224 (1864); "Smith v. Commonwealth," 669–74.
74. Smith v. Commonwealth; "Smith v. Commonwealth" 669–74.
75. Smith v. Commonwealth; "Smith v. Commonwealth," 669–74.

76. "Intemperance and Insanity," *American Journal of Insanity* 23 (July 1866), 6–45.
77. "Intemperance and Insanity," 6–45. Chipley's comments are limited to the decision of the appeal judge. He acknowledges in a later discussion of his paper in the same issue that he is unfamiliar with the testimony in the case. "Proceedings of the Association," *American Journal of Insanity* 23 (July 1866), 133.
78. "Proceedings of the Association," 111–15, 132–33.

Chapter 5: "They Are Simply Drunk"

1. Mariana Valverde, *Diseases of the Will: Alcohol and the Dilemmas of Freedom* (Cambridge: Cambridge University Press, 1998), 1–5. For additional background see Gerald N. Grob, *Mental Institutions in America: Social Policy to 1875* (New York: The Free Press, 1973); David Rothman, *The Discovery of the Asylum: Social Order and Disorder in the New Republic* (Boston: Little, Brown, 1971).
2. Valverde, *Diseases of the Will*, 2.
3. William L. White, "The Lessons of Language: Historical Perspectives on the Rhetoric of Addiction," in *Altering American Consciousness: The History of Alcohol and Drug Use in the United States, 1800–2000*, ed. Sarah W. Tracy and Caroline Jean Acker (Boston: University of Massachusetts Press, 2004): 33–60; "On a Particular Form of Insanity," *American Journal of Insanity* 8 (July 1851): 4. For the importance of the shift from "intemperance" to "inebriety" to "dipsomania" to describe alcohol consumption, see Sarah Whitney Tracy, "The Foxborough Experiment: Medicalizing Inebriety at the Massachusetts Hospital for Dipsomaniacs and Inebriates, 1833–1919" (PhD diss., University of Pennsylvania, 1992), 10–53; Valverde, *Diseases of the Will*, 46–50.
4. Albert Ernest Wilkerson, "A History of the Concept of Alcoholism as a Disease" (PhD diss., University of Pennsylvania, 1966), 3. See also E. M. Jellinek, *The Disease Concept of Alcoholism* (New Haven, CT: Hillhouse Press, 1960).
5. Andrew McFarland, "Editorial," *Chicago Medical Examiner* 3 (December 1862): 766–67.
6. Isaac Ray, *Contributions to Mental Pathology: A Facsimile Reproduction with an Introduction by Jacques M. Quen, MD* (1873; repr., Delmar, NY: Scholars, 1973), 35.
7. "Contemporary Literature," *Quarterly Journal of Psychological Medicine and Medical Jurisprudence* 2 (January 1868): 147–51.
8. Stephen Rogers, "The Influence of Methomania upon Business and Criminal Responsibility," *Quarterly Journal of Psychiatric Medicine and Medical Jurisprudence* 3 (April 1869): 330–31.
9. T. H. Tanner, "Dipsomania," *American Journal of Insanity* 19 (October 1862): 246–47.
10. John Ordronaux, "Is Habitual Drunkenness a Disease?" *American Journal of Insanity* 30 (April 1874): 430–43.
11. Wilkerson, "History of the Concept," 3.
12. "The Murder of Swanston," *New York Times*, November 14, 1857.
13. "The Murderer of Swenson Brought to the City," *New York Times*, October 23, 1857; "Trial of Rodgers for the Murder of Swanston, in Tenth-Avenue," *New York Times*, November 13, 1857; "Trial of Rodgers for the Murder of Swanston—Verdict

of Guilty—An Exciting Scene in Court," *New York Times*, November 14, 1857; "The Tenth Avenue Murder," *New York Herald*, October 21, 1857; "The Murder of Swanston"; "Appalling Increase of Crime," *New York Times*, November 23, 1857. Swanston was initially misidentified as "Swenson"; Rogers's name is spelled "Rodgers" in the press, but official transcripts used "Rogers," which is the spelling I have used here.

14. "Trial of Rodgers for the Murder of Swanston, in Tenth-Avenue"; "Decision of the Court of Appeals of the State of New York, in the Case of James Rogers, Convicted of Murder," *American Journal of Insanity* (January 1859): 258–71.
15. "The Murderers in the Tombs," *New York Times*, January 14, 1858.
16. "The Murder of Swanston."
17. "The Convicts and Prisoners in the Tombs—Interview with Rodgers, Cangemi, Holmes," *New York Times*, November 23, 1857; "Execution of James Rodgers To-day, for the Murder of Mr. Swanston," *New York Times*, November 12, 1858; "Supreme Court—General Term," *New York Times*, December 9, 1857; "Decision of the Court of Appeals," 259–60.
18. The People, Plaintiffs in Error v. Rogers, Defendant in Error, 18 N.Y. 9 (N.Y. Lexis 101 1858).
19. "Intemperance and Insanity," *American Journal of Insanity* 23 (July 1866): 8–9; "Decision of the Court of Appeals," 258–60."
20. "Appalling Increase of Crime"; "The Murderer James Rodgers," *New York Times*, May 27, 1858; "Execution of James Rodgers."
21. "Another Rodgers in the Field," *New York Times*, July 9, 1858.
22. "Horrible Tragedy," *Daily Morning News*, January 3, 1859; Wallace Putnam Reed, *History of Atlanta, Georgia* (Atlanta: D. Mason, 1889), 298–99; Franklin M. Garrett, *Atlanta and Environs: A Chronicle of Its People and Events, 1820s–1870s* (Athens: University of Georgia Press, 2011), 448–49; "Choice v. State (31 Ga. 424.), In the Supreme Court of Georgia, August Term, 1860," in *The Adjudged Cases on Insanity as a Defence to Crime*, ed. John Davison Lawson (Saint Louis: F. H. Thomas, 1884), 538–56.
23. "Choice v. State," 550.
24. "Choice v. State," 538–43.
25. "Choice v. State," 538–56. For a discussion of the use of this decision as precedent, see Lawrence P. Tiffany, "The Drunk, the Insane, and the Criminal Courts: Deciding What to Make of Self-induced Insanity," *Washington University Law Quarterly* 69 (January 1991): 221–42.
26. Charles J. G. Griffin, "John Brown's 'Madness," *Rhetoric and Public Affairs* 12 (Fall 2009): 377. Griffin also notes Virginia Governor Henry Wise "needed Brown to be seen as sane by the public because only then did his actions provide tangible proof of Northern designs on the interests of the South."
27. Reed, *History of Atlanta*, 299; Garrett, *Atlanta and Environs*, 449; "Georgia Legislature," *Daily Morning News*, November 19, 1859; "By Telegraph," *Daily Morning News*, December 5, 1859.
28. "Shocking Case of Infanticide—A Mother Throws Her Child into the Canal," *Rochester Daily Union and Advertiser*, July 10, 1865; "The Case of Infanticide,"

Rochester Daily Union and Advertiser, July 11, 1865; "Arrest of the Woman Who Drowned Her Infant," *Rochester Daily Union and Advertiser*, July 17, 1865; "Ann Barry Committed to Answer for Murder—She Confesses Her Guilt," *Rochester Daily Union and Advertiser*, July 20, 1865.

29. "Arrest of the Woman Who Drowned Her Infant"; "Trial of Ann Barry, for the Murder of Her Infant Child by Drowning," *Rochester Daily Union and Advertiser*, February 21, 1866; "Trial of Ann Barry, for the Murder of Her Infant Child by Drowning," *Rochester Daily Union and Advertiser*, February 23, 1866.
30. Sarah Barringer Gordon, "Law and Everyday Death: Infanticide and the Backlash against Woman's Rights after the Civil War," in *Lives in the Law*, ed. Austin Sarat, Lawrence Douglas, and Martha Merrill Umphrey (Ann Arbor: University of Michigan Press, 2002), 55–81.
31. Scott C. Martin, *Devil of the Domestic Sphere: Temperance, Gender, and Middle-Class Ideology, 1800–1860* (DeKalb: Northern Illinois University Press, 2010), 15–17.
32. Quoted in Harry Gene Levine, "Temperance and Women in 19th-Century United States," in *Alcohol and Drug Problems in Women: Research Advances in Alcohol and Drug Problems*, vol. 5, ed. Oriana Josseau Kalant (New York: Plenum Press, 1980), 33–34. The rest of the title of Doner's autobiography is worth mentioning: *The Life of Thomas Doner: Having Lost Both Arms through Intemperance, He Wrote His Book with His Teeth As a Warning to Others.*
33. *Confessions of a Female Inebriate or Intemperance in High Life by a Lady* (Boston: William Henshaw, 1842). See preface to Isaac F. Shepard, "Confessions of a Female Inebriate (1842)," in *Drunkard's Progress: Narratives of Addiction, Despair, and Recovery*, ed. John W. Crowley (Baltimore: Johns Hopkins University Press, 1999), 69–70.
34. *Confessions of a Female Inebriate*, 25–26.
35. Martin, *Devil of the Domestic Sphere*, 15–38.
36. "Trial of Ann Barry," February 21, 1866. There was some dispute that the confession was made "under a threat or promise"; Gordon, "Law and Everyday Death," 63.
37. "The Child Murder," *Rochester Daily Union and Advertiser*, July 18, 1865; "Ann Barry Committed to Answer for Murder."
38. "Trial of Ann Barry," February 21, 1866.
39. "Trial of Ann Barry for the Murder of her Infant Child by Drowning," *Rochester Daily Union and Advertiser*, February 20, 1866; "Trial of Ann Barry," February 23, 1866. A brief account of the trial also appears in R. Gregory Lande, *The Abraham Man: Madness, Malingering, and the Development of Medical Testimony* (New York: Algora, 2012), 74–75.
40. "Trial of Ann Barry," February 23, 1866.
41. "Trial of Ann Barry," February 23, 1866; "Drunkenness and Crime," *American Journal of Insanity* 24 (April 1868): 489–91.
42. "Conclusion of the Trial of Ann Barry—Verdict of Murder in the Second Degree—Sentenced to State Prison for Life," *Rochester Daily Union and Advertiser*, February 26, 1866; "Trial of Ann Barry," February 20, 1866.
43. "Twentieth Annual Meeting of the Association of Medical Superintendents of American Institutions for the Insane, *American Journal of Insanity* 23 (July 1866): 134–35.

44. For more on the M'Naghten case, see Roger Smith, *Trial by Medicine: Insanity and Responsibility in Victorian Trials* (Edinburgh: Edinburgh University Press, 1981); Daniel N. Robinson, *Wild Beasts and Idle Humours: The Insanity Defense from Antiquity to Present* (Cambridge, Massachusetts: Harvard University Press, 1996), 161–75; Charles Rosenberg, *The Trial of the Assassin Guiteau: Psychiatry and the Law in the Gilded Age* (Chicago: University of Chicago Press, 1968), 102–3. For an example of "irresistible impulse" see the ruling on the case of Abner Rogers in Leonard W. Levy, *The Law of the Commonwealth and Chief Justice Shaw* (Cambridge, MA: Harvard University Press, 1957), 212–17; Isaac Ray, "The Law of Insanity," *American Law Review* 4 (1869): 236–52.
45. Louis E. Reik, "The Doe-Ray Correspondence: A Pioneer Collaboration in the Jurisprudence of Mental Disease," *Yale Law Journal* 63 (1953): 185–87; John Reid, "Understanding the New Hampshire Doctrine of Criminal Insanity," *Yale Law Journal* 69 (1960): 367–420; John Starrett Hughes, *In the Law's Darkness: Isaac Ray and the Medical Jurisprudence of Insanity in Nineteenth-Century America* (New York: Oceana Publications, 1986), 97–101.
46. Reik, "Doe-Ray Correspondence," 187.
47. Reid, "Understanding the New Hampshire Doctrine," 373–74; Reik, "Doe-Ray Correspondence," 188–91, 191n.
48. "Murder and Robbery," *Lowell Daily Citizen and News*, May 9, 1868; "Thomas Brown; Thursday; Pike," *The Quincy Whig*, May 12, 1868; "Pike the Murderer," *Lowell Daily Citizen and News*, May 13, 1868; "The Murder at Hampton Falls—Confession of the Murderer," *New York Times*, May 14, 1868; "The Hampton Falls Tragedy," *Springfield Weekly Republican*, May 16, 1868; "New Hampshire," *Lowell Daily Citizen and News*, October 12, 1868.
49. "Murderer Condemned," *Boston Daily Journal*, October 31, 1868.
50. "Supreme Judicial Court," *Portsmouth Journal of Literature and Politics*, October 31, 1868.
51. "Supreme Judicial Court."
52. T. Edwards Clark, "The Dangerous Classes of the Community," *Quarterly Journal of Psychiatric Medical and Medical Jurisprudence* 1 (October 1867): 218. Note that Richard Dugdale first undertook his study of the Jukes in 1874, see Richard Dugdale, *The Jukes: A Study of Crime, Pauperism, Disease and Heredity* (New York: G. P. Putnam's Sons, 1877).
53. "Supreme Judicial Court"; "Murderers in the New Hampshire State Prison," *Concord Patriot*, November 3, 1868; On hereditary theories of insanity, see Isaac Ray, M.D., *A Treatise on the Medical Jurisprudence of Insanity* (New York: Arno Press, 1976, 1871): 172–73.
54. Rogers, "Influence of Methomania," 323–50.
55. "Supreme Judicial Court."
56. "Murderer Condemned"; "Supreme Judicial Court"; "A New Hampshire Murderer Condemned to Be Hanged," *New York Herald*, November 2, 1868; "Sentence of Murderer," *New Hampshire Patriot and State Gazette*, November 4, 1868; "Josiah L. Pike," *Jackson Citizen*, November 10, 1868.

57. "Supreme Judicial Court of New Hampshire. State v. Pike," *American Law Register* 20 (April 1872): 233–59; Isaac Ray, "The Law of Insanity," *American Law Review* 4 (1869): 245–47.
58. State v. Pike, 49 N.H. 399 (N.H. Lexis 33 1870).
59. State v. Pike, 49 N.H. 399; "Supreme Judicial Court of New Hampshire. State v. Pike," 235–42.
60. The New Hampshire doctrine was formulated through the decisions of three cases—Boardman v. Woodman (1865), State v. Pike (1869), and State v. Jones (1871). Interest in the doctrine was renewed in the 1950s with the application of what would be known as the Durham rule as a modification to the still-controversial M'Naghten test of right and wrong. See Reid, "Understanding the New Hampshire Doctrine," 367–420.
61. "The Death Penalty," *Hartford Daily Courant*, November 10, 1869.
62. Janet A. Tighe, "Francis Wharton and the Nineteenth Century Insanity Defense: The Origins of a Reform Tradition," *American Journal of Legal History* 27 (July 1983): 223–53; James C. Mohr, *Doctors and the Law: Medical Jurisprudence in Nineteenth-Century America* (New York: Oxford University Press, 1993), 37–38.
63. Francis Wharton, *A Treatise on Mental Unsoundness, Embracing a General View of Psychological Law*, vol. 1 in Wharton and Stillé's *Medical Jurisprudence*, 3rd ed. (Philadelphia: Kay and Brother, 1873), vii–xviii.
64. "State v. Johnson (40 Conn. 136.), in the Supreme Court of Errors of Connecticut, April Term, 1873," in *The Adjudged Cases on Insanity as a Defence to Crime*, ed. John Davison Lawson (Saint Louis: F. H. Thomas, 1884), 603–8.
65. "State v. Johnson," 603–11.

Chapter 6: An Apology for Sin and for Crime"

1. Theodore L. Mason, "Anniversary Address," *Quarterly Journal of Inebriety* 1 (December 1876): 17.
2. A. Jaffe, "Reform in American Medical Science: The Inebriety Movement and the Origins of the Psychological Disease Theory of Addiction, 1870–1920," *British Journal of Addiction* 73 (June 1978): 142–43; Arnold Jaffe, *Addiction Reform in the Progressive Age: Scientific and Social Responses to Drug Dependence in the United States, 1870–1930* (New York: Arno Press, 1976), 30–33. For an overview of inebriety in this period, see also *The Disease of Inebriety from Alcohol, Opium and Other Narcotic Drugs, Its Etiology, Pathology, Treatment and Medico-Legal Relations (1893)* (New York: Arno Press, 1981). Although the book was published by the American Association for the Study and Cure of Inebriety, the bulk of the work has been attributed to T. D. Crothers.
3. Mason, "Anniversary Address," 2–6; T. D. Crothers, "Inebriate Tramps in New York State," *Quarterly Journal of Inebriety* 1 (March 1877): 117.
4. Mason, "Anniversary Address," 18–19; For similar attempts to differentiate between vice and the disease of inebriety, see N. S. Davis, "Pathology of Drunkenness—Is It a Disease or a Moral Delinquency?" *Chicago Journal of Nervous and Mental Disease* 2 (October 1875): 503–4.

5. Paul R. Shipman, "A Sketch of the Life of Joseph Parrish," *Journal of Inebriety* 12 (April 1890): 141–59; Joseph Parrish, *Alcoholic Inebriety: From a Medical Standpoint with Cases from Clinical Records* (1883; repr., New York: Arno Press, 1981), 12–39.
6. George M. Beard, *American Nervousness: Its Causes and Consequences* (New York: G. P. Putnam and Sons, 1881), vi–viii; George M. Beard, *Stimulants and Narcotics: Medically, Philosophically and Morally Considered* (New York: G. P. Putnam and Sons, 1871); Tom Lutz, *American Nervousness, 1903: An Anecdotal History* (Ithaca, NY: Cornell University Press, 1991), 3–7.
7. George M. Beard, "Causes of the Recent Increase of Inebriety in America," *Quarterly Journal of Inebriety* 1 (December 1876): 28–29, 36. For more on this view of inebriety, see Michele Rotunda, "Savages to the Left of Me, Neurasthenics to the Right, Stuck in the Middle with You: Inebriety and Human Nature in American Society, 1855–1900," *Canadian Bulletin of Medical History* 24 (Spring 2007): 49–65.
8. Franklin D. Clum, *Inebriety: Its Causes, Its Results, Its Remedy* (1888; repr., New York: Arno Press 1981), 75.
9. F. G. Gosling, *Before Freud: Neurasthenia and the Medical Community, 1870–1910* (Chicago: University of Illinois Press, 1981); Anson Rabinbach, "Neurasthenia and Modernity," in *Incorporations*, eds. Jonathan Crary and Sanford Kwinter (Cambridge, MA: MIT Press, 1992), 178–89.
10. Charles E. Rosenberg, "The Place of George M. Beard in Nineteenth Century Psychiatry," *Bulletin of the History of Medicine* 36 (1962): 245–59; Charles E. Rosenberg, *The Trial of the Assassin Guiteau: Psychiatry and the Law in the Gilded Age* (Chicago: University of Chicago Press, 1968), 227, 249–51.
11. Barbara Weiner and William White, "The *Journal of Inebriety* (1876–1914): History, Topical Analysis, and Photographic Images," *Addiction* 102 (2007): 16–17; Edward M. Brown, "'What Shall We Do with the Inebriate?': Asylum Treatment and the Disease Concept of Alcoholism in the Late Nineteenth Century," *Journal of the History of the Behavioral Sciences* 21 (January 1985): 48–49.
12. Mariana Valverde, *Diseases of the Will: Alcohol and the Dilemmas of Freedom* (Cambridge: Cambridge University Press, 1998), 70.
13. Janet Ann Tighe, "A Question of Responsibility: The Development of American Forensic Psychiatry, 1838–1930" (PhD diss., University of Pennsylvania, 1983), 235–36.
14. Thomas D. Crothers, "What Shall We Do with the Inebriate?" *Alienist and Neurologist* 2 (1881), 175; Mason, "Anniversary Address," 19–20; Brown, "What Shall We Do," 50–51. For a broader study of the complex social negotiations between physicians, policy makers, patients and their families, see Sarah W. Tracy, *Alcoholism in America from Reconstruction to Prohibition* (Baltimore: Johns Hopkins University Press, 2005).
15. "Lunacy and Inebriety," *New York Times*, December 4, 1869.
16. "Edward Charles Spitzka, M.D.," *Journal of Nervous and Mental Disease* 41 (April 1914): 209–11; Rosenberg, *Trial of the Assassin Guiteau*, 71–74, 155–57; Tighe, "A Question of Responsibility," 234–37, 251–59.
17. E. C. Spitzka, *Insanity: Its Classification, Diagnosis and Treatment* (New York: E. B. Treat, 1889), 251–53.

18. T. D. Crothers, "Inebriety and Its Symptomology," *Quarterly Journal of Inebriety* 2 (September 1878): 196.
19. Janet A. Tighe, "The New York Medico-Legal Society: Legitimating the Union of Law and Psychiatry (1867–1918)," *International Journal of Law and Psychiatry* 9 (1986): 231–43.
20. T. D. Crothers, *The Trance State in Inebriety—Its Medico-Legal Relations* (New York: The Case, Lockwood and Brainard, 1882), 13–39. A number of the inebriety physicians wrote on similar states including Beard. See for example, George M. Beard, "Are Inebriates Automatons?" *Quarterly Journal of Inebriety* 3 (January 1879): 8–18; Parrish, *Alcoholic Inebriety*, 63–74; Frederick W. Mann, "Alcoholic Hallucination," *American Journal of Inebriety* 46 (April 1890): 439–50.
21. Crothers, *The Trance State in Inebriety*, 13–39.
22. "Alcoholic Trance," *Science*, November 19, 1881, 545–46. For another conflict involving similar issues, see the disagreement between Edward Mann and Charles Dana over the definition of dipsomania and inebriety: Edward C. Mann, "Inebriety as a Disease," *North American Review* 148 (January 1889): 135–36; John Cotton Dana, "Dipsomania and Original Sin," *North American Review* 148 (May 1889): 646–47.
23. Edward C. Mann, "The Attitude of Legal Medicine vs. the Disease of Alcoholic Inebriety," in *Medical Jurisprudence of Inebriety, Being Papers Read before the Medico-Legal Society of New York and the Discussion Thereon* (New York: Medico-Legal Journal Association, 1888), 29–34.
24. T. L. Wright, "Personal Responsibility as Affected by Alcoholic Influence," in *Medical Jurisprudence of Inebriety, Being Papers Read before the Medico-Legal Society of New York and the Discussion Thereon* (New York: Medico-Legal Journal Association, 1888), 74–81.
25. William Tucker, "The Hereditary Effects of Intemperance, as It Effects Responsibility, Legal and Moral," in *Medical Jurisprudence of Inebriety, Being Papers Read before the Medico-Legal Society of New York and the Discussion Thereon* (New York: Medico-Legal Journal Association, 1888), 82–87.
26. "Hillsboro Crusade Sketches," in *Drugs in America: A Documentary History*, ed. David F. Musto (New York: New York University Press, 2002), 87–94; T. Edwards Clark, "The Dangerous Classes of the Community," *Quarterly Journal of Psychological Medicine and Medical Jurisprudence* 1 (October 1867): 218–19; Catherine Gilbert Murdock, *Domesticating Drink: Women, Men and Alcohol in America, 1870–1940* (Baltimore: Johns Hopkins University Press, 1998), 16; E. C. Spitzka, "The Increase of the Alcohol Habit," *The Forum* 6 (1888): 101–8; K. Austin Kerr, *Organized for Prohibition: A New History of the Anti-Saloon League* (New Haven, CT: Yale University Press, 1983).
27. Rosenberg, *Trial of the Assassin Guiteau*, 76–79, 238–41.
28. "Executed!" *Newark Morning Register*, January 4, 1884; "Jas. B. Graves," *Newark Morning Register*, January 4, 1884.
29. "Terrible Tragedy: Double Murder Last Night," *Newark Morning Register*, June 16, 1881.
30. "The Martin Trial," *Newark Morning Register*, October 13, 1881.

31. "Terrible Tragedy"; "Shocking Double Murder," *Newark Daily Advertiser*, June 16, 1881.
32. "Newark's Double Tragedy, *New York Times*, June 17, 1881; "Shocking Double Murder"; "Terrible Tragedy"; "The Nassau Street Tragedy," *Newark Daily Advertiser*, June 18, 1881; "Wednesday Night's Murder," *Newark Morning Register*, June 17, 1881.
33. "Newark's Double Tragedy."
34. "Editorial Mention," *Newark Morning Register*, June 18, 1881.
35. "Terrible Tragedy."
36. Murdock, *Domesticating Drink*, 142–43.
37. "Terrible Tragedy"; "The Nassau Street Tragedy"; "The Martin Murder Trial," *Newark Daily Advertiser*, October 11, 1881.
38. "The Martin Murder Trial."
39. "The Martin Murder Trial."
40. "Tried for a Double Murder," *Newark Daily Advertiser*, October 10, 1881; "The Martin Murder Trial"; "The Martin Trial," *Newark Morning Register*, October 12, 1881.
41. "The Martin Trial," *Newark Morning Register*, October 14, 1881.
42. See for example, Madelon Powers, *Faces along the Bar: Lore and Order in the Workingman's Saloon, 1870–1920* (Chicago: University of Chicago Press, 1998); Elaine Frantz Parsons, *Manhood Lost: Fallen Drunkards and Redeeming Women in the Nineteenth-Century United States* (Baltimore: The Johns Hopkins University Press, 2003); Mary Douglas, ed., *Constructive Drinking: Perspectives on Drink from Anthropology* (Cambridge: Cambridge University Press, 1987).
43. "Insanity as a Defence—Burden of Proof—Intoxication," *Criminal Law Magazine and Reporter* 3 (1882): 48.
44. "The Martin Trial," *Newark Morning Register*, October 15, 1881; "Close of the Murder Trial," *Newark Morning Register*, October 15, 1881.
45. "Robert Martin," *Newark Morning Register*, March 6, 1882; "Martin the Murderer," *Newark Morning Register*, February 11, 1882.
46. "Shocking Double Murder."
47. "Both Sentenced to Be Hanged," *New York Times*, November 25, 1883.
48. "Kissam in His Own Defense," *New York Times*, January 27, 1881; "Murder in the Second Degree," *New York Times*, January 29, 1881. Race as well as class was likely a factor in this case. See Scott C. Martin, Devil of the Domestic Sphere: Temperance, Gender, and Middle-Class Ideology, 1800–1860 (DeKalb: Northern Illinois University Press, 2010), 34–35 for perceptions of female intemperance among immigrants, the working class, and African Americans. Additional research on the Kissam case might prove useful.
49. "Pleading for Robert Martin," *New York Times*, March 21, 1882; "Writ of Error for Martin," *Newark Daily Advertiser*, March 22, 1882.
50. "Robert Martin," *Newark Morning Register*, March 1, 1882.
51. "Opinion," *New Jersey Law Journal* 5 (April 1882): 99.
52. "Inebriety and Crime," *New York Times*, September 13, 1888; T. D. Crothers, "Should Inebriates Be Punished By Death for Crime?" *Medical Record* (October 20, 1888): 473–75.
53. "Treatment of Inebriates Legally," *Times and Register* 21 (August 9, 1890): 126; *The Disease of Inebriety*, 265–66.

54. "Inebriety and Crime"; Crothers, "Should Inebriates Be Punished," 473–75; *The Disease of Inebriety*, 265–94; "Martin, the Murderer," 2.
55. "Inebriety and Crime"; Crothers, "Should Inebriates Be Punished," 473–75; *The Disease of Inebriety*, 265–94.
56. James B. Graves v. State, Supreme Court of New Jersey, 45 N.J.L 203 (N.J. Lexis 47 1883); James B. Graves, plaintiff in error, v. State, defendant in error, Court of Errors and Appeals of New Jersey, 45 N.J.L. 347 (N.J. Lexis 80 1883); E. C. Spitzka, "The Case of the Insane Murderer Graves, Recently Executed in Newark," *American Journal of Neurology and Psychiatry* 3 (April 1884): 108n.
57. "Murder in Cold Blood," *Newark Morning Register*, December 21, 1881; "A Brutal Murder," *Newark Daily Advertiser*, December 21, 1881. These accounts put Eddie's age at thirteen; some later accounts state that he was fourteen. In the court transcript, his father states he was thirteen, "James B. Graves vs. The State of New Jersey," New Jersey Supreme Court, April 8, 1882, 19.
58. "Murder in Cold Blood."
59. William H. Shaw, *History of Essex and Hudson Counties New Jersey* (Philadelphia: Everts and Peck, 1884), 296; "The Graves Trial," *Newark Daily Advertiser*, January 20, 1882.
60. "New Jersey Supreme Court: James B. Graves vs. The State of New Jersey," *New Jersey Court of Errors and Appeals* 80 (1883): 120–21.
61. "New Jersey Supreme Court," 123. The prosecutor in the case made a request to the judge that all females be excluded from the court room when the journal was read. The judge stated he only had the power to exclude children, see "The Graves Murder Trial," *Newark Daily Advertiser*, January 23, 1882.
62. "New Jersey Supreme Court," 123–25. For more on the idea that masturbation was associated with mental illness through much of the nineteenth century, see James Whorton, "The Solitary Vice: The Superstition That Masturbation Could Cause Mental Illness," *Western Journal of Medicine* 175 (July 2001): 66–68.
63. "The Graves Case," *Newark Morning Register*, January 24, 1882; "Editorial Mention," *Newark Morning Register*, January 24, 1882.
64. "Editorial Mention," *Newark Morning Register*, December 24, 1881.
65. "At the Jail," *Newark Sunday Register*, December 30, 1883; Spitzka, "The Case of the Insane Murderer Graves," 101.
66. Spitzka, "The Case of the Insane Murderer Graves," 91–92.
67. "Crime and Insanity," *Newark Daily Advertiser*, January 24, 1882.
68. Spitzka, "The Case of the Insane Murderer Graves," 103, 110–11. He also attempted to further discredit Hunt by pointing out that in his editorial of January 4, he had questioned the results of the autopsy before the report was even made (114).

Epilogue

1. Clark Bell, "The Medical Jurisprudence of Inebriety," in *Medical Jurisprudence of Inebriety, Being Papers Read before the Medico-Legal Society of New York and the Discussion Thereon* (New York: Medico-Legal Journal Association, 1888), 1–11.
2. James B. Jacobs, *Drunk Driving: An American Dilemma* (Chicago: University of Chicago Press, 1989), 74–77.

3. Montana v. Egelhoff 518 U.S. 337 (1996).
4. Montana v. Egelhoff.
5. Montana v. Egelhoff.
6. Ronald J. Allen, "Montana v. Egelhoff—Reflections on the Limits of Legislative Imagination and Judicial Authority," *Journal of Criminal Law and Criminology* 87 (Spring 1997): 651.
7. Montana v. Egelhoff.
8. Brett G. Sweitzer, "Implicit Redefinitions, Evidentiary Proscriptions, and Guilty Minds: Intoxicated Wrongdoers after *Montana v. Egelhoff*," *University of Pennsylvania Law Review* 146 (November 1997): 279.

INDEX

Page references in *italics* refer to figures.

MICHELE ROTUNDA received her PhD from Rutgers, the State University of New Jersey, and is currently an assistant professor of history at Union County College. She is a lifelong New Jersey resident and currently resides in Montclair.